LEGAL INFORMATION ONLINE ANYTIME

24 hours a day

www.nolo.com

AT THE NOLO.COM SELF-HELP LAW CENTER, YOU'LL FIND

- Nolo's comprehensive Legal Encyclopedia filled with plain-English information on a variety of legal topics
- Nolo's Law Dictionary—legal terms <u>without</u> the legalese
- Auntie Nolo—if you've got questions, Auntie's got answers
- The Law Store—over 250 self-help legal products including Downloadable Software, Books, Form Kits and eGuides
- Legal and product updates
- Frequently Asked Questions
- NoloBriefs, our free monthly email newsletter
- Legal Research Center, for access to state and federal statutes
- Our ever-popular lawyer jokes

Quality LAW BOOKS & SOFTWARE FOR EVERYONE

Nolo's user-friendly products are consistently first-rate. Here's why:

- A dozen in-house legal editors, working with highly skilled authors, ensure that our products are accurate, up-to-date and easy to use
- We continually update every book and software program to keep up with changes in the law
- Our commitment to a more democratic legal system informs all of our work
- We appreciate & listen to your feedback. Please fill out and return the card at the back of this book.

OUR "NO-HASSLE" GUARANTEE

Return anything you buy directly from Nolo for any reason and we'll cheerfully refund your purchase price. No ifs, ands or buts.

An Important Message to Our Readers

This product provides information and general advice about the law. But laws and procedures change frequently, and they can be interpreted differently by different people. For specific advice geared to your specific situation, consult an expert. No book, software or other published material is a substitute for personalized advice from a knowledgeable lawyer licensed to practice law in your state.

2nd edition

101 Law Forms for Personal Use

by Attorneys Robin Leonard & Ralph Warner
with the editors of Nolo

Keeping Up to Date

To keep its books up-to-date, Nolo issues new printings and new editions periodically. New printings reflect minor legal changes and technical corrections. New editions contain major legal changes, major text additions or major reorganizations. To find out if a later printing or edition of any Nolo book is available, call Nolo at 510-549-1976 or check our website at http://www.nolo.com.

To stay current, follow the "Update" service at our website at http://www.nolo.com/update. In another effort to help you use Nolo's latest materials, we offer a 35% discount off the purchase of the new edition of your Nolo book when you turn in the cover of an earlier edition. (See the "Special Upgrade Offer" in the back of the book.)

SECOND EDITION   OCTOBER 2001

Editor   MARCIA STEWART

Illustrations   MARI STEIN

Cover Design   TONI IHARA

Book Design   TERRI HEARSH

Proofreading   ROBERT WELLS

Index   JEAN MANN

Printing   CONSOLIDATED PRINTERS, INC.

Warner, Ralph.
   101 law forms for personal use / by Ralph Warner & Robin Leonard. -- 2nd ed.
     p. cm.
   Rev. ed. of: 101 law forms for personal use / by Robin Leonard & Ralph Warner with the editors of Nolo Press. 1st ed. 1998.
   Includes index.
   ISBN 0-87337-708-7
   1. Forms (Law)--United States--Popular Works.   I. Title: One hundred and one law forms for personal use. II. Warner, Ralph E. III. Leonard, Robin. 101 law forms for personal use. IV. Title.

KF170.S74 2001
347.73'55--dc21

00-069569

For information on bulk purchases or corporate premium sales, please contact the Special Sales Department. For academic sales or textbook adoptions, ask for Academic Sales. Call 800-955-4775 or write to Nolo at 950 Parker Street, Berkeley, CA 94710.

Acknowledgments

This book is a compilation and modification of some of the forms that exist in several other Nolo publications, plus several new ones. It couldn't have been written without the editorial assistance and support of Nolo's editorial department, particularly: Amy DelPo, Steve Elias, Ella Hirst, Shae Irving, Beth McKenna, Shannon Miehe, Janet Portman, Mary Randolph, Barbara Kate Repa and Marcia Stewart. Thanks to Teresa Bruns for her research assistance. Terri Hearsh labored long and hard to make the book both attractive and functional. Mari Stein provided the wonderful artwork.

Table of Contents

2 Basic Estate Planning

3 Things to Do After Death: Documents for Executors

4 Renting Residential Real Estate

5 Borrowing or Lending Money

6 Buying a House

7 Buying or Selling a Car, Dog or Other Personal Property

8 Renting Personal Property and Storing Goods

13 Living Together

14 Settling Legal Disputes

15 Miscellaneous Forms for Personal Use

Appendices

A Using the Forms CD-ROM

B Tear-Out Forms

Index

Introduction

How to Use This Book

This book provides 101 ready-to-use forms and contracts for a variety of everyday legal and practical transactions that most Americans can safely handle without formal legal help. Among the forms included are those necessary to write a simple will, settle minor legal disputes, prepare a power of attorney document, lend or borrow money, rent a place to live, request your credit report and sell a used car. Forms are also included to hire someone to do home repairs, to care for your children and for a variety of other purposes.

The Importance of Getting Contracts in Writing

The most important rule when making any business agreement or transaction is this: Get it in writing. In a few situations—such as a contract to buy or sell real estate—you must have a written agreement for it to be legally enforceable. Similarly, a contract that can't be performed within one year of when it's made must be written.

But even when an oral contract is legal, there are many practical reasons why you want to write it down. Two years from now, you and the other people involved in any transaction are likely to have significantly different recollections about what you agreed to. So putting your agreement into black and white is an important memory aid. But a well-drafted contract has several other important benefits. For one, it serves as a framework for settling disputes. If this proves impossible and a court contest ensues, it will be far easier to prove the terms of a written contract than an oral one.

Another important benefit of drafting a written agreement is that the act of putting a contract together can help you and the other parties focus on all key legal and practical issues, some of which might otherwise be overlooked. By starting this process with a well-designed form—like those in this book—you increase your chances of creating a thorough document.

Many of the forms in this book are primarily designed for your personal use, such as the Apartment-Finding Service Checklist or Loan Comparison Worksheet. But other forms in the book, such as the Elder Care Agreement, are contracts, designed for two or more parties to create a legally enforceable agreement. Unlike commercial contracts used to buy a house or sign up with a health maintenance organization, which almost always consist of pages full of hyped-up legalese, the contracts in this book are written in everyday (but legal) language. They are designed to describe and define a transaction, such as designating a temporary guardian for your child, with a reasonable level of specificity—without sacrificing the important virtues of clarity and simplicity.

The jargon-free nature of our contracts does not jeopardize their enforceability. In general, as long as two parties—business entities or people—exchange promises to each do something of benefit for the other, a valid contract is formed. A contract will usually be enforced unless any of the following is true:

- **The terms are too vague.** The contract must be clear and detailed enough so that an arbitrator or judge can sensibly decide who is right. For example, a house painting agreement that says "John the Painter shall paint Sally the Homeowner's house" provides so little guidance that it is next to worthless and probably would not be enforced. At the very least, to be enforceable the contract should state how much John is to be paid for his work. Of course, you'll want to go beyond creating a contract that defines who and what is involved to create one that anticipates problems likely to arise under it. To be of real value, it should include key details such as the type and color of paint to be used, the work schedule, how and when payment is to be made and what happens if John and Sally disagree about a key issue.
- **The contract involves an illegal purpose.** A contract formed to accomplish something that the law prohibits is not enforceable in a court. For instance, if two people who sign a contract

to transfer an illegal gambling operation later have a falling out, the agreement will not be enforced by a judge.

- **Enforcement would be grossly unfair.** The contracts you make using the forms in this book are unlikely to be challenged on the grounds of fairness. But know that in extreme situations, if a contract is both unfair and the result of one party's superior bargaining position (such as a one-sided premarital agreement between a millionaire and an unsophisticated recent immigrant), a court might not enforce it. If you keep in mind that the best contracts substantially benefit both parties, you will have no problems.

A. Filling in the Contracts and Forms

The 101 forms in this book are designed to be used as needed; we don't expect you to read the book from start to finish. But we do ask one thing: Read the introductory material at the beginning of any chapter from which you will use a form, as well as the instructions for completing the form itself.

You can use the forms provided in this book in at least three ways:

1. **Use the Forms CD-ROM.** All the forms are contained on the accompanying disk. If you have access to a computer, the most efficient approach is to fill in and print a desired form using the computer's word processing program, customizing the form as needed.

2. **Use the tear-out form.** You can certainly get the job done the old-fashioned way—by photocopying a form out of the book and filling it in with a typewriter or pen. *Don't*, however, use the original tear-out form from the book, or you'll be left without a clean copy. Although you'll be fine filling in some forms for your personal use by hand, such as the Property Worksheet, we suggest that you type the agreements whenever possible. While typing is not legally required, a printed document usually carries more weight than a

handwritten one and is more legible. But if convenience or cost dictate that you fill a contract or form in by hand, do it neatly and you should be fine.

⚠️ **You must retype the tear-out will.** As explained in Chapter 2, Basic Estate Planning, you cannot just tear out the will form, fill it in and sign it. Instead, use the disk that comes with this book (or a typewriter if you don't have access to a computer) to prepare a fresh will that contains only the clauses you want. If you are writing a will, be sure to read the instructions in Chapter 2 carefully, including how wills must be signed and witnessed.

3. **Use the forms in this book to evaluate similar forms and contracts.** If someone drafts a contract and presents it to you to sign, you can use a corresponding form in this book as a checklist to make sure that the proposed contract has all the recommended ingredients. If it doesn't, use the form in this book as a model to suggest modifications or additions.

B. Editing the Forms

Many of the forms in this book may meet your needs perfectly. All you will need to do is fill in a few blanks and sign it. But for some forms, you'll want to make some changes—such as adding or deleting language or clauses. Here's how.

⚠️ **Be sure your changes are clear, easy to understand and legal.** If you add a list of property or work specifications to a contract, your contract should still be fine. But if you delete one of our clauses, and substitute your own, make sure your language is easy to understand, free from ambiguity and consistent with the rest of the contract. Also, if you have any doubt about the legal validity of language you want to add or delete—especially if significant amounts of money or property or the personal rights of the other person are involved—have the changes checked by a lawyer.

1. Selecting From Several Choices

Many of our forms contain one or more clauses which ask you to choose among several options, such as the method of payment for the work being performed under a Home Repairs Agreement or Child Care Agreement (see sample below). When you see a clause like this, simply check the correct box on the tear-out form and provide any requested additional information.

On several of our forms, you may encounter some slightly awkward language, such as ☐ Yes ☐ No or "his/hers." In either case, you can easily clean the form up by deleting words that don't apply or substituting more appropriate language (assuming you're using the forms on disk). If you're filling in a tear-out form, leaving the unneeded words in will not affect the validity of the contract. If you prefer, however, you can ink out the portion that does not apply.

2. Deleting Clauses or Phrases

Some individual clauses or phrases in our forms and agreements may not apply to your situation. If you

are using the forms on the disk, making changes is easy—simply delete those clauses and renumber the remaining as appropriate.

If you are using the tear-out forms, draw lines through the clause you want to delete and have all parties put their initials next to it. If you are deleting a complete clause, you'll need to renumber the clauses to avoid confusion. For example, if you do not want your lease to include a clause on extended absences of tenants (Clause 16 of Form 22, Fixed-Term Residential Lease), make the modifications as shown below.

3. Adding Clauses or Language

Adding extra terms to a contract is easy if you're using the forms on disk: Simply add the new language or clauses and renumber the remaining clauses as appropriate.

If you are using the tear-out forms, and want to add words to a clause, use the space provided. If we didn't leave enough room, or if you want to add a new clause, you should prepare a separate addendum sheet or attachment. See "How to Prepare an Attachment Page" below for details.

Example of Clause With Several Options (Clause 2 of Home Repairs Agreement)

2. Payment

In exchange for the work specified in Clause 1, Homeowner agrees to pay Contractor as follows *[choose one and check appropriate boxes]:*

☐ $ _____ , payable upon completion of the specified work by ☐ cash ☐ check.

☐ $ _____ , payable by ☐ cash ☐ check as follows:

_____ % payable when the following occurs: _____

_____ % payable when the following occurs: _____

_____ % payable when the following occurs: _____ .

☐ $ _____ per hour for each hour of work performed, up to a maximum of $ _____ ,

payable at the following times and in the following manner: _____

_____ .

Example of How to Delete Clause (Clause 16 of Form 22, Fixed-Term Residential Lease)

~~Clause 16. Extended Absences by Tenant~~

_MS_ ~~Tenant will notify Landlord in advance if Tenant will be away from the premises for _____~~ ~~or more consecutive days. During such absence, Landlord may enter the premises at times reasonably~~ ~~necessary to maintain the property and inspect for needed repairs.~~

Clause ~~17~~ 16. Possession of the Premises

  a. _Tenant's failure to take possession._

  If, after signing this Agreement, Tenant fails to take possession of the premises, Tenant will still be responsible for paying rent and complying with all other terms of this Agreement.

How to Prepare an Attachment Page

If you need to add anything to a tear-out copy of one of the forms or agreements in this book, take the following steps.

1. If you want to add words to a clause, and there is not space to insert the new language into the specific clause of the agreement, you can refer to it as an attachment, by adding the words: "Clause [number] continued on Attachment A [or B or C and so on] of [name agreement or form]"

EXAMPLE: Clause 1 of the General Bill of Sale provides space for you to list the items you're selling. If there is not enough room to list all these items on the tear-out, write the words "Clause 1 Continued on Attachment A of the General Bill of Sale."

Similarly, if you want to add a new clause, insert the words "Agreement Continued on Attachment A of [name agreement or form]" after the last clause of the agreement and before the place where the agreement gets signed.

Use a separate attachment each time you need more room.

2. Make your own Attachment form, using a sheet of blank white $8^1/_2$" by 11" paper. At the top of the form, write "Attachment A [or B or C and so on] to [name agreement or form] between [insert names of all parties]" for the first attachment, and so on. Then add the words "a continuation of [name clause]" if you're continuing a clause, or "an addition to," if you're adding a new clause.

EXAMPLE: "Attachment A to General Bill of Sale between Beth Spencer and Rich Portman. A continuation of Clause 1."

3. Type or print the additional information on the attachment.
4. Have both parties sign or initial the attachment at the bottom of each page.
5. Staple all attachments to the end of the main agreement or form.

C. Describing People, Property and Events

Some forms ask you to name people or describe events or property. Here's the best way to do this.

People. Where you are asked to insert the name, address and other identifying information for a person, use that person's legal name—the name on a driver's license—and home street address. If a person commonly uses two names (not including a nickname), include both, for example, "Alison Johnson aka Alison Walker-Johnson."

Property. To identify property, such as a defective computer you're returning with a Request for Refund or Repair of Goods Under Warranty (Form 88), be as specific as you can. There are no magic words. Your objective is simply to identify the property clearly so that no misunderstanding will arise later. Normally, this means listing the make, model, type, color, identifying number if the item has one and any other identifying characteristics that come to mind. For instance, if you are requesting repair of a computer under warranty, you might say "Power Macintosh 7200, ID # 445556, 80 MB hard disk."

Events. Take a similar approach when describing events, such as payment for a housecleaner (Form 82). As long as you identify the date, time (if appropriate) and location, and include a clear description of what happened or what is supposed to happen, your description should be adequate.

D. Signing the Forms

Each form has specific signing instructions, including who must sign, how many copies to make, whether or not notarization is required or recommended and any requirements for a spouse to sign or for witnesses.

! Always keep your signed copy in a safe place, along with any related documents or correspondence. You may need this at some point—for example, if you end up in court over a dispute concerning an agreement or contract.

1. Notarization

Where we suggest that you have the document notarized, we have written [Notary Seal] at the end of the form. Notarization means that a person authorized as a notary public certifies in writing that:

- You're the person you claim to be, and
- You've acknowledged under oath signing the document.

Very few legal documents need to be notarized or witnessed. Notarization and witnessing are usually limited to documents, such as a power of attorney involving real estate, that are going to be recorded at a public office charged with keeping such records —for example, a county land records office or register of deeds. Occasionally—but very rarely— state laws require witnesses or notaries to sign other types of documents.

If you want to have a form notarized, everyone who has to sign the form must appear together in front of the notary. The notary will want proof of your identity, such as a driver's license that bears your photo and signature. The notary will watch each of you sign and then will complete an acknowledgment, including a notarial seal. Notarization language can vary from state to state, and you will want to use the language required in your state. A sample of typical notarization language (this is included on the power of attorney forms in Chapter 1) is shown below.

You can often find a notary at a bank, lawyer's office, real estate office or title insurance office. Most charge under $20 for notarizing a document.

Notarization is always an option. If there is no mention of notarization in the signing instructions for a form, it is not required or recommended. However, even if we don't suggest you have a form notarized, you may choose to—simply because it adds a measure of legal credibility.

Sample Notarization Language

Certificate of Acknowledgment of Notary Public

State of _____ }
                                              } ss
County of _____ }

On _____, _____, before me, _____,
a notary public in and for said state personally appeared _____,
personally known to me (or proved on the basis of satisfactory evidence) to be the person whose name is
subscribed to the within instrument, and acknowledged to me that he or she executed the same in his or
her authorized capacity and that by his or her signature on the instrument, the person, or the entity upon
behalf of which the person acted, executed the instrument.

WITNESS my hand and official seal.

_____

Notary Public for the State of _____

My commission expires _____

[NOTARY SEAL]

2. Spouse's Signature

If you'll be asked to sign a contract, such as a promissory note, that makes you liable for a debt, the other person may ask that your spouse sign as well. This is most likely to happen, for example, if you're borrowing money to buy property that both spouses will use or to help finance a new business venture. For more details, see the discussion of promissory notes in Chapter 5.

E. Resolving Disputes

Sadly, you may have a legal dispute involving one of the forms or contracts in this book. For example, maybe your partner reneges on an agreement to share property (Form 85) when you split up or you're upset with the treatment of your dog contrary to your pet care agreement (Form 4). One way to resolve a dispute is through a court fight. This is usually a bad way, given that trials are typically expensive, prolonged and emotionally draining. It usually makes far more sense to attempt to resolve disputes through other means, including the following:

Informal negotiation. The parties to the dispute try to voluntarily work out their differences through open discussions. which often result in each compromising a little to put the matter to rest. It may make sense to have a trusted mutual friend informally negotiate an agreement.

Mediation. The parties try to achieve a voluntary settlement with the help of a neutral third party, a mediator. With mediation, the two of you get together to talk face to face about your disagreements, with a neutral mediator working to help you craft your own solution. No one has the power to impose a solution with mediation—rather, you must work out your own agreement voluntarily. Mediation is inexpensive, quick, confidential and effective the majority of the time. Depending on your situation, you may want to contact a community mediation agency that offers mediation, usually by trained community volunteers.

Arbitration. If mediation fails to resolve a dispute, arbitration is the next best choice. With arbitration, the parties allow a neutral third party, an arbitrator, to arrive at a binding decision in order to resolve the dispute. Normally, the decision is solely up to the arbitrator and the parties agree beforehand to abide by his or her decision. In some situations, however, the parties establish certain rules in advance of the arbitration—for example, a limit on the amount of money that can be awarded. Where limits are set by the parties, the arbitrator is bound by them.

Arbitration is almost always speedier and usually much less expensive than litigation.

Ideally, you'd like to be able to settle disputes informally. Unfortunately, however, even when everyone tries in good faith, they don't always reach a compromise. Therefore, a dispute resolution clause (see the one shown below) lets you agree in advance on a framework mandating non-court alternatives such as mediation and arbitration for resolving disputes. This dispute resolution clause is already in several of the forms in this book. If it's not on a particular form, and you want to add it, you can find it the file **DISPUTE.** To add the dispute clause, simply follow the directions in Section B, above, as to adding a clause.

This dispute resolution clause allows the parties to make one of three choices:

Dispute Clause

Disputes

[choose one]

☐ **Litigation.** If a dispute arises, any party may take the matter to court.

☐ **Mediation and Possible Litigation.** If a dispute arises, the parties will try in good faith to settle it through mediation conducted by *[choose one]:*

☐ _____ *[name of mediator].*

☐ a mediator to be mutually selected.

    The parties will share the costs of the mediator equally. If the dispute is not resolved within 30 days after it is referred to the mediator, any party may take the matter to court.

☐ **Mediation and Possible Arbitration.** If a dispute arises, the parties will try in good faith to settle it through mediation conducted by *[choose one]:*

☐ _____ *[name of mediator].*

☐ a mediator to be mutually selected.

    The parties will share the costs of the mediator equally. If the dispute is not resolved within 30 days after it is referred to the mediator, it will be arbitrated by *[choose one]:*

☐ _____ *[name of arbitrator].*

☐ an arbitrator to be mutually selected.

Judgment on the arbitration award may be entered in any court that has jurisdiction over the matter.

Costs of arbitration, including lawyers' fees, will be allocated by the arbitrator.

- **Litigation.** You go to court and let a judge or jury resolve the dispute.
- **Mediation and possible litigation.** You agree to let a mediator help you reach a voluntary settlement of the dispute. If mediation doesn't accomplish this goal, either of you can take the dispute to court. You can name the mediator when you prepare the form or agree on one when the need arises.
- **Mediation and possible arbitration.** You start by submitting the dispute to mediation. If mediation doesn't lead to a settlement, you submit the dispute to arbitration. The arbitrator makes a final decision that will be enforced by a court, if necessary. You can name the arbitrator when you prepare the form or agree on one when the need arises.

 Information on mediation and other methods of resolving disputes, is available online through Nolo's free online Legal Encyclopedia at http://www.nolo.com, under the heading "Lawsuits and Mediation." An excellent source for more thorough information is *How to Mediate Your Dispute,* by Peter Lovenheim. If you do end up fighting a case in court, read *Represent Yourself in Court*, by Bergman and Berman-Barrett. If your case is worth less than a few thousand dollars, you may choose small claims court. In that case, see *Everybody's Guide to Small Claims Court,* by Ralph Warner. All titles are published by Nolo.

F. Do You Need a Lawyer?

Most of the contracts used in this book involve relatively straightforward transactions. Just as you routinely negotiate deals to lend money to a friend or hire someone to paint your kitchen without formal legal help, you can just as safely complete the basic legal paperwork needed to record your understanding.

But like most generalizations, this one isn't always true. Creating a solid written agreement—

especially where a lot of money or property is at stake—will occasionally mean obtaining the advice of a lawyer. Fortunately, even when you seek a lawyer's help, the forms and information included here will let you keep a tight rein on legal fees. You'll have gotten a running start by learning about the legal issues and perhaps drawing up a rough draft of the needed document, allowing you and your lawyer to focus on the few points that may not be routine.

Ideally, you should find a lawyer who comes highly recommended from personal referrals. Look for someone who's willing to answer a few questions, or possibly to review a completed contract draft, but who respects your ability to prepare the routine paperwork. Adopting this approach should keep the lawyer's fee to a minimum. For more advice on finding and working with a lawyer, see the Lawyers and Legal Malpractice section under "Lawsuits and Mediation" in Nolo's online Legal Encyclopedia at http://www.nolo.com.

G. Icons Used in This Book

As you've read this Introduction, you no doubt encountered a few icons, alerting you to specific information. Here's a list of the icons used in this book.

 A practical tip or good idea.

 A warning about a potential problem.

 Resources that give more information about the issue discussed in the text.

 Related topics covered in this book

An alert that notarization of the form is recommended or required. ■

Delegating Authority to Care for Children, Pets and Property

Human beings can be distinguished from the rest of the animal kingdom in one fundamental way: the ability to reason or make decisions. Many of the key decisions adults make affect the care of their children, finances and property. And sometimes, when we know we won't be available to make these decisions, we appoint a person we trust to do so. This chapter includes a temporary guardianship authorization, a power of attorney for finances and several forms you can use to delegate decision-making to others in a few common situations.

When it comes to care of your children, be sure you choose the right person. While it's important to prepare a sound agreement authorizing someone to care for your children when you can't, even the best legal document won't help much if you don't choose a good caretaker. So be sure you pick someone you trust completely to follow your wishes for your child's care.

Form 1: Temporary Guardianship Authorization for Care of Minor

You may find it necessary to leave your child in the care of another adult for a few days, weeks or months. If so, you should give the caretaker permission to authorize medical care for your child and to make other important decisions on his or her behalf. This includes school-related decisions—for example, if your child needs approval to go on a field trip, or your child becomes ill and needs to be picked up from school.

When you complete a temporary guardianship authorization, you are establishing what the law calls an "informal guardianship." By contrast, a formal guardianship requires court approval and is used most often when a child will be in a guardian's care for a long period of time—for example, when a young child moves in with her grandparents because her parents have died. A formal guardianship

permits the guardian to make more extensive decisions for a child, such as taking the child out of one school and registering her at another.

An informal or temporary guardianship is most often used in these two situations:

- You will be traveling or otherwise unavailable for a relatively short period of time—for example, due to a hospital stay—and will leave your child in another adult's care.
- Your child lives with you and a stepparent who has not legally adopted your child. Because you travel frequently, the stepparent commonly functions as the primary caregiver.

If you have more than one child, you should prepare a separate temporary guardianship authorization for each child.

Authorizing medical care. When you make a temporary guardianship authorization, you should also consider making an "Authorization for Minor's Medical Treatment, " discussed just below (Form 2). Although the temporary guardianship form gives the temporary guardian explicit permission to authorize medical examinations, X-rays, hospital care and other necessary treatments, the medical treatment authorization form allows you to spell out your child's medical history and needs in more detail. The two forms work well together. Whichever forms you complete, you should speak with the doctor's office so that they know that the person you name as temporary guardian has your permission to make healthcare decisions for your child.

Signing Instructions

The parent(s) and the temporary guardian must sign the Temporary Guardianship Authorization for Care of Minor document for it to be valid. Print out two copies of the form (or enough for each person who will be signing the form to have their own copy). The parent(s) and the temporary guardian should sign and date all copies of the authorization form. Give one of the signed documents to the temporary guardian. Keep the other signed document for your own records and store it in a safe place.

This form contains a space for the acknowledgment of a notary public. To have a form notarized, you must go to the notary before signing it. (See the Introduction, Section D1, for general advice on having a form notarized.) Notarization will add a measure of legal credibility, but it isn't always necessary. For example, you probably don't need to have your temporary guardianship authorization form notarized if you will be leaving your child with a grandparent for a few days. But if you will be away from your child for a long time—especially if your child stays with a non-relative—it's a good idea to visit a notary. Practically speaking, a notarized form is likely to be more readily accepted by others.

date both. Give one of the signed documents to the person who has permission to authorize medical treatment for your child. Keep the other signed document for your own records and store it in a safe place.

This form contains a space for the acknowledgment of a notary public. To have a form notarized, you must go to the notary before signing it. (See the Introduction, Section D1, for general advice on having a form notarized.) Notarization will add a measure of legal credibility, but it isn't always necessary. Practically speaking, a notarized form is likely to be more readily accepted by others.

Form 2: Authorization for Minor's Medical Treatment

A medical care authorization permits an adult that you name to authorize necessary medical or dental care for your child. This can help you rest easier when your child is participating in sports or other organized activity outside of your supervision. You should provide this authorization to an adult who will be caring for your child when you are away, including babysitters and temporary guardians. This form provides details on your child's doctor, dentist, insurance, allergies, ongoing medical conditions such as diabetes or asthma, as well as information on how to reach you while your child is in another's care.

If your child is participating in a specified activity, such as a basketball league or dance lessons, the sponsoring organization will most likely give you its own medical authorization to fill out. But if the organization doesn't give you a form, you should take the time to complete this one.

Signing Instructions

You (the parent(s)) must sign the Authorization for Minor's Medical Treatment document for it to be valid. Print out two copies of the form and sign and

Form 3: Authorization for Foreign Travel With Minor

Your child might not be permitted to travel outside the United States with someone other than his parent or legal guardian unless that person has documentation showing his legal relationship to your child and his authority to travel with your child. If you are planning such a journey for your child, you should prepare an authorization for foreign travel. This form provides necessary proof that you have given consent for your child to leave the country with another adult. It also provides information about the child's travel plans and contact information for you (the parents).

If you have more than one child who will be traveling outside the country with another adult, you should prepare a separate authorization form for each child.

Before your child departs on his or her travels with another adult, you should check travel rules carefully. Start by calling the embassy or consulate for the foreign country your child will be traveling to. Ask if the country has any rules or regulations governing adults traveling in their country with an unrelated minor. Chances are good that the country does not, but it's always good to ask. If there are special requirements, you and the child's adult traveling companion can prepare for them in advance.

Authorizing medical care. This form does not permit the person traveling with your child to authorize medical care for him or her. To ensure that your child receives any necessary medical treatment while traveling, you should also complete the Authorization for Minor's Medical Treatment (Form 2), discussed just above.

Signing Instructions

You (the parent(s)) must sign the Authorization for Foreign Travel With Minor document for it to be valid. Print out two copies of the form. You and your child's other parent (if any) should sign and date both copies of the document. If you and your child's other parent are divorced or separated, you must still obtain the signature of the second parent before authorizing your child to leave the country with another adult. This will eliminate the possibility that foreign authorities will detain the travelers, suspecting a violation of child custody laws.

Give one of the signed documents to the person who has permission to travel with your child. Keep the other signed document for your own records and store it in a safe place.

Your foreign travel authorization should be notarized. To have a form notarized, you must go to the notary before signing it. (See the Introduction, Section D1, for general advice on having a form notarized.) The acknowledgment of a notary public will give the form a greater degree of legitimacy, especially in the eyes of a foreign government. This could help if problems arise during the trip.

Form 4: Pet Care Agreement

If you're going on a trip or will be otherwise unable to care for your pet for a period of time, you might leave your animal in the care of a neighbor or friend. If you do so, it's a good idea to make a written agreement describing the arrangement and setting out clear instructions for your pet's care. With this form, you can specify your pet's needs (including food, medication, exercise and grooming), veterinarian contact information, special instructions such as vaccination due dates, how you can be reached, how you will reimburse the caregiver for any expenses involved in caring for your pet and more. This will greatly reduce the chances of a misunderstanding that might hurt your pet—or your relationship with the caregiver. And if you do find yourselves involved in a dispute, this agreement contains a provision stating that you and the pet caregiver agree to select a mutually agreeable third party to help you mediate the dispute and that you will share equally any costs of mediation. The Introduction, Section E, describes mediation and other dispute resolution procedures.

Payment for pet food and vet bills. When a friend cares for your pet while you are away, you may think it unnecessary to reimburse him for a few dollars worth of pet food. Think again—you are already asking for a big favor, one that is only likely to be extended again if you are scrupulous about the details. Even if your friend has several animals of his own and ten bags of pet food in his garage, bring along more than enough chow to feed your pet while you will be away, plus some extra cash for unexpected expenses. Also, if your pet is prone to illness or recovering from an illness or injury, arrange for payment of your vet bills in advance, or ask to be billed. Otherwise, leave your credit card number with your vet in case your pet needs care while you are away. Finally, make sure you complete an authorization form for your vet, specifying that your pet is under the care of your friend while you are away and that this friend has the authority to arrange any necessary care decisions. Your vet may have an authorization form for you to fill out, or he may ask you to write a simple letter authorizing the pet caregiver to make any necessary decisions.

Signing Instructions

The pet owner and caregiver must sign the Pet Care Agreement for it to be valid. Print out two copies of the agreement. You should each sign and date both copies. Give the pet caregiver one of the signed documents and keep the other one for your own records.

Form 5: Authorization to Drive a Motor Vehicle

Lending your vehicle to a friend or even a relative isn't always as simple as handing over the keys. If the person who borrows your car is pulled over by the police or is involved in an accident, he or she will want to quickly prove that you agreed to the use of your car. If the borrower can't show that you gave permission, he or she may be detained while police investigate whether the vehicle is stolen. Completing this authorization form provides the important legal proof that you've given someone else permission to drive your vehicle.

This form provides a place to list important information, such as your insurance policy number, that will help ensure that your guest driver (and car) are taken care of in the event of an accident or other mishap. If you want to set any restrictions on when or where the car may be used—for example, limiting driving to a specific geographic area—you can do so.

This motor vehicle authorization form is designed for a car, but it will work fine for a motorcycle, truck or other motor vehicle, such as a motorboat.

Signing Instructions

You (the vehicle owner) must sign your Authorization to Drive a Motor Vehicle form to make it valid. Print out two copies of the authorization document. Sign and date both copies. Give one of the signed originals to the person who will be driving your car or other vehicle. Keep the other for your own records.

Form 6: Power of Attorney for Finances (Full Power)

A power of attorney is a legal document in which you give another person legal authority to act on your behalf. In legal jargon, you're called "the principal," and the person to whom you give this authority is called your "attorney-in-fact." In this context, "attorney" refers to anyone authorized to act on another's behalf; it's most definitely not restricted to lawyers. Most importantly, your attorney-in-fact (including any alternates you choose to name) should be someone you trust completely to act in your best interests—such as a spouse, relative or close friend—who has enough common sense and experience to carry out the task(s) you assign.

You can use Clause 5 of this power of attorney form to give your attorney-in-fact as much or as little authority as you choose. For example, you can give your attorney-in-fact the authority to handle all of your business and financial matters for you while you are out of town or just real estate transactions.

If you want to authorize someone to handle only a single transaction, such as selling your house or car, use the Power of Attorney for Finances (Limited Power) (Form 7), discussed below.

You will notice that Clause 6 of this power of attorney form allows you to fill in "special instructions" for your attorney-in-fact. While the list of powers you can grant in Clause 5 is comprehensive and should cover all of your basic needs, you may want to use Clause 6 to add restrictions or additions to these powers. For example, some people use the special instructions section to forbid the attorney-in-fact from selling their home, to restrict the attorney-in-fact's ability to sell or encumber a small business, to permit the attorney-in-fact to make gifts to others or to require the attorney-in-fact to make periodic financial reports to business associates or relatives. That said, however, you'll want to be judicious in your use of special instructions. If you add too many, you run the risk of making your document confusing. Whatever instructions you do include should be as specific as possible.

⚠ **If you live in the District of Columbia** and you are granting power over your real estate, you should not use this power of attorney form. Your power of attorney must contain special language that is not included here.

This power of attorney form is designed to be used for a pre-established period (see Clause 4)—for example, while you are on vacation. You specify when the attorney-in-fact's authority begins and ends. Don't make a power of attorney that will last for longer than a year. If you want someone to manage your finances for longer than that, you should make a new document periodically so that financial institutions and others won't question the form's validity.

You have the legal right to revoke or terminate your power of attorney at any time. (You can use the Notice of Revocation of Power of Attorney, Form 8, below, for that purpose.) If you become incapacitated while the power of attorney is in effect, your attorney-in-fact's authority automatically ends.

This power of attorney form includes language (Clause 11) designed to reassure third parties that they can accept the document without risk of legal liability. This "indemnification" clause clearly states that a third party may rely on the document without worry—in other words, that he or she may conduct business with your attorney-in-fact as you have instructed—unless the third party knows that you have revoked the document.

💡 **Financial institutions may have their own power of attorney forms.** If you're giving your attorney-in-fact authority to deal with a bank, brokerage firm or other financial institution, find out whether it has its own power of attorney form. If it does, you'll probably want to use that form in addition to this broader power of attorney form. Doing so will reduce hassles for your attorney-in-fact because a financial institution will know what powers its own form grants, and will have no need to quibble with your document.

Conventional Versus Durable Power of Attorney

Forms 6 and 7 are typically referred to as "conventional" power of attorney documents. As you may know, there is another type of power of attorney, called a durable power of attorney, that remains in effect even if you become incapacitated and can no longer make decisions for yourself. These are commonly signed in advance of need by older and ill people who realize that at some point they may require help managing their affairs. Because state laws vary in this area, if you want a durable power of attorney, you will need more extensive information. One excellent resource is *Quicken Lawyer Personal Deluxe* software, which lets you create a valid will, durable power of attorney for finances, healthcare directives and final arrangements document using your computer.

Signing Instructions

A Power of Attorney for Finances is a serious document, and to make it legally valid and effective you must observe certain formalities when you sign it. Specifically, you must have your power of attorney form notarized, and, in some states, you may need to sign your document in front of witnesses. (See "States That Require Witnesses for a Power of Attorney," below.) In a few situations, you may also be required to put a copy of your power of attorney in the public records. (See "Putting Your Power of Attorney on Public Record," below.)

If you live in California, Georgia, Pennsylvania or Wisconsin, your attorney-in-fact must sign the power of attorney before taking action under the document. In all other states, the attorney-in-fact's signature is not required, but it's a fine idea to include it anyway. The attorney-in-fact's signature acts as assurance that the attorney-in-fact has read and fully understands the document, and is willing to assume the responsibility of acting prudently and honestly on your behalf. For this reason this power of attorney form includes a blank for the attorney-in-fact to sign.

When you print your document, you will notice several blank lines at the top, following the words "RECORDING REQUESTED BY AND WHEN RECORDED MAIL TO." If you won't be recording your document, you can ignore these lines completely. If you do need to put your document on file in the public records, you will fill in your name and address when you go to the clerk's office

You must sign your power of attorney in the presence of a notary public for your state. When you sign, you must also fill in the blank lines above your signature that ask for the date and the state and county where you finalize the document. In some states, notarization is required by law to make the power of attorney valid. But even where law doesn't require it, custom does. A power of attorney that isn't notarized may not be accepted by people your attorney-in-fact needs to deal with.

If you will have your form witnessed (see "States That Require Witnesses for a Power of Attorney," below), everyone who has to sign the form must appear together in front of the notary. The notary will watch each of you sign and then he or she will complete an acknowledgment, including a notarial seal.

For more information on finding and using a notary, see the Introduction, Section D1.

Give the original, signed and notarized document to the attorney-in-fact. He or she will need it as proof of authority to act on your behalf. Make a copy for yourself and store it in a safe place. If you wish, you can give copies of your power of attorney to the people your attorney-in-fact will need to deal with—for example, banks or government offices. If your financial power of attorney is already in their records, it may eliminate hassles for your attorney-in-fact later. Be sure to keep a list of everyone to whom you give a copy.

Revoking a power of attorney. If you later revoke your power of attorney, you must notify each institution of the revocation. We include a formal notice of revocation form below (Form 8).

Putting Your Power of Attorney on Public Record

If you will give your attorney-in-fact power to buy, sell or mortgage your real estate (or engage in transactions involving your probate-avoiding living trust that contains real estate), put a copy of the document on file in the land record office of the county where the property is located. This office is called the local County Recorder, Land Registry or Register of Deeds office. The process of filing your document is called "recording" or "registration" in some states. If your document isn't in the public records, your attorney-in-fact won't be able to sell, mortgage or transfer the property. Even if your power of attorney doesn't grant power over real estate, you can go ahead and record it. Officials in some financial institutions may be reassured by seeing that you took the extra step to formalize your document.

Recording a document is usually easy. You may even be able to do it by mail, but it's safer to go in person. For a small fee, the clerk will usually assign a reference number to your power of attorney and make a copy for the public record. In a few counties, however, you are required to file an original document with the land records office. In this case, you'll need to make a second original power of attorney, being sure to sign and finalize it in the exact same manner as the first. To save yourself some effort, you may want to call the land records office before you make your document and find out whether you'll need to prepare a second original document for filing. If so, you can do them both at the same time.

Form 7: Power of Attorney for Finances (Limited Power)

A limited power of attorney for finances lets you appoint someone (called your "attorney-in-fact") to help you with one or more clearly defined tasks involving your finances or property. For example,

States That Require Witnesses for a Power of Attorney

Most states don't require a power of attorney to be signed in front of witnesses. The few states that do and the number of witnesses required are listed below. Witness requirements normally consist of the following:

- Witnesses must be present when you sign the document in front of the notary.

- Witnesses must be mentally competent adults.
- The person who will serve as your attorney-in-fact can't be a witness.

Choose witnesses who will be easily available if they are ever needed. It's obviously a good idea to choose witnesses who live nearby and will be easy to contact.

State	Number of Witnesses	Other Requirements	State	Number of Witnesses	Other Requirements
Arizona	1	Witness may not be your attorney-in-fact, the spouse or child of your attorney-in-fact or the notary public who acknowledges your document.	**Michigan**	2	Witnesses are necessary only if your power of attorney is to be recorded. Neither witness may be your attorney-in-fact.
Arkansas	2	Neither witness may be your attorney-in-fact.	**Ohio**	2	Neither witness may be your attorney-in-fact.
Connecticut	2	Neither witness may be your attorney-in-fact.	**Oklahoma**	2	Witnesses may not be your attorney-in-fact, or anyone who is related by blood or marriage to you or your attorney-in-fact.
District of Columbia	2	Witnesses are necessary only if your power of attorney is to be recorded. Neither witness may be your attorney-in-fact.	**Pennsylvania**	2	Neither witness may be your attorney-in-fact.
Florida	2	Neither witness may be your attorney-in-fact.	**South Carolina**	2	Neither witness may be your attorney-in-fact.
Georgia	2	Neither witness may be your attorney-in-fact. In addition, one of your witnesses may not be your spouse or blood relative.	**Vermont**	2	Witnesses are necessary only if your power of attorney is to be recorded. Neither witness may be your attorney-in-fact.
Illinois	1	Witness may not be your attorney-in-fact.	**Wisconsin**	2	Witnesses may not be your attorney-in-fact, anyone who is related to you by blood or marriage or anyone entitled to inherit a portion of your estate under your will.

you may want to name a relative or close friend to monitor certain investments while you are on vacation or in the hospital for a short stay—and sell them, if necessary. Or you may need someone to sign business or legal papers for you while you are unavailable. If your needs really are definable in this way, it makes good sense to use the restricted document, Form 7, rather than the broader power of attorney set out in Form 6. Even though the longer document is just as legal, it's not wise to clutter your power of attorney with a lot of unnecessary language or to give your attorney-in-fact unnecessary powers.

To create your limited power of attorney, you'll enter some basic information about you (the "principal") and your attorney-in-fact, followed by the exact powers you want to grant—such as selling your car, signing loan papers while you're out of town or monitoring your investments. Be as specific as possible—for example, if you want someone to sell your car for a minimum of $15,000 cash only, spell this out. Include relevant bank account numbers and complete descriptions of any property the attorney-in-fact may deal with.

After you print the form, you will see the information and instructions you specified, plus language designed to reassure third parties that they can accept the document without risk of legal liability. This "indemnification" clause clearly states that a third party may rely on the document without worry—in other words, that he or she may conduct business with your attorney-in-fact as you have instructed—unless the third party knows that you have revoked the document.

⚠ **This is not a durable power of attorney for finances.** A durable power of attorney form gives your attorney-in-fact broad authority to handle your finances if you become incapacitated and unable to handle your own affairs. This limited power of attorney is the form to use when you want someone to handle a single transaction for you at a set time. For more details, see "Conventional Versus Durable Power of Attorney," above.

Signing Instructions

A Power of Attorney for Finances is a serious document, and to make it effective, you must observe certain formalities when you sign it. To make your document legally valid, follow the instructions that accompany Form 6. They explain the requirements for notarizing your document and, if necessary, having it witnessed.

⚠ **Record your power of attorney if real estate is involved.** As discussed above (Form 6), if your attorney-in-fact will have the power to buy, sell or encumber your real estate, you must record the document at the County Recorder's, Land Registry or Register of Deeds office in the county in which the real estate is located.

Form 8: Notice of Revocation of Power of Attorney

You can use a Notice of Revocation of Power of Attorney form in two situations:

- You want to revoke your power of attorney prior to the termination date set out in the document.
- Your power of attorney has ended as specified in the document, but you want to be absolutely sure that all institutions (such as banks, stockbrokers and insurance companies) and people (such as your attorney or accountant) who have received it know that it is no longer in force.

Signing Instructions

Sign and date the Notice of Revocation in front of a notary public for your state as explained in the discussion of Form 6, Power of Attorney for Finances (Full Power).

If you recorded your Power of Attorney, record the Notice of Revocation. If you put your power of attorney on file in the public records office and it hasn't expired on its own, you should also record your Notice of Revocation. Otherwise, people who don't actually know of your revocation are entitled to continue to deal with your attorney-in-fact on your behalf. ■

CHAPTER

2

Basic Estate Planning

Making plans for what will happen to your property after you die is called estate planning. Generally, if you die without a will or other legal means for transferring property, your property will be distributed to certain close relatives—your spouse, children, parents and siblings—under state "intestacy" laws.

Making a will is an important estate planning step. For many people, coupled with naming beneficiaries for retirement plans, insurance policies and other investments, a will is the only estate plan they need. Whether or not that is true for you depends on your circumstances. Generally speaking, the more wealth you possess, the more you'll want to consider legal issues beyond the scope of a will, such as avoiding probate—the court-supervised process of gathering and distributing a deceased person's assets—and reducing death taxes. And, depending on your situation, you may want to provide for a disabled child, establish a fund for grandchildren or make charitable gifts.

This chapter introduces the concept of estate planning and provides some useful worksheets and some bare-bones will forms. Resources listed in the chapter explain where to go for more extensive information.

at your death. For example, if you have a retirement account (such as an IRA or 401(k)) or insurance policy, you have probably named a beneficiary and alternate beneficiary. If you own real estate, you may hold it in joint tenancy with right of survivorship, meaning that the other joint owner will automatically inherit your share at your death. If you've already named someone to take an asset after your death, write down the beneficiary's name on the Property Worksheet under "Name of Any Existing Beneficiary."

Signing Instructions

There are no signing instructions for the Property Worksheet. Simply fill it out and use it when preparing your will or other estate planning document.

Nolo publishes *Personal RecordKeeper*, a comprehensive software program designed to keep track of all your property (investments, memorabilia), key addresses (friends, business contacts) and the location of important items (safe deposit box key, family pictures, old tax returns). It can both help to organize your life and provide a roadmap to the final arrangements you have made for after your death.

Form 9: Property Worksheet

Before you write a will or other estate planning document, you may find it helpful to make an inventory of your property, including real estate, cash, securities, cars, personal property such as household goods and business personal property, such as a company you own or the right to receive royalties. Filling out the Property Worksheet can jog your memory to make sure you don't overlook important items.

Describe each asset on the Property Worksheet under the appropriate section of the "Property" column. If an asset, such as a house or car, is jointly owned, specify the percentage you own.

Even if you haven't made a will, you may have already named someone to get some of your property

Form 10: Beneficiary Worksheet

Like the Property Worksheet, the Beneficiary Worksheet is a tool that can help you get ready to draft your estate planning documents. On the Beneficiary Worksheet, list each item of property you want to leave as a distinct gift. Then list the beneficiary or beneficiaries you want to get each item. If you name more than one beneficiary to share a specific gift, state the percentage share each is to receive. It is also highly advisable to name an alternate beneficiary or beneficiaries for each gift, in case your first choice dies before you do. If you've already named a beneficiary for some of your property, be sure to check the box in the margin on the Beneficiary Worksheet next to the particular item. (See

"Common Property That May Already Have Beneficiaries.")

In addition to naming beneficiaries, list all debts you want to forgive at your death. For example, if you loaned your best friend $10,000 and he pays you back with interest $100 a month, it will take him many years to pay off the debt. If he still owes you money when you die, you can forgive or waive the balance due. This means that your heirs cannot go after your friend for the rest.

Finally, list a "residuary" beneficiary or beneficiaries. This is one or more people or organizations who will get everything you don't leave to a specific beneficiary. Do this even if you are sure you have identified all your property and named a beneficiary to receive it; there is always a chance that between the date you make your will and your death, you'll acquire additional property.

Common Property That May Already Have Beneficiaries

As noted in the discussion for the Property Worksheet, you may have already planned the eventual disposition of much of your property before you prepare a will. Here are some examples of property for which you may have already named a beneficiary:

- bank accounts, naming (on a form provided by the bank) a payable-on-death beneficiary
- real estate, holding it with someone else in joint tenancy, in tenancy by the entirety or (in community property states) as community property with your spouse
- securities, registering them in transfer-on-death form if your state law allows it
- retirement accounts, naming a beneficiary (on a form provided by the account custodian) to take whatever is still in the account at your death, and
- life insurance policies, naming a beneficiary (on a form provided by the company) to receive the proceeds at your death.

Do you need to use the Beneficiary Worksheet? If you plan to leave all your property to one or a very few people (for example, "all property to my spouse, or if she predeceases me, to my children in equal shares"), there is no need to complete the Beneficiary Worksheet. You already know who will get your property at your death, and you can turn to the will forms that follow.

Signing Instructions

There are no signing instructions for the Beneficiary Worksheet. Simply fill it out and use it when preparing your will or other estate planning document.

Forms 11 and 12: Bare-Bones Wills

A simple or "bare-bones" will:

- is easy to make
- lets you leave your property to anyone you wish, and
- is easy to change or revoke; you're not stuck with it if you change your mind later.

Anyone who is 18 or older (19 if you live in Wyoming) and of sound mind can make a valid will. (The legal term for someone who makes a will is "testator.") You have to be very far gone before your will can be invalidated on the grounds that you were mentally incompetent. Or put another way, if you're reading and understanding this book, your mind is sound enough.

In addition to designating who will receive your property, your will is also where you appoint the person you want to supervise its distribution after your death (your executor). And if you have minor children, a principal purpose of your will may be to name a guardian for them—someone to raise your children in the event you die and the other parent isn't available to raise the children.

This chapter contains two bare-bones forms, which can be used by residents of all states except Louisiana. These wills are a good choice if you suddenly want a will on the eve of a long trip or don't want to spend much time on estate planning right now.

Unless you have a very simple estate plan for leaving your property, however, you'll probably want to draft a more extensive will for the long term. Precisely because these bare-bones forms are short, simple and easy to use, they do not include a lot of options. For example, they do not let you create a trust to hold property that may be left to children or young adults.

If you have children, use Form 12, the Will for Adult With Child(ren). Otherwise, use Form 11, the Will for Adult With No Child(ren).

⚠ **Do not just fill in and sign your tear-out will. You must retype it.** Unlike the forms in the rest of this book, will forms cannot just be torn out, filled in and signed. To prepare a legally valid will, you must use the disk that comes with this book (or a typewriter if you don't have access to a computer) to print out a fresh will which eliminates all the clauses you don't need. Then sign this will in front of witnesses following the instructions below. If you simply fill in the blanks and sign it, your will may not be valid.

Nolo Resources on Estate Planning

Nolo publishes several books and software products containing more sophisticated—but still easy-to-use—information on wills and living trusts. A living trust is the document used most often to avoid probate, the process of distributing a person's property under court supervision.

- *Plan Your Estate,* by Denis Clifford and Cora Jordan, is a comprehensive estate planning book, covering everything from basic estate planning (wills and living trusts) to sophisticated tax-saving strategies (AB trusts and much more). If you haven't yet decided how to approach your estate planning tasks, this is Nolo's best resource.

- *Quicken Lawyer Personal Deluxe* interactive software lets you make a more sophisticated will than the ones contained here. For example, with *Quicken Lawyer Personal Deluxe* you can choose among three ways to provide property management for children should you die before they are competent to handle property themselves. In addition, *Quicken Lawyer Personal Deluxe* allows you to express your last wishes for your funeral and burial and contains both a healthcare directive (living will) and durable

power of attorney for finances valid in your state.

- *Living TrustMaker* software lets you create a revocable living trust to avoid probate. The program creates an individual trust or a trust for a married couple. Especially if you haven't taken advantage of other probate-avoidance techniques, a living trust may offer a safe and efficient way to save your survivors many thousands of dollars.

- *Nolo's Will Book,* by Denis Clifford, provides step-by-step instructions and forms to create a detailed will. Its will is similar in scope and sophistication to *Quicken Lawyer Personal Deluxe.* The book comes with a disk, which you can use with any standard word processing program to make drafting and printing out the will easy.

- *8 Ways to Avoid Probate,* by Mary Randolph, explains important and often overlooked ways to avoid probate. It is now possible to avoid probate for many kinds of property without creating a living trust. If you vaguely know you should be paying attention to probate avoidance, but dread thinking about it, start with this small but thorough book.

Leaving property. Use "Specific Gifts," (Clause 3 on Form 11, Clause 4 on Form 12 of the will), to leave specific items of property. When you list the items in your will, describe them so that your executor—and anyone else—will know exactly what you meant. There is no need to use formal legal descriptions unless they are really necessary to identify the property. Here are some examples of good property descriptions:

- "my house at 435 76th Avenue, Chicago, Illinois"
- "all household furnishings and possessions in my house at 435 76th Avenue, Chicago, Illinois"
- "$10,000 from my savings account, No. 44444, at First National Bank, Chicago, Illinois."

When you leave property, any encumbrances on it—for example, a mortgage—pass with the property. In other words, the beneficiary takes the debt as well as the property.

If you want to leave everything to just one beneficiary, or a group of them—your spouse or your three children, for example—leave the "Specific Gifts" part of the will blank. Instead, use "Residuary Estate" (Clause 4 of Form 11, Clause 5 of Form 12). Since "residuary" simply refers to the rest of your estate and you have made no gifts, it's easy to see that everything will go to the person or persons you name as your residuary beneficiary(ies). Similarly, if you wish to leave a few small specific gifts (for example, family memorabilia or $10,000) to named individuals, with everything else going to one or several persons (for example, to be divided among your three children), use Clause 3 (Form 11) or Clause 4 (Form 12) to make your specific gifts and the Residuary Estate clause to leave everything else to your children.

Naming your executor. In your will, you must name the person you want to be in charge of winding up your affairs after your death. This person is called your executor (the term "personal representative" is used in some states). The executor must shepherd your property through probate, the court process of distributing the property of a deceased person, if it's necessary, and must see that your property is distributed according to the wishes expressed in your will.

Many people name their spouse or a grown child as executor. The executor usually doesn't need special financial or legal expertise. The important thing is that the person you choose is completely trustworthy and will deal fairly with other beneficiaries.

Signing Instructions

Your signature on your will must be witnessed. When you are ready to sign it, gather together three adults who aren't beneficiaries of your will. Your witnesses do not need to read your will. You simply state, "This is my will." The witnesses (in unison or individually) respond, "She says it's her will." Then you sign and date your will while the witnesses watch. Finally, each witness signs while the other witnesses watch. Be sure to store your will in a safe place.

⚠ **If you're married, your spouse may be able to claim a share of your estate.** In most states (all except Arizona, California, Idaho, Louisiana, Nevada, New Mexico, Texas, Washington and Wisconsin—which follow the community property system), a surviving spouse has the right to reject what he or she might take through a will and instead claim a share of the deceased spouse's entire estate. In most states, that share is from one-third to one-half of the estate. The details get tricky fast. The point is, if you plan to leave your spouse at least half of your property, you don't need to worry about it. But if you don't, see a lawyer and don't try to use the forms in this book.

Form 11: Will for Adult With No Child(ren)

This is the will to use if you don't have children. Use Form 12 if you do. Remember, these forms can be used by residents of all states except Louisiana.

Read the introduction to Bare-Bones Wills (above) for brief but important instructions on filling out the form correctly, so that you will create a legally valid will that accomplishes what you want.

Form 12: Will for Adult With Child(ren)

If you have children, you have some special issues to consider before you make your will.

Heading off claims. You should mention each of your children in your will, even if you don't leave them any property through the will. That's because, although children are not usually entitled to claim any property from a parent's estate, they do have certain rights if it appears that they were unintentionally overlooked. By listing all of your offspring, you head off any argument that you accidentally forgot any of them.

Custody of minor children. If you have minor children, use your will (Clause 8) to name the person you want to raise the children if you die and the other parent is unavailable to raise them. This person is called their "personal guardian." It is also wise to nominate an alternate personal guardian, in case the first choice can't serve.

If you and the other legal parent die (or are otherwise out of the parenting picture) before your kids reach 18, meaning a guardian must be appointed, a judge will review your choice. If no one objects, the person you name will be routinely appointed. But in an unusual situation, a judge who is convinced that naming a different personal guardian is in the best interests of the child has the authority to do so.

⚠ **With this will form, you cannot name different guardians for different kids.** The bare-bones will form in this book requires that you name the same personal guardian for all of your minor children. If for some reason you want to name a different person as guardian for different children, use *Nolo's Will Book* or *the Quicken Lawyer Personal Deluxe* software program.

Property left to children. Minors cannot legally own property outright, free of supervision, beyond a minimal amount—up to about $3,000 in most states. By law, an adult must be legally responsible for managing any significant amount of property owned by a minor child. So if your children might eventually take property through your will—even if they're only alternate beneficiaries—you should arrange for an adult to supervise any property they might own. You can do this easily in your will.

Form 12 gives you a choice of two methods to provide for adult supervision for gifts to your children:

- **Name a custodian for each child.** The custodian will manage any property slated for the child until the child turns 21 (in most states). A custodian is authorized under your state's Uniform Transfers to Minors Act (UTMA). (See Clause 10 of the will.)

- **Name a property guardian.** You should always name a property guardian and successor property guardian in your will, even if you appoint a custodian under the Uniform Transfers to Minors Act. The property guardian will be formally appointed by a court and will manage any property not left through your will (and so not covered by the UTMA custodianship)—for example, property the minor gets from someone else.

Uniform Transfers to Minors Act. All states except South Carolina and Vermont have adopted the Uniform Transfers to Minors Act (UTMA). This law authorizes you to appoint an adult custodian and successor custodian in your will to supervise property you leave to a minor. The custodianship ends, and any remaining property must be turned over to the child outright, at the age the UTMA specifies. In most states, this is either 18 or 21, but a few, including California and Alaska, allow you to choose age 25. Our form sets the ending age at the oldest age allowed in your state, which in the majority is 21.

Because the custodian has almost complete discretion over management of the property, it is essential that you name someone who is both totally honest and has good financial management skills. The custodian also has a legal duty to act prudently, and always in the best interests of the child. Normally, no court supervision is required.

You can name UTMA custodians for as many children as you wish. In addition, you can name different custodians for different children. When preparing your will, you'll first list all gifts you leave, including gifts to your minor or young adult children. Then you'll complete a separate UTMA clause for each child.

Other Property Management Options

The Will for Adult With Child(ren) does not offer two other fairly common—but legally more complicated—ways to arrange for a minor's property to be managed by an adult:

- A family pot trust that will hold property left to all your minor children, allowing the trustee you name to spend it as needed. For example, if one child had an expensive medical problem, the trustee could spend more for that child and less for others.
- A trust for each child. This option is primarily of value for people with larger estates who do not want adult children to take control of money outright until they are in their middle or late twenties. It gets around the fact that in most states a custodianship under the terms of the Uniform Transfers to Minors Act ends at age 21.

These options are available in *Quicken Lawyer Personal Deluxe* software and in *Nolo's Will Book*.

Form 13: Will Codicil

A codicil is sort of a legal "P.S." to a will. In a codicil, you can revoke a clause in your will and then substitute a new clause. Or you can simply add a new provision, such as a new gift of an item of property.

A codicil must be executed with all of the formalities of a will. It must be typed or computer-printed (start with "First Codicil to the Will of _____," leaving off our title), then dated and signed by you in front of three witnesses. You don't have to use the same witnesses who signed your will, but none of the witnesses should be people named as a beneficiary in your will or codicil.

Today codicils are less commonly used than they were in the days when wills were laboriously copied by hand or typed on a typewriter. With almost universal access to computers, it's usually easier—and less likely to confuse—to prepare a whole new will. Nevertheless, codicils can still be sensibly used to make limited changes to a will—for example, when you want to change who receives one item. ■

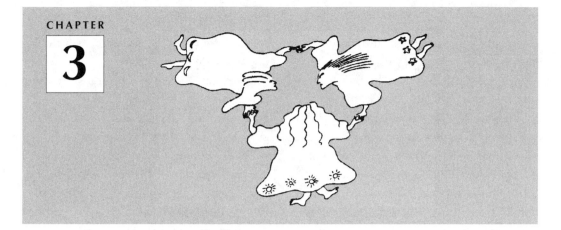

CHAPTER

3

Things to Do After Death: Documents for Executors

After a death, someone must step in and wind up the deceased person's affairs. An executor—also called personal representative or administrator—is the person named in the will, or appointed by the court, who has legal responsibility for safeguarding and handling the deceased person's property, seeing that debts and taxes are paid and distributing what is left to beneficiaries as directed by the will. This chapter contains a number of simple forms and letters you can use if you are named as someone's executor, including forms to notify the deceased's creditor and the Social Security Administration of the death.

How to Probate an Estate, by Julia Nissley (Nolo), gives California residents step-by-step instructions for handing an estate after someone has died. Also *Quicken Lawyer Personal Deluxe* software has several documents for executors as well as a full range of estate planning documents.

These forms are not applicable in all situations. The forms in this chapter cannot be used to claim benefits under an insurance policy or retirement plan. You will need to contact the appropriate companies to complete their forms in order to request benefits.

Form 14: Request for Death Certificate

As the executor or personal representative of the estate of someone who has died, you will need to handle many tasks, such as terminating leases and credit cards, notifying banks, the post office and so forth. No matter what your specific duties, if you will be contacting agencies, businesses or organizations about the death, you will need certified copies of the death certificate. You can ask the mortuary you deal with to obtain copies of a death certificate (and add the cost to the bill). Otherwise, you can use this form to request the forms yourself.

Where to send the request for death certificate form. Before you send in a request, call the local vital statistics office or county health department in the county where the decedent died and ask where

to send your request and the cost of obtaining a copy of a death certificate.

If several weeks have passed since the death, you can also obtain copies by writing to your state's vital statistics office. To find out where to write in your state and how much the copies cost (about $5 to $15 each, depending on the state), go to the website of the National Center for Health Certificates at http://www.cdc.gov/nchs and click on the link "How to Obtain Birth, Marriage and Death Certificates."

Information to include in your request. You will need the name of the deceased and place of death. The deceased person's place of birth and Social Security number are optional, but they can be very helpful for identification purposes. Be sure to indicate your relationship to the deceased person whose death certificate you are requesting, such as a spouse. Some states restrict access to death records to those who are related to the deceased, or to people who have a legal role in the deceased's affairs, such as the executor. Check with your state's vital records office to find out what restrictions they might have.

Reason for the request. Most states now require you to include the reason why you are requesting the death certificate. This form tells the vital records office that you need the death certificate in order to wind up the affairs of the deceased's estate. Be sure to indicate the number of copies you want. Most people need to order at least ten copies to handle all their responsibilities as executor.

Check state rules on providing death certificates. Many vital records offices restrict the purposes for which they will release records. If you are requesting the death certificate for any reason other than taking care of a deceased's estate—for example, genealogical research—do not use this form. Also, many states are changing their laws about releasing death certificates and other vital records, and they are sometimes adding special requirements (for example, several states now require that the person requesting the death certificate send in a photocopy of his or her driver's license or other photo identification with the request). Before you mail in your request, it is important to check with your state's office of vital statistics about any special requirements you must follow.

Signing Instructions

Sign and date your Request for Death Certificate. Mail it to the appropriate agency, along with a check for the amount you specified in your request and a stamped self-addressed envelope (use a business-sized envelope). Keep a copy of the form for your records.

Form 15: Notice to Creditor of Death

After someone dies, their estate representative needs to notify creditors of the death and close the deceased person's credit accounts. That's the purpose of this form. You can send this notice to credit card issuers, department stores, banks, mortgage companies and other businesses from which the deceased bought on credit or had an account (such as a local pharmacy or furniture store).

You will need to provide the deceased's date of death and the appropriate account number on this notice. You may also need to attach a document showing your appointment as exector or administrator.

If a formal probate court proceeding is conducted, you'll also probably have to follow special rules for notifying creditors—such as publishing a notice to creditors in a local newspaper. Check with the lawyer who is handling the probate proceedings, or, if you are handling probate on your own, ask the probate clerk at the county courthouse for the rules.

Signing Instructions

As estate representative, you should sign this Notice to Creditor of Death and mail one to each of the deceased's creditors. The creditor who receives this notice should sign and date it—and mail a copy to you in the stamped, self-addressed envelope you enclose. Keep the completed copy you receive for your records. You may later need it as proof that you properly notified the creditor of the death.

Reconcile the deceased person's records. This notice asks the creditor to forward information to you about any remaining balance owed by the deceased. Once you hear back from the creditor, check the information sent by the creditor against the deceased person's records.

Form 16: Notice to Stop Social Security Payments After a Death

If a deceased person was receiving Social Security benefits, the executor or personal representative must notify the Social Security Administration (SSA) of the death and return checks issued for the month of death and thereafter. Complete this form to provide the Social Security Administration with the required "stop payment" notice. If you don't know the street address of the SSA office from which the Social Security checks originated, call the SSA helpline at 800-772-1213, or check their website at http://www.ssa.gov/regions.

Along with this notice, take the check in person or mail it your local SSA office and get a receipt. If the Social Security checks were being deposited directly into the decedent's bank account, you should notify the bank by telephone to return the funds to Social Security, in addition to notifying Social Security of the death.

Signing Instructions

As estate representative, you should sign and date this Notice to Stop Social Security Payments and mail it to the appropriate Social Security office, along with any returned checks. The Social Security agent who receives the notice should sign and date it— and mail a copy to you in the stamped, self-addressed envelope you enclose. If you hand-deliver the notice and check, you should get a copy at that point. Keep the completed copy you receive from the Social Security Administration. You may later need it as proof that you properly notified the agency of the death.

Form 17: General Notice of Death

If you are named in a will or appointed by the court to handle the estate of someone who has died, you may want to notify businesses and organizations that aren't creditors—that is, they aren't owed any money—of the death. For example, you might want to send a simple notice communicating the fact that someone has died to charities to which the deceased person has donated regularly, magazine publishers and mail-order businesses that frequently send catalogs.

If you want to get the deceased's name deleted from junk mail lists, use Form 74, Notice to Remove Name from List.

It's easier to send a form than to write individual letters to each organization or business. You can also send this form to individuals who need to be notified of the death—unless they are friends or relatives who merit a personal call or note from someone who was close to the deceased.

Do not use this general notice of death form for creditors and government agencies. Many need specific information about the deceased, such as the accounts owing or type of benefits received. For example, if the deceased person was receiving Social Security benefits, you must notify the agency of the death—and return any unused benefit checks. (You can use Form 16 for this purpose.)

Signing Instructions

Sign and date your General Notice of Death and mail it to the business or organization you wish to notify of someone's death. Keep a copy of the notice for your records. If you are sending many copies, you may simply want to keep a record of everyone on your mailing list, rather than copies of every notice sent.

Form 18: Notice to Deceased's Homeowner's Insurance Company

Use this form if the deceased person owned a home that he or she insured. The form notifies the insurance company of the death and asks that you, the estate representative, be added as a "named insured" to the homeowners' insurance policy.

If you are both a co-owner of the home and the executor of the deceased person's estate, do not use this form. Instead, call the insurance company and tell them that the decedent has died.

As the executor for someone who owned (or co-owned) and insured a home, you will want to be added as a named insured to that policy as soon as possible. This status will give you all the protections and rights that the deceased person had under the policy. This means that you will be covered if you or anyone is injured on the premises due to your carelessness. And you will be able to make claims for property damage, if necessary. As a named insured, you also have the right to increase coverage or change policy limitations. For example, if you discover that the home and its contents are underinsured, you can make changes in the coverage. Finally, if the insurance company makes a payment after a claim has been made under the policy—for example, paying for the results of a wind-damaged roof—you will be a co-payee on the check. This is important because these payments are part of the estate and you will need to receive and account for them.

After you are added as a named insured, you'll want to discuss with the insurance agent or broker how best to continue insurance coverage for the deceased's home. You may want to add coverage or increase coverage limits, particularly if you discover that the home was underinsured. You may also want to add riders for jewelry or other special items.

To complete this form, you will need the following information:

- The deceased person's full name and Social Security number. If the deceased's name is different on the insurance policy, be sure to note that.
- The deceased's date of death. (If you don't know the date of death, look on the death certificate.)
- The name of the insurance company that issued the policy and the complete address of their home office.
- The homeowners' policy number.
- A certified copy of the deceased person's death certificate (see Form 14 to request a death certificate).

Signing Instructions

Sign and date the Notice to Deceased's Homeowner's Insurance Company. Make two photocopies of the signed notice. Mail the original and one copy to the insurance company office, along with a stamped, self-addressed envelope and a certified copy of the deceased person's death certificate. Keep the second copy of the notice for your records.

Form 19: Notice to Deceased's Vehicle Insurance Company

Use this form if the deceased person owned and insured one or more automobiles, trucks, motorcycles, motor homes or trailers. The notice informs the insurance company of the death of the insured person and asks them to add you, the executor, to the insurance policy.

As the executor for someone who owned (or co-owned) an insured vehicle, you will want to be added as a "named insured" to that policy as soon as possible. This status will give you all the protections and rights that the deceased person had under the policy. Most important, you will be permitted to add or delete coverage or adjust policy limits, if appropriate. Also, you will be named as a co-payee (along with others insured under the policy) in any

payment from the company. Since these payments are part of the estate, you'll want to receive and account for them.

Many people own more than one vehicle. Each one will be insured under a separate policy. Even if the deceased person used the same company for multiple policies, you should send a separate notice for each policy.

After you are added as a named insured, you'll want to discuss with the insurance agent or broker how best to continue insurance coverage for the deceased's vehicles. You may want to add coverage or increase coverage limits; and if the deceased was rated a poor risk, you may even want to ask for a reduction in premiums.

Even if you do not expect that the vehicle will be used, you must insure it in case of a fire or other calamity. A parked car in a home garage, for example, will not be covered by the homeowner's policy if there is a fire—you need an auto policy or other insurance coverage. When the vehicle is distributed or sold and is no longer part of the estate, you can easily cancel the insurance you have purchased.

To complete this form, you will need the following information:

- The deceased person's full name and Social Security number. If the deceased's name is different on the insurance policy, be sure to note that.
- The deceased's date of death. (If you don't know the date of death, look on the death certificate.)
- Vehicle year, make and model.
- The name of the insurance company that issued the policy and the complete address of their home office.
- The vehicle insurance policy number.
- The latest billing statement from the insurance company.
- A certified death certificate for the person who has died (see Form 14 to request a death certificate), and
- A certified copy of your driving record (available from your state's department of motor vehicles).

Document your role as executor. When the insurance company contacts you, they may require proof of your status as the executor. Be prepared to send them a copy of the court order that names you as the executor. If you do not have a court order by the time the insurance company calls you, ask them what other proof they will accept.

Signing Instructions

Sign and date the Notice to Deceased's Vehicle Insurance Company. Make two photocopies of the signed notice. Mail the original and one copy to the insurance company office, along with a stamped, self-addressed envelope. Remember to enclose a certified copy of the deceased person's death certificate and a state-certified copy of your driving record. Keep the second copy of the notice for your records. ■

CHAPTER

4

Renting Residential Real Estate

Whether you rent (or own) property, you probably understand just how bad a failed landlord-tenant relationship can be. But there is an excellent way to get any land-lord-tenant relationship off to a good start and mini-mize the possibility of future misunderstandings and legal problems: Put all agreements and concerns in writing. This chapter includes a lease and the prin-cipal forms you'll need to do this, plus a few forms that will be helpful at move-out time. Most of these forms are geared toward tenants, although we indicate when conscientious landlords will also find them useful.

To learn the details of landlord-tenant law, see the following Nolo books and software:

From the landlord's point of view:

- *Every Landlord's Legal Guide*, by Marcia Stewart, Ralph Warner and Janet Portman. This 50-state book provides extensive legal and practical infor-mation on leases, tenant screening, rent, security deposits, privacy, repairs, property managers, discrimination, roommates, liability, tenancy termination and much more. It includes more than 25 legal forms and agreements as tear-outs and on disk.
- *LeaseWriter* (CD-ROM for Windows/Macintosh). This full stand-alone software program generates a customized legal residential lease or rental agreement, plus more than a dozen key documents and forms every landlord or property manager needs. It includes instant access to state-specific landlord-tenant information and extensive online legal help.

From the tenant's point of view:

- *Every Tenant's Legal Guide*, by Janet Portman and Marcia Stewart. This book gives tenants in all 50 states the legal and practical information they need to deal with their landlords and protect their rights when things go wrong. It covers all impor-tant issues of renting, including signing a lease, getting a landlord to make needed repairs, fighting illegal discrimination, protecting privacy rights, dealing with roommates, getting the security deposit returned fairly, moving out and much more.

Form 20: Apartment-Finding Service Checklist

Many landlords list their rental property with a homefinders' service that provides a centralized list-ing of rental units for a particular geographic area. Using one of these services can be an efficient way for a tenant to search for a place to live, especially in metropolitan areas. Prices of apartment-finding services vary, but typically tenants pay a flat fee, such as $50 to $100 for a one-month membership. In some tight rental markets, you may also have to pay the service a percentage of your monthly rent if you find an apartment through them. Check newspaper ads or look in the Yellow Pages under "Apartment-Finding and Rental Services." Many of the larger agencies have online sites.

Do a little investigating. Many homefinding services do a good job of helping people to find a place to rent, but some are sloppy and a few are actually crooked. Unscrupulous companies have been caught selling either outdated rental lists—most or all of the apartments have already been rented—or lists no different from what is in a newspaper. So before you sign up with an apartment-finding service, check with the Better Business Bureau and local consumer organi-zations to be sure the service is reputable and worth the money. Also, especially in urban areas, pay close attention to the geographical scope of any service you are considering. Some may be excellent in one area but not others.

Form 20, the Apartment-Finding Service Check-list, offers you a good way to organize and collect the information you need before pulling out your checkbook and signing up with a service. Use it to jot down the type, number and locations of listings typically available, membership costs and additional services such as roommate referrals

Signing Instructions

There are no signing instructions for the Apartment-Finding Service Checklist. Simply fill one out each time you start collecting information on a different homefinding service. Keep a copy in your file.

Form 21: Rental Application

Landlords routinely use rental applications to screen potential tenants and select those who are likely to pay the rent on time, keep the unit in good condition and not cause problems. Form 21 includes a wide variety of information, including the applicant's rental, employment and credit history and personal references. Conscientious landlords will insist on checking out this information before signing a lease or rental agreement.

If you own or manage rental property, you can use this rental application to help screen potential tenants. Before doing so, be sure all applicants sign the rental application authorizing you to verify the information and references and to run a credit check. Also, use the "Notes" section at the end of the application to write down legal reasons for refusing an individual—for example, negative credit history, insufficient income or your inability to verify information. You will want this kind of record in order to survive a fair housing challenge if a disappointed applicant files a discrimination complaint.

⚠ Make sure you understand how discrimination laws work. Many types of discrimination are illegal, including race, religion, national origin, sex, familial status, disability and, in some states, sexual orientation or marital status. For more information on legal and illegal reasons to reject a tenant, see the resources listed at the beginning of this chapter.

Savvy tenants will also find Form 21 useful when looking for a new place to live. If you're a tenant, we suggest you complete this rental application in advance of apartment-hunting—providing information about your employment, income, credit background and rental housing history. Take a copy of the completed application along when you see a potential rental unit. This is almost guaranteed to impress a landlord or his rental agent.

Signing Instructions

There are no signing instructions for the Rental Application. If you're a landlord, give a copy to each tenant applying for your rental property. Be sure the tenant fills it in completely and signs it before you call references or run a credit check.

If you're a tenant, complete the application in advance of apartment-hunting. You can either give your application to prospective landlords or use the information you've pulled together on Form 21 to complete the landlord's application.

Form 22: Fixed-Term Residential Lease

Form 23: Month-to-Month Residential Rental Agreement

Leases and rental agreements often look so similar they can be hard to tell apart. That's because both cover nitty-gritty issues, such as the amount of rent and deposits you must pay and the number of people who can live in the rental unit. The big difference is the length of the tenancy. A *rental agreement* typically lasts only from one month to the next (although week-to-week agreements are possible in many states). The agreement automatically self-renews unless terminated by either the landlord or tenant, by giving the proper amount of written notice (typically 30 days). By contrast, a *lease* almost always covers a longer, fixed term, such as one year. With a fixed-term lease, the landlord can't raise the rent or change other terms of the tenancy until the lease runs out (unless the lease itself allows future changes or the tenant agrees in writing). In addition, a landlord, can't terminate the tenancy before the lease expires, unless the tenant fails to pay the rent or violates another significant term of the lease or the law.

Form 22 is a fixed-term lease. Form 23 is a month-to-month rental agreement. We believe both are fair and balanced from both the landlord and tenant viewpoint.

Several blanks of these forms have legal implications:

Clause 15, Landlord's Right to Access. This tries to balance the tenant's right of privacy against the landlord's right to enter the rental unit to make repairs or for other reasons. A landlord always has the right to enter a rental unit in case of genuine emergency, such as fire. But to show the unit to prospective tenants or to make repairs, many states require 24 hours' written notice. Some states have no notice requirements or simply require the landlord to give the tenant "reasonable notice." Arizona, Delaware, Hawaii, Kentucky, Rhode Island, Vermont and Washington require two days' notice of landlord's entry. In all other states, we believe 24 hours' notice is a workable standard, and therefore recommend that you adopt it in completing Clause 15.

Clause 19, Payment of Court Costs and Attorney Fees in a Lawsuit. Under the law of many states, a clause providing that a landlord will be entitled to attorney fees and court costs in a legal dispute will be read by a court to go both ways. This means that if the tenant wins, she will be entitled to attorney fees and court costs, even if the lease or rental agreement doesn't specifically say so.

For tenants, a landlord's attorney fees clause often makes it easier to find a lawyer willing to take a case that does not have the potential for a hefty money judgment. That's because with an attorney fees clause, a winning lawyer will get paid by the landlord, rather than rely on the tenant's pocketbook. On the other hand, tenants who are confident about representing themselves may prefer not to have an attorney fees clause, reasoning that a landlord who can't recover attorney fees in a lawsuit may be more willing to compromise, rather than go to court.

Landlords usually prefer to include an attorney fees clause unless they intend to do all or most of their own legal work in any potential eviction or other lawsuit. In that situation, if a tenant wins, the landlord will have to pay the tenant's legal fees; if the landlord wins, the tenant will owe nothing because the landlord didn't hire an attorney.

State Laws Vary Concerning Many Key Issues

All states have laws regulating residential landlord-tenant relationships. Typically, these laws include establishing the maximum amount allowed for a security deposit and the deadline for returning it, the amount of notice required to change or end a month-to-month tenancy, tenants' privacy rights, late rent charges, a tenant's right to install locks and disclosures regarding the condition of property. For details, see the Nolo resources listed at the beginning of the chapter.

Some states require that leases include certain language. Alaska, Florida, Georgia, Kentucky, Maryland, Michigan, North Carolina, Tennessee and Washington require landlords to give tenants written information on various aspects of the security deposit, such as where it is held, interest payments and when the deposit may be withheld. Even if it's not required, you may want to provide details on security deposits in the space provided in Clause 8 of Forms 22 and 23.

Also, local rent control ordinances may require that your lease include specific language, such as the address of the local rent control board. Check your local ordinance for more information.

Federal law requires landlords to disclose known lead-based paint hazards in the rental premises. In addition, some states require landlords to make other disclosures about the property, such as flood hazards, before a new tenant signs a lease or rental agreement. Clause 20 is the place to make these kinds of disclosures.

Signing Instructions

Print out two copies of the Lease (or Rental Agreement)—one for the landlord and one for the tenant(s). The landlord and every tenant should sign and date both copies in the spaces indicated. The landlord should keep one signed copy and the tenant(s) the other. (Co-tenants, if any, may make their own copies of the tenant's signed document.) Store your document in a safe place.

Form 24: Landlord-Tenant Agreement to Terminate Lease

If you're a tenant with a long-term lease, ideally, you'll sign a lease for just the amount of time you need a rental. But despite your best efforts to plan ahead, you may want to move before your lease is up.

One option is to simply move out without sweating the legalities. Leaving before a fixed-term lease expires, without paying the remainder of the rent due under the lease, is called breaking the lease. With a little luck, it may not cost you much—in most states, the landlord is required to re-rent the property reasonably quickly. If the landlord does so (and doesn't attempt to hide the fact that he has a new rent-paying tenant), your financial liability will be limited to paying the rent for the brief time the unit was vacant.

Nevertheless, if you plan to leave early, you don't just have to move out and hope your landlord plays fair and gets a new tenant quickly. For a variety of reasons, the landlord may drag his feet, claim he couldn't find a new tenant or rent the unit to a tenant who pays less rent than you did—meaning you're liable for the difference. Fortunately, there are steps you can take to minimize your financial responsibility—as well as help avoid receiving a bad reference from the landlord next time you're apartment hunting.

First, consider simply asking the landlord to cancel the lease using Form 24. If you and the landlord both sign and date this form, your obligations for rent beyond the termination date end. (You are still responsible for unpaid back rent and any damage you've caused beyond normal wear and tear.) Why would a landlord voluntarily agree to let you off the hook? If you have been a steady and considerate tenant, it's possible that you'll be treated in kind, especially if the landlord has a new tenant standing

by who will pay a higher rent. If the landlord initially balks at canceling the lease, you might bring her around by offering to pay an extra month's rent in exchange for the lease cancellation.

In addition, in some states, landlords must allow early termination of a lease under certain conditions. For example, in Delaware you need give only 30 days' notice to end a long-term lease if you must move because your present employer has relocated or because of health problems—yours or a family member's. In New Jersey, a tenant who has suffered a disabling illness or accident can break a lease and leave after 40 days' notice. Some states, such as Georgia, allow members of the military to break a lease because of a change in orders. If you have a good reason for a sudden move, check your state's law.

If you can't get the landlord to cancel the lease outright, your best approach is usually to find a new tenant to sign a new lease at the same or higher rent and who will be ready to move in as soon as you leave. If you follow this approach, you should owe nothing additional since the landlord won't be able to argue that a suitable replacement tenant couldn't be found.

If the landlord won't accept the tenant you find. Keep careful records of all prospective tenants you find, especially their credit histories—you can use the Rental Application (Form 21). If the landlord sues you for back rent, present these records to the judge as proof the landlord failed in her responsibility to limit (mitigate) your damages by accepting a suitable replacement tenant.

If the landlord accepts the new tenant, you and the landlord should cancel your lease by completing Form 24. The landlord and the new tenant can sign their own lease, and you won't be in the picture.

Signing Instructions

Print out two copies of the Landlord-Tenant Agreement to Terminate Lease form—one for the landlord and one for the tenant(s). The landlord and every tenant should sign and date both copies. The landlord should keep one signed copy and the tenant(s) the other. (Co-tenants, if any, may make their own copies of the tenant's signed document.)

Form 25: Consent to Assignment of Lease

If you are a tenant who wants to move out permanently, but the landlord won't cancel your lease or sign a new lease with a tenant you find, your next best option may be to "assign" your lease to a new tenant (called an "assignee") who is acceptable to the landlord. With an assignment, you turn over the remainder of your lease to someone else. You can do this with Form 25. Unless the landlord agrees otherwise, you remain in the picture as a guarantor of rent payments in case the new occupant (the assignee) fails to pay. Having a second source for the rent is one reason a savvy landlord might agree to an assignment but not a cancellation.

A landlord can voluntarily waive his right to look to you as the guarantor of the assignee's rent, something that is not uncommon when the new tenant has excellent credit. Clause 4 of Form 25 releases you from this worrisome obligation, essentially putting you in the position of someone who has terminated the lease. If the landlord balks at the release, and you are reasonably sure of your replacement's ability to pay the rent, you may not be risking much if you cross out Clause 4 and remain theoretically responsible for the rent.

Signing Instructions

Print out three copies of the Consent to Assignment of Lease form—one for the landlord, one for the tenant and one for the assignee. Each person should sign and date all copies in the spaces indicated. The landlord should keep one signed copy and the tenant and assignee the others.

Form 26: Landlord-Tenant Checklist

Legal disputes between tenants and landlords have justly gained a reputation for having the potential to be almost as nasty as a bad divorce. And like a failed marriage, disputes often continue after the legal relationship is over. This is most likely to occur when a landlord keeps all or part of a tenant's security deposit, claiming the place was left filthy or damaged.

Fortunately, using Form 26, a landlord and tenant can work together to minimize deposit-related disputes by jointly inspecting the rental unit at both the start and end of the tenancy. The idea is to identify damage, dirt, mildew and obvious wear and tear before the tenant moves in (use column 1) and inspect the unit again in the company of the landlord or property manager just before the tenant moves out (use columns 2 and 3).

In the "additional explanation" section at the end of the form, note any areas of disagreement. (Incidentally, to avoid a court battle over security deposit deductions, many wise landlords and tenants try to compromise any disputed damage claims when doing the final inspection.) Tenants should read and check off the box on the bottom of the third page of the form regarding smoke detectors and fire extinguishers.

Signing Instructions

After completing the Landlord-Tenant Checklist at move-in time, make two copies. The landlord and tenant should sign and date both copies and each keep one copy. Review the Checklist again at move-out time.

Take photos at move-in and move-out to avoid disputes. You'll be able to compare "before" and "after" pictures, rather than just have landlord's word against tenant's. If you end up in court fighting over the security deposit, documenting your point of view with photos will be invaluable visual proof. Tenants should consider taking along a friend or colleague as a potential witness to the condition of the rental unit at move-in or move-out time—someone who will be available to testify in court on your behalf if necessary.

Form 27: Notice of Needed Repairs

Landlords are legally required to offer their tenants livable premises when they originally rent a unit and to maintain their rental property in decent condition throughout the rental term. In most states, the legal jargon used to describe this obligation is the "landlord's legal duty to adhere to the implied warranty of habitability."

Tenants have the right to a decent place to live even if they move into a place that's clearly sub-standard (below reasonable habitability standards), or even if the lease comes right out and says that the landlord doesn't have to provide a habitable unit. Or put another way, almost all courts have rejected the sleazy argument that a tenant waives the right to a livable place because he is so desper-ate for a place to live that he accepts a substandard rental unit.

If there's a problem with the physical condition of your rental unit, you'll want to notify your land-lord or manager as soon as possible so that it can be promptly fixed. The best approach is to put every repair and maintenance request in writing, using Form 27, keeping a copy for yourself. You may find it easier to call your landlord first, particu-larly in urgent cases, but be sure to follow up with a written repair request.

Be as specific as possible regarding the problem —whether it's plumbing, heating, security, weather-proofing or other defects. Note the effects of the problem on you, what you want done and when. For example, if the thermostat on your heater is always finicky and sometimes doesn't function at all, explain how long you've been without heat and how low the temperature has dipped—don't simply say "the heater needs to be fixed." Be sure to note the date of the request and how many requests, if any, have preceded this one; keep records of all repair requests.

If you are a landlord, it's a good idea to give tenants copies of Form 27 and encourage them to immediately report plumbing, heating, weather-proofing or other defects or safety problems. Be sure to note details as to how and when the problem was fixed, including reasons for any delay, on the bottom of the tenant's repair request form. Keep copies of all completed forms in your tenant files.

Signing Instructions

There are no specific signing instructions for this Notice of Needed Repairs form. Tenants should simply sign the document and keep a copy for their records. If your landlord has an on-site office or a resident manager, deliver the repair request person-ally. If you mail it, consider sending it certified mail (return receipt requested) or use a delivery service that will give you a receipt establishing delivery. Besides keeping a copy of every written repair request, keep notes of oral communications, too.

If your landlord ignores your requests and your rental is unlivable, you'll have to undertake stronger measures, such as calling state or local build-ing or health inspectors, moving out, withholding the rent or repairing the problem yourself. These remedies, available only in certain situations according to your state's laws, are thoroughly discussed in the Nolo books listed at the beginning of this chapter.

Form 28: Tenant's Notice of Intent to Move Out

If you have a month-to-month tenancy, in most states and for most rentals you must provide 30 days' notice to your landlord if you want to move out. In some states, if you pay rent weekly or twice a month, you can give written notice to terminate that matches your rent payment interval. For example, if you pay rent every two weeks, you may need to give only 14 days' notice.

In most states, you can give notice at any time during the month (unless your rental agreement says otherwise). If you pay your rent on the first, you don't have to give notice on that date so that your tenancy will end on the last day of the month. For example, if you pay rent on the first of the month but give notice on the tenth, you will be obliged to pay for only ten days' rent for the next month, even if you move out earlier. To calculate the amount, prorate the monthly rent.

Check the Nolo resources listed at the beginning of the chapter for specific requirements as to how and when notice must be provided.

Signing Instructions

Tenants should sign and date the Tenant's Notice of Intent to Move Out form and give or mail it to the landlord. Be sure to check your state rules to make sure you are meeting any specific notice requirements.

If you give oral notice, follow up in writing with this form. If you know your landlord or manager well, you may wish to tell him that you'll be moving. Fine, but immediately follow up with written confirmation. The law almost always requires written notice. You can use Form 28 for this purpose.

Form 29: Demand for Return of Security Deposit

Getting cleaning and security deposits returned can be a problem for tenants. To avoid trouble, or to positively deal with it when it's unavoidable, use Form 26, the Landlord-Tenant Checklist, to make a written and photographic record of what the place looks like when you move in and when you move out. Be sure you leave the rental in good condition, give proper notice and are paid up in rent when you leave. And don't forget to give the landlord your new address.

Depending on the law of your state, you should normally receive your deposits back within 14 to 30 days of moving out. If you don't, you should send a written request using the Demand for Return of Security Deposit. If this doesn't work, you may need to sue the landlord in small claims court. (Some state security deposit statutes require tenants to make a written request; and, in some states, small claims court rules require you to make a demand letter before you can sue.)

Your demand letter should state the date you moved out of the rental and lay out the reasons your landlord owes you deposit money. Refer to any statutory deadlines and tangible evidence supporting your demand, such as photos or a before-and-after Landlord-Tenant Checklist. Form 29 makes it clear that if the landlord does not promptly return your deposit by a specified date (we suggest seven to ten days), you plan to go to small claims court.

In many states, if a landlord withholds a deposit without giving the tenant a good reason for doing so (for example, to cover specific damage or unpaid rent), in writing, within the required time, the tenant may sue for the amount of the wrongly withheld deposit, plus an extra amount for punitive damages if the landlord intentionally failed to return the deposit on time. Check your state law for specifics and refer to them in any correspondence with your landlord. For example, California landlords have three weeks to return the security deposit with an itemized statement of deductions.

Signing Instructions

Sign your Demand for Return of Security Deposit letter and send it certified mail (return receipt requested) to the landlord, or use a delivery service that will give you a receipt establishing delivery. Keep a copy of your letter and all related correspondence. You'll need this if you end up in a court dispute over your security deposit.

Going to Small Claims Court

Hopefully your Demand for Return of Security Deposit letter will spur action on the landlord's part and you'll get your deposit back. If it doesn't you may need to file in small claims court. Depending on the state, you can sue for $2,500 to $7,500, which should cover most deposit cases. You can sue your landlord for your security deposit and for interest (if it's required in your state or city). In many states you can also sue for extra punitive damages if the landlord intentionally failed to return the deposit on time.

Small claims court is inexpensive (usually $10 to $50) to file a case; you don't need a lawyer, and disputes usually go before a judge (there are no juries) within 30 to 60 days. Small claims courts are informal places, intended to be used by regular folks presenting their own cases.

For detailed advice on filing (or defending) a case in small claims court, see *Everybody's Guide to Small Claims Court*, by Ralph Warner (Nolo).

CHAPTER

5

Borrowing or Lending Money

This chapter contains several promissory notes you can use when you borrow money from or lend money to a friend, relative or someone else who isn't a commercial customer. (Banks and other institutional lenders follow many legal rules and must use forms with far more fine print.) This chapter also includes a loan comparison worksheet to keep track of information you collect on different loans (whether from a personal or commercial lender), a form to authorize a lender to check the borrower's credit and "demand" letters for use when trying to collect an overdue payment or bad check.

Form 30: Loan Comparison Worksheet

A good consumer shops around before making a significant purchase. There is no reason to act otherwise when you are looking to borrow money. A loan from one bank may come with very different terms than a loan from a credit union or finance company —or even from a different bank across town. And a loan from your former college roommate or your Aunt Charlotte may be very different still.

The cost of a loan doesn't only depend on how much interest you pay. Long-term loans will carry a higher rate of interest than will short-term loans (the lender runs the risk that inflation will erode the real value of the interest it receives for a longer period, so it passes some of this risk on to you in the form of a higher interest rate). But short-term loans are not necessarily cheaper. That's because application and other up-front fees, which can vary considerably from one lender to the next, also must be taken into consideration to compute the cost of a loan. Fortunately, this isn't true of all short-term loans, so be sure to shop around. When you apply for a commercial loan, you must be told the annual cost of the loan. This is stated as the annual percentage rate, or APR. You can use that figure to compare the annual cost of different loans.

APR isn't the entire story, especially for adjustable rate loans or loans with a balloon payment or other features. For a full comparison of loans, use this worksheet to record the terms of any loans you are considering, whether to buy a car or computer

system, pay down your credit cards or just take a well-deserved vacation. See "Basic Loan Terms Explained" before you start collecting information on different loans.

Because mortgage loans involve far more considerations than these loans, use Form 51 (Mortgage Rates and Terms Worksheet) in Chapter 6, when shopping around for a mortgage.

Signing Instructions

There are no signing instructions for the Loan Comparison Worksheet. Simply fill one out each time you start collecting information on different loans.

Form 31: Authorization to Conduct Credit Check

Commercial lenders—banks, credit unions and finance companies—will always check a loan applicant's credit before agreeing to lend money. If you're thinking of lending someone money, it makes good sense to do the same. First, you'll need the borrower's authorization to do this. Some employers, financial institutions and credit sources may want to see this kind of signed authorization before providing information on the borrower. That's the purpose of Form 31. The borrower should complete all sections, including details on their employment and credit history.

Doing a credit check to learn whether or not the person is likely to repay you in full and on time puts you in a good position to say "no" to someone with poor credit. While checking a person's credit and saying "no" may put a strain on a personal relationship, making a loan to someone who can't handle it is more likely to cause long-term problems. When a personal loan isn't repaid, the result is often the loss of a friendship or a serious family tension.

Signing Instructions

The person borrowing money should sign and date the Authorization to Conduct Credit Check. The

Basic Loan Terms Explained

To be able to understand your loan agreement, you'll need to know the meaning of a few terms.

Adjustable rate. The interest rate charged by the lender that is set initially, usually fairly low, and then fluctuates (usually meaning it increases) every several months.

Balloon payment. A lump sum payment made at the end of a loan to cover the remaining balance. For example, you borrow $10,000 for five years at 6% interest. The monthly payments are $193.33. You can only afford to pay about half that amount. So the lender lets you pay $100 a month. At the end of five years, you owe a balloon payment of $6,511.53. Balloon payments are usually bad deals. Borrowers often get into trouble by focusing on the low monthly payments rather than the large and often unaffordable sum due at the end of the loan term.

Cap. On an adjustable rate loan, the cap refers both to the maximum amount the interest rate can increase each year and the ultimate maximum a interest rate can reach. For example, an adjustable rate loan that begins at 4% may have an annual cap of $1/2$% and a lifetime cap of 7%. This means that at the beginning of the second year, the rate will be $4^1/2$%. If the loan continues to increase $1/2$% each year, it will reach its lifetime cap or 7% at six years, and never go up again.

Collateral. Property a borrower pledges as security for repayment of a loan. Sometimes it's the item being purchased, such as when you finance the purchase of your car. Other times the collateral is property the borrower already owns that he pledges as security on a new loan. If the borrower defaults, a lender can take the collateral without first suing the borrower and obtaining a judgment.

Cosigner. A creditworthy person who agrees to be fully liable for repayment of a loan if the borrower defaults.

Credit check. A lender obtaining a copy of the borrower's credit report from a credit reporting agency in order to verify the borrower's credit-worthiness.

Credit insurance. Insurance coverage offered by some lenders to pay off a loan in the event the borrower becomes disabled or dies.

Fixed rate. The interest rate charged by the lender that is established at the outset and will never change.

Grace period. The number of days a borrower has after a loan payment is due to make the payment without being charged a late fee. For example if your loan payments are due on the 1st of the month, you may have a grace period until the 10th, meaning that the lender will accept your payment until that date without penalizing you.

Late Fee. The fee a lender charges when a borrower pays late. See "Grace period."

Loan application fee. Nuisance fees charged by lenders for the privilege of lending money. These include credit checks, appraisals on collateral and loan processing fees.

Loan discounts. Incentives offered by a lender to reduce a borrower's loan interest rate. For example, you might be offered a $1/2$% discount if you set up a direct payment from your checking account or if you maintain a checking account with the lender with a minimum balance of $1,000.

Points. Real estate loans usually come with points, an amount of money equal to a percentage of your loan. This money is paid to the lender simply for the privilege of borrowing money.

Prepayment penalty. A penalty imposed on a borrower for paying off a loan early. It's usually expressed as a flat fee or a percentage of the interest the lender lost by your prepaying.

person lending money should keep the original and give the borrower a copy.

Form 32: Monthly Payment Record

Especially if a loan will be repaid over many months or years, it's easy to forget if and when every payment has been made. This is especially likely if the debtor misses several payments because of an emergency and then makes them up a little at a time. In this case, the amounts will be different each month. Use Form 32, Monthly Payment Record, to keep track of payments made under installment notes, such as the promissory notes (Forms 33-37) included in this chapter.

Signing Instructions

There are no signing instructions for the Monthly Payment Record. The lender simply records payments due and made every month.

Forms 33-37: Promissory Notes

A promissory note is nothing more than legal jargon for a written promise to pay money to someone. As with all legal documents, promissory notes often contain loads of needless hyped-up legalese. Because the notes in this chapter are designed to be used primarily between family and friends—and because, lawyers notwithstanding, there is no law against using plain English—we prefer to keep the language simple.

The primary function of a promissory note is to serve as written evidence of the amount of a debt and the terms under which it will be repaid, including the interest rate (if any). One is typically signed when money is borrowed or something is bought on credit. Perhaps in the best of all possible worlds, such evidence would not be needed. One friend would lend another $1,000, the two people would shake hands, and that would be it. But because the "best possible world" and the "real world" are often barely on speaking terms when it comes to loan

repayment, here are several important reasons why all promissory notes should be put in writing:

- You are assured that the borrower and lender have agreed to the same terms, including the repayment schedule and interest rate.
- You specify exactly what those terms are.
- Both parties have a written document with which to refresh their memories if need be.

This chapter contains five promissory notes, each designed to deal with a somewhat different repayment scenario:

- Form 33: Promissory Note—Installment Payments With Interest
- Form 34: Promissory Note—Installment Payments With Interest and Balloon Payment
- Form 35: Promissory Note—Installment Payments Without Interest
- Form 36: Promissory Note—Lump Sum Payment With Interest
- Form 37: Promissory Note—Lump Sum Payment Without Interest.

All of these notes are for unsecured loans—meaning that the borrower does not pledge any property, such as a house or car, as collateral to guarantee repayment. This means if the borrower doesn't repay the loan, the lender must sue in court to get a judgment, which then makes her eligible to collect by use of wage or property attachments. You can add a security provision using Form 39, which gives the lender the right to force the sale of property pledged as collateral, such as a house or car, if the borrower doesn't repay.

Signing Instructions for Promissory Notes

The borrower(s) must sign the Promissory Note for it to be valid. (There may be two borrowers—for example, if a husband wife are jointly borrowing money. See "Does a Borrower's Spouse Need to Sign a Promissory Note?") Print out one copy of the form. The borrower(s) should sign and date only one copy of the document in the space provided. This signed original should be given to the lender. The borrower(s) should keep a copy of the signed document for their own records.

The promissory note forms contain a space for the acknowledgment of a notary public. You may want to have the borrower sign the promissory note in front of a notary public. This may even be required in some states; even if it is not, notarization adds a measure of legal credibility to your promissory note. See the Introduction, Section D1, for general advice on having a form notarized.

Does a Borrower's Spouse Need to Sign a Promissory Note?

In a promissory note, a borrower signs a contract that makes him or her liable for a debt. The lender may ask that the borrower's spouse sign as well. This is most likely to happen, for example, if someone is borrowing money to buy property that both spouses will use or to help finance a new business venture. Keep in mind that a lender may not require a borrower's spouse to sign if the borrower is applying for a loan on his or her own and no jointly held or community property is involved.

By having the borrower's spouse sign, a second person becomes legally liable for repaying the debt. Normally, if only the borrower signed the contract and didn't repay it, the other party to the agreement could get a judgment against the borrower but not his or her spouse. This means that the creditor would be able to seize property that the borrower owns in his or her own name, but not property that the borrower and his or her spouse own in both of their names or that the spouse owns in his or her name, unless the borrower lives in a community property state such as California. (See "Who Pays the Debts in Community Property States?" for more details.) But if the borrower and his or her spouse both sign a contract and then default, the other party can sue and get a judgment against both people. That judgment can be enforced by seizing the couple's joint bank account, putting a lien on jointly owned real estate, seizing property in the borrower's name alone and seizing property in the spouse's name alone.

If the borrower's credit is questionable, consider requiring a cosigner. You can add a cosigner clause to your promissory note by using Form 38.

Who Pays the Debts in Community Property States?

Arizona, California, Idaho, Louisiana, Nevada, New Mexico, Texas, Washington and Wisconsin follow the community property system. (In Alaska, a couple can choose to have their property treated as community property by preparing a written agreement.) In these states, a married couple's property is generally considered community (joint) regardless of whose name it's in or who paid for it. In addition, all debts incurred during the marriage—even if only one spouse signed the loan papers—are considered community (joint) debts unless a creditor was explicitly told that only one spouse would be liable for the debt.

In most situations, the rights of creditors to seize property after getting a judgment for nonpayment of a debt depend on whether the property is considered community or separate.

- **Community Property.** Usually, property earned or acquired by either spouse during the marriage—except property acquired by gift or inheritance or defined as separate under a premarital agreement—is considered community property. A creditor can go after all community property to pay for either a community debt or a separate debt.

- **Separate Property.** This is property a spouse owned before getting married, acquired during the marriage by gift or inheritance or agreed in writing to be kept separate. It's also property acquired using separate assets. For example, if a woman owned a house when she got married, sold it and used the proceeds to buy stock, the stock is her separate property. For community debts, a creditor can seek reimbursement from either spouse's separate property. For example, the wife's separate debts, a creditor can go after her separate property and all community property, including her husband's share.

Form 33: Promissory Note—Installment Payments With Interest

Form 33 allows for repayment in installments rather than all at once, and charges interest. Charging a friend or family member interest strikes some people as being ungenerous. In our opinion, this view is based on a misconception as to the function of interest, which is to fairly compensate the lender for the use of his money. Think of it this way. Suppose Joan lends Harry $5,000 for a year, interest-free. If Joan had put the money in a certificate of deposit, she would have earned the going rate of interest. By giving Harry the money interest-free, Joan ends up paying for the privilege of lending the money to Harry.

Interest charged on money lent to friends and relatives tends to run between 5% and 10%. If you wish to charge a higher rate of interest, check your state law to see if the rate is legal; it may constitute the crime of usury. How much interest is appropriate? In an effort to be generous to a relative or friend, many lenders charge interest at somewhat less than the market rate, sometimes as little as—or just slightly more than—they would receive if they purchased a bank certificate of deposit for the same time period. This is a great deal for the borrower; after all, even if Harry qualified to borrow from a bank or other commercial lender, he would have to pay a much higher rate of interest than Joan would receive if she put the money in a CD.

Charging interest adds a level of complication when it comes to figuring out the amount of the monthly payments. For this, you will need an amortization calculator or software program. You can find one at http://www.nolo.com/calculator. You plug in the loan amount, interest rate and number of months the borrower will take to repay the loan. The calculator gives you the monthly payment amount.

If the borrower decides to pay off the principal sooner than the promissory note calls for under the installment plan, you will have to recalculate the payments based on the new outstanding balance. This is easy to do with the amortization calculator.

Legal Terminology of Promissory Notes

Here we translate some legal terms into plain English.

Acceleration. Our promissory notes accelerate the borrower's responsibility to make all necessary loan payments if he misses one or more regularly scheduled payments. You specify the number of days—typically 30 or 60—the borrower has to pay before you exercise this option. Without this provision you can't sue for loan installments not yet due, even though the borrower has missed several payments and it is obvious he has no plans to repay.

Attorney fees. Our promissory notes include a clause providing that a lender will be entitled to attorney fees and court costs in a legal dispute. Under the laws of many states, this type of clause will be read by a court to go both ways. This means that if the borrower wins, she will be entitled to attorney fees and court costs, even if the loan papers don't specifically say so.

Buyer in due course. This is a person who buys or otherwise legally receives a promissory note from a lender. The borrower's obligation to repay the note doesn't change just because the lender sells the note to someone else.

Joint and several liability. This means that if there is more than one borrower, all borrowers are liable for repaying 100% of the loan. If Chuck and Laura borrow $5,000 from Miguel and default, Miguel can go after either Chuck or Laura for the full $5,000. Neither can claim that he or she is liable for only $2,500.

Form 34: Promissory Note— Installment Payments With Interest and Balloon Payment

Form 34 is similar to Form 33 in that the loan is required to be repaid in installments with interest.

But there's an additional twist; individual payments are lower than they otherwise would be, with the shortfall made up by one large balloon payment at the end of the loan term. To see how this works, let's take a look at an example. You lend a friend $10,000 at 7% interest and want the money paid back in three years. Using an amortization calculator, you discover that your friend would have to pay you $308.78 each month to pay it back over that time.

Your friend can't afford to pay that amount each month now, but knows he will receive some money in about three years when a trust matures. So you propose the following: Your friend can borrow $10,000 from you at 7% and repay it over three years. But to make his payments affordable now, you agree to amortize the loan as though it were to be paid off in ten years, meaning your friend's monthly payments are only $116.11, far less than $308.78. You agree to take these low payments for 36 months and at the end, your friend will make you one large payment, called a balloon payment, of the remaining principal. That amount is $7,693.

Form 35: Promissory Note— Installment Payments Without Interest

Use Form 35 if the borrower will repay you in installments, but you won't charge interest. When the parties involved in the transaction are family members or close friends, the amount borrowed is relatively small and the probability of repayment is high, lenders sometimes prefer to use an interest-free installment note.

Be aware that if the IRS learns of an interest-free loan, it can impute interest. This means that the lender will be assumed to have earned interest and will be required to report that interest as income on her tax return. For most personal loans, this won't be a problem because uncharged interest can be treated as a tax-free gift, as long as the total amount given to the borrower in a calendar year is $10,000 or less.

Form 36: Promissory Note—Lump Sum Payment With Interest

This note is normally used when the borrower won't be able to repay the loan for a period of months or years. For example, you might borrow money from a friend to help you open a small business. You aren't likely to have the cash flow for at least six months or a year to repay the loan. In such a situation, your friend might agree to be repaid in a lump sum in two years.

The easiest way to determine the amount of annual interest which will be due on the loan is to use simple, not compound, interest. Multiply the amount of the loan by the annual interest rate. For instance, if the loan is for $4,000, and your annual interest rate is 10%, the annual amount of interest on the loan is $400. To determine the total amount of interest due, multiply the annual interest amount by the time period of the loan. In our example, if the loan is for two years, the interest due would be $800.

If you need to compute the interest for a period of months rather than years, compute the interest for one year, divide by 12, and then multiply the result by the number of months. For example, assume the $4,000 loan is for an 18-month period. Take the annual interest amount ($400), divide by 12 ($33.33) and multiply by 18 ($600).

If the loan is paid back before it is due, Clause 2 gives the lender two choices:

- Charge the full interest. This is not unreasonable, given that you committed yourself to being without the amount of the entire loan for the time indicated.
- Pro-rate the interest to correspond to the actual period of time the loan was outstanding. Returning to the $4,000 loan example, if you originally figured interest at 10% for two years ($800) but the loan was paid back in 18 months, simply charge the 18-month figure ($600) instead.

Form 37: Promissory Note—Lump Sum Payment Without Interest

This promissory note, which calls for a lump sum loan repayment and no interest, is about as basic as you can get. This sort of note is normally used by people with a close personal relationship when the person lending the money is primarily interested in helping out the borrower and expects nothing in return except, eventually, the return of the amount borrowed.

If the IRS learns of the loan, it can impute interest. This means that the lender will be assumed to have earned interest and will be required to report that interest as income on her tax return. For most personal loans, this won't be a problem because uncharged interest can be treated as a tax-free gift, as long as the total given to the borrower by the lender is $10,000 or less in a calendar year.

Form 38: Cosigner Provision

A cosigner is someone who promises to repay a loan if the primary debtor defaults. If you'll be lending money to someone with a questionable (or no) credit history or a background of sporadic employment, you might require one or more cosigners, such as a parent or friend. (If there is more than one cosigner, each is 100% liable to repay the note if the borrower fails to.)

Federal law requires that commercial lenders give cosigners a notice of their potential liability when they agree to cosign a debt. Although this is not required for personal loans between friends and relatives, we believe full disclosure of the risks of cosigning is a good idea and so we incorporate much of that notice language in Form 38.

Signing Instructions

After filling in the top of the Cosigner Provision, staple it to your promissory note and then have the cosigner complete sign and date it. The lender should keep the original and give each cosigner a copy, along with a copy of the promissory note.

Forms 39-42: Security Agreements

If you lend money to someone who does not repay it, in general, your only recourse to get paid is to sue the person, obtain a court judgment and then take property that can legally be seized to satisfy a debt.

There is an easier way: You can attach a security agreement to the promissory note. In a security agreement, property belonging to the borrower, such as a car or computer, is specified as collateral for repayment of the loan. If the borrower doesn't repay the loan, you can take the property, sell it and use the proceeds to satisfy what is owed. You don't have to go to court. However, you do have to follow proper procedures when you take back (repossess) the property.

Sometimes, a dishonest borrower will try to use the same piece of collateral to secure more than one debt. The result is that if the unscrupulous borrower later defaults on these secured loans, the lenders will find themselves competing to sell the collateral and use the proceeds to satisfy their debts. This raises the legal question of how secured creditors can protect themselves. The answer is that they must be the first to file evidence of their claim with the correct recording agency.

This chapter includes four different forms relating to security interests:

- Form 39, Security Agreement Provision for Promissory Note
- Form 40, Uniform Commercial Code (U.C.C.) Financing Statement
- Form 41, Release of U.C.C. Financing Statement
- Form 42, Release of Security Interest.

Creating a security interest is a multi-step process. First you must add Form 39 to your promissory note. If the collateral is personal property, such as a car, the security agreement must be filed with the appropriate state agency using the U.C.C. Financing Statement, (Form 40). If the collateral is real property, such as a house, the borrower must sign a mortgage or deed of trust before a notary public, which then must be recorded with the county land records office.

The Difference Between a Mortgage and a Deed of Trust

When someone borrows money from a lender to finance a home, the legal instrument recorded at the county land record's office is a deed of trust. When the borrower executes a deed of trust, he gives the trustee (often a title company) the right to sell the property, with no court approval, if he fails to pay the lender on time. By contrast, a mortgage normally involves only a borrower and a lender, and depending on the laws of the state where the property is located, often requires a more complicated judicial foreclosure proceeding if payments aren't made.

Here is deed of trust language translated into English.

Beneficiary. The lender is the beneficiary of the deed of trust; if the borrower defaults and the trustee sells the house, the beneficiary is paid from the proceeds.

Trustee. The trustee, usually a title insurance company, doesn't exercise any control over the house as long as the borrower keeps payments current. If the borrower defaults, however, the trustee can sell the house and use the proceeds to pay off the trust beneficiary (the lender).

Trustor. The trustor is the borrower. As trustor, the borrower signs a deed of trust giving the trustee the power to sell the house and turn the proceeds over to the beneficiary (the lender) if the borrower defaults on the loan.

Form 39: Security Agreement Provision for Promissory Note

You can use Form 39 to identify the security interest, such as a car, house or valuable personal property, as a part of your contract. Choose the sample language on the form that is most appropriate for your situation and delete the others.

Signing Instructions

After completing the Security Agreement Provision, staple it to your promissory note. The borrower (owner of the collateral) should sign and date the form. The lender should keep the original and give the borrower a copy, along with a copy of the promissory note.

Form 40: U.C.C. Financing Statement

Use the U.C.C. Financing Statement to record your security interest if the collateral identified in your security agreement is personal property.

Do not use this form if the collateral identified in your security agreement is real property, such as a house. In this case you should file a mortgage or deed of trust with the county land records office, not a U.C.C. Financing Statement.

Once you have completed the security agreement (Form 39), contact the appropriate state agency— most likely the motor vehicles department if the collateral is a car, boat or similar vehicle, or the Secretary of State for most other property, such as electronics equipment or a computer system. Ask for a copy of your state's rules for filing a U.C.C. statement, and find out if your state has any special form you must use. If it does, use the state form (not this one). Otherwise, use Form 40.

Signing Instructions

The borrower(s) should sign and date the U.C.C. Financing Statement. The lender should keep the original and give the borrower a copy. The lender should attach the promissory note with security interest and file these with the appropriate state office, such as the Secretary of State. Leave the section at the bottom of the form blank; the Filing Officer will complete this.

Form 41:   Release of U.C.C. Financing Statement

When a borrower pays off a loan, she obviously wants the public record to reflect that her property is no longer encumbered (held hostage) in favor of the lender. To do this, you will need to file Form 41 with the public agency, such as the Secretary of State, where you filed a U.C.C. Financing Statement. That will let prospective lawyers, creditors and credit rating agencies know that the lender no longer claims an interest in the borrower's collateral.

This form should correspond to your original U.C.C. Financing Statement. Therefore, make sure the description of property listed as collateral is identical and the other information makes it clear which U.C.C. Financing Statement is being released.

Signing Instructions

The borrower(s) should sign and date the Release of U.C.C. Financing Statement. The lender should keep the original and give the borrower a copy. The lender should file this release with the appropriate state office, such as the Secretary of State. Leave the section at the bottom of the form blank; the Filing Officer will complete this.

Note: Make sure your state does not have special U.C.C. form requirements before using this one.

Form 42:   Release of Security Interest

If the collateral for your loan is real, not personal, property, you should have filed a mortgage or deed of trust with the county land records office, not a U.C.C. Financing Statement with the state. For real property, you must file a Release of Security Interest when the borrower pays off the loan. That will let prospective lawyers, creditors and credit rating agencies know that the lender no longer claims an interest in the borrower's collateral.

This form should correspond to your original mortgage or deed of trust. Make sure the property description is identical and the other information makes it clear which mortgage or deed of trust is being released.

Signing Instructions

The lender should sign and date the Release of Security Interest and give the borrower a copy. The lender should file this release with the appropriate land records office.

Form 43:   Agreement to Modify Promissory Note

If someone who borrows money from you falls behind on repayment, give a call to find out what's wrong. Offer whatever help you can to get the person back on track. Sometimes this will require no more than being willing to extend the repayment period for a few months. In other instances you might take interest-only payments or rewrite the loan at a lower interest rate. Whatever you agree on, you must put it in writing. You can use Form 43 for that purpose.

Signing Instructions

The borrower(s) who signed the promissory note should sign and date the Agreement to Modify Promissory Note, and indicate the location (city or county) where this agreement is being signed. The lender should keep the original signed document and give a copy to the borrower(s).

Form 44:   Overdue Payment Demand

If someone who owes you money (under a promissory note) falls behind on repayment despite your efforts to work out a new repayment plan, your next step is to send the borrower a formal demand letter. You can use Form 44 in such a situation. It serves as a formal notice to the borrower demanding repayment. It states that if you do not hear from the borrower within 15 days, you will enforce your rights under the promissory note, including possibly filing a lawsuit to collect the debt.

⚠️ **Be careful not to make any threats that you don't intend to keep.** Although the federal and state fair debt law probably don't apply to you, it's still a good idea to be fair, yet firm, in trying to persuade the borrower to pay you back.

Signing Instructions

Sign the Overdue Payment Demand and send it to all borrowers and all cosigners by certified mail (return receipt requested). Keep a copy for your records. You may later need this if you end up suing the borrower to collect the money owed.

If you are writing a demand letter to request the return of a security deposit, use Form 29 in Chapter 4.

Form 45: Demand to Make Good on Bad Check

This form is similar to Form 44 in that it's used when someone who owes you money is not meeting her obligation to pay you and has ignored all your efforts to resolve the problem informally. The difference is that this form is for use when the person who owes you money writes you a bad check, a slightly more complicated legal situation. Use

Form 45 to make a formal written demand for payment on a bad check.

Although writing a bad check is a crime in every state, rarely is a person prosecuted for writing bad checks. Even in the unlikely event that a district attorney is willing to bring charges, there's a good chance the person would avoid a trial by agreeing to attend a diversion program for bad check writers and making restitution—that is, paying up.

In most states, you'll want to deal with getting a bad check in a civil, not criminal, manner. The person who receives a bad check can usually sue for extra damages (above and beyond the amount of the check) if she isn't paid within 30 days of making a formal written demand for payment.

A clause is included in the Demand to Make Good on a Bad Check stating that if you sue over the bad check, you may file a lawsuit and ask for the maximum monetary damages allowed under state law. This is often two or three times the amount of the check. You can find a chart of maximum damages permitted by your state at Nolo's online Legal Encyclopedia at http://www.nolo.com/encyclopedia/articles/dc.

Signing Instructions

Sign this Demand to Make Good on Bad Check and deliver it personally to the person who wrote you the bad check. Alternatively, send this certified mail (return receipt requested) or use a delivery service that will give you a receipt establishing delivery. Keep a copy for your records. You may later need this if you end up filing a lawsuit to collect payment. ■

CHAPTER

6

Buying a House

No doubt about it—buying a house is one of the largest and most important investments you'll ever make. And as with any big investment, careful planning and organization are necessary to get the best house for your money. The forms in this chapter help you accomplish this by providing:

- an efficient method to help you identify house features most important to you and systematically evaluate and record relevant information about each house you see (Forms 46, 47 and 48)
- a systematic procedure for determining how much house you can afford—in terms of both the down payment and monthly mortgage payments (Forms 49 and 50), and
- a simple way to keep track of information you collect on different loans and efficiently compare features such as interest rate and loan costs (Form 51).

This chapter also includes a useful moving checklist (Form 52) to help plan your move.

Real Estate on the Web

You can find a wide range of house-buying resources in the Real Estate section of Nolo's online Legal Encyclopedia at http://www.nolo.com. Here you will find a compilation of the best websites and other information on buying a house, such as:

- comparing interest rates and applying for a mortgage
- screening houses that meet your needs
- gathering information on schools, crime and other neighborhood information to help with relocation decisions
- checking sales prices of comparable property to make a realistic offer,
- arranging house inspections, and
- finding a real estate agent, home inspector or other professional.

Nolo publishes *How to Buy a House in California*, by Ralph Warner, Ira Serkes and George Devine, an excellent resource on all aspects of house buying. Although it's written specifically for Californians, who have the benefit of many laws concerning disclosure of defects, the information on most topics, including looking for a house, negotiating with a seller, financing the purchase and closing escrow, applies to anyone buying.

Form 46: Ideal House Profile

When you're looking for a house, it's easy to become confused by the huge array of choices. This is understandable, given that houses themselves are so different. Then, there's the issue of location— houses come in all sorts of neighborhoods, school districts and potential hazard zones (fire, earthquake and flood, to name a few). And, of course, price and purchase terms are crucial considerations for most homebuyers. To cope with all these and at least a dozen other important variables, it's essential to establish your priorities in advance and stick to them.

The Ideal House Profile will help simplify house-hunting. It lists all major house features such as number of bedrooms, type of yard, sales price and location. Use it to identify the essential items you're looking for (must have) in a house. Since price is an obvious consideration for most people, fill in the top section first. For example, under *Upper price limit*, you might note $400,000, and a *Maximum down payment* of $60,000. And if you have two kids, you might note that three bedrooms and excellent public schools are also mandatory priorities.

In most cases, it will be obvious where to note your priorities. For example if extreme quiet is important (you don't want to be near a freeway off-ramp) or you want walking access to a park, list these under *Desired neighborhood features*. If you're not sure where to list a particular "must have" such as a hot and dry climate, ocean view or garage parking, put it in the *Other desired features* category on the Ideal House Profile.

Once you've run through your list of "must haves," jot down features that you'd like but that aren't crucial to your decision of whether or not to buy. For example, under *Type of yard and grounds*, you might note patio and flat back yard in the "Hope to Have" column. Or under *Number and type of rooms*, you might list finished basement or master bedroom with bath.

Be sure to list your *Absolute no ways* (you will not buy a house that has any of these features) at the bottom of the form. Avoiding things you'll always hate, such as a house in a flood zone or in a poor school district, or one that's too far from where you work, can be even more important than finding a house which contains all your mandatory priorities.

Be sensitive to your spouse's (partner's) major concerns. If you're buying with another person, prepare your list of priorities together, so that each person's strong likes and dislikes are respected.

Can any of your priority items be added after you move in? A new kitchen, deck, patio and sometimes even an extra room, can also be added a few years down the road. Of course, replacing a small dark yard with a large sunny one can't be done.

Signing Instructions

There are no signing instructions for the Ideal House Profile. Simply fill it out and use it to help narrow your house search.

Getting more neighborhood information. If you're moving to a new area, you may not have a good sense of what particular cities and neighborhoods are like. Before finalizing a decision to buy, you'll want to take steps to get more information. For example, if under your "Must Have" column you've written "excellent public schools," you need in-depth information about the school system in each community you

are considering. It's fine to ask a real estate agent. Also, take the time to talk to people in the area whose kids currently attend its schools, or ask for help from a reference librarian at an area public library. And don't forget to check the wealth of community and neighborhood information available online. (See "Real Estate on the Web," above.)

Form 47: House Priorities Worksheet

Now it's time to use the information collected in Form 46 to create a House Priorities Worksheet which will help you see how each house you visit stacks up with your priorities. Start by making several copies of this worksheet to allow for mistakes or the eventual scaling back of your priority list if it turns out you can't afford all the features you would like. Then, enter relevant information on a master copy of Form 47 under each major category—"Must have," "Hope to have" and "Absolute no ways."

Once you have completed your House Priorities Worksheet to your satisfaction, make several copies. Take one with you each time you visit a house. For each house you see, fill in the top of the worksheet. Enter the address, asking price, name and phone number of the contact person (listing agent or seller, if it's for sale by owner) and the date you saw the house. As you walk around each house and talk to the owner or agent, enter a checkmark if the house has a desirable or undesirable feature. Also make notes next to a particular feature if it can be changed to meet your needs (an okay kitchen could be modernized for $25,000). Add comments at the bottom, such as "potential undeveloped lot next door" or "neighbors seem very friendly." If you look at a lot of houses, taking notes such as these will help make sure you don't forget important information.

You should seriously consider only those houses with all of your "must haves" and none of your "no ways."

Signing Instructions

There are no signing instructions for the House Priorities Worksheet. Simply fill it out and use it to help narrow your house search.

💡 **Set up a good filing system.** As the list of houses you look at grows, you will need a method to keep track of the information you collect. Failing to adopt a good system may lead to revisiting houses you've already seen and rejected or making decisions based on half-remembered facts. For each house that seems like a possible prospect, make a file that includes a completed House Priorities Worksheet, the information sheet provided at the open house, the Multiple Listing Service information, ads and your notes. You can also use your computer to set up a simple database with key details on each house you see.

Form 48: House Comparison Worksheet

If, like many people, you look at a considerable number of houses over an extended period of time, you may soon have trouble distinguishing or comparing their features. That's where Form 48, the House Comparison Worksheet, comes in. Across the top of the form, list the addresses of the three or four houses you like best. In the left column, fill in your list of priorities and "absolute no ways" from your Ideal House Profile and House Priorities Worksheet. Then put a check on the line under each house that has that feature to allow for a quick comparison.

Signing Instructions

There are no signing instructions for the House Comparison Worksheet. Simply fill it out and use it to help focus your house search.

Form 49: Family Financial Statement

When planning to buy a house, one of your most important tasks is to determine how much you can afford to pay. To do this, begin by preparing a thorough family financial statement, which includes:
- your monthly income
- your monthly expenses, and
- your net worth (your assets minus your liabilities).

We use the word "family" as shorthand for the economic unit that will buy a house. For these purposes, an unmarried couple or a single person is just as much a family as is a married couple with three kids.

Preparing a family financial statement begins the process of learning how much house you can afford —in terms of both the down payment and monthly mortgage payments. It also gives real estate people and potential lenders a good sense of your general financial situation. And if you haven't been pre-approved for a mortgage loan when you make a purchase offer, a financial statement can be extremely helpful to convince the seller that you're a serious bidder. This may be crucial, especially if there's more than one prospective buyer. The person who can best convince the seller she's financially able to swing the deal with no glitches often prevails, even if her offer isn't the highest.

⚠️ **Don't list incorrect or incomplete information on your Family Financial Statement.** A lender will surely check with credit reporting agencies, and usually with employers and banks, to verify your information, meaning that listing bogus or exaggerated information is likely to be discovered and held against you. If necessary, a far better approach is to take the time to clean up a bad or erroneous credit file before you start house hunting.

Directions for Completing the Family Financial Statement

Top. Indicate the name(s), address(es), home phone number(s), employer's name(s) and address(es) and work phone number(s) for yourself and any co-borrower. A co-borrower includes a spouse, partner, friend or non-spouse relative with whom you are purchasing the house.

Worksheet 1: Income and Expenses

This worksheet shows you how much disposable income you have each month, a key fact in determining how big a mortgage you can qualify for. In columns 1 and 2, you and any co-borrower each list your monthly income and expenses. Total them in column 3.

IA. Monthly gross income. List your gross monthly income from all sources. Gross income means total income before amounts such as taxes, Social Security or workers' compensation are withheld.

  1. Employment. This is your base salary or wages plus any bonuses, tips, commissions or overtime you regularly receive. If your income is irregular, take the average of the past 24 months. If you have more than one job, include your combined total.

  2. Public benefits. Include income from Social Security, Disability, Aid to Families with Dependent Children (AFDC), Supplemental Security Income (SSI) and other public programs.

  3. Dividends. Include all dividends from stocks, bonds and similar investments.

  4. Royalties. If you have continuing income from the sale (licensing) of books, music, software, inventions or the like, list it here.

  5. Interest and other investment income. Include interest received on savings or money market accounts, or as payments on rental property. If the source of the income has costs associated with it (such as the costs of owning rental property), include the net monthly profit received.

  6. Other. Include payments from pensions, child or spousal support or separate private maintenance income. Specify the source.

IB. Total monthly gross income. Total items 1–6. This is the figure which lenders use to qualify you for mortgages.

IIA. Monthly nonhousing expenses. List what you spend each month on items such as child care and clothing. These won't interest the lender as much as they are important to you in evaluating how much house you can afford. Here are some notes clarifying specific items. Also, see Form 63, Daily Expenses, for advice on computing average monthly expenses.

  3. Food. Include eating at restaurants, as well as at home.

  6. Personal. Include costs for both personal care (haircuts, shoe repairs and toiletries) and personal fun (attending movies; buying CDs and lottery tickets; subscribing to newspapers). Also, include any regular personal loan payments.

  7. Education. Include monthly payments for education loans here, plus educational payments, such as your child's private school tuition.

  9. Transportation. Include costs for both motor vehicles (include monthly car loan payments, but exclude insurance) and public transit. You can include monthly upkeep for a vehicle and a reasonable amount for repairs; if you do, expressly say so.

  10. Other. Specify such expenses as regular monthly credit card payments, charitable or religious donations and savings deposits or child or spousal support payments.

IIB. Current housing expenses. If you currently own a home, list the mortgage and interest, taxes, insurance and utilities, including gas, electricity, water, sewage, garbage, telephone and cable service. If you rent, include your monthly rent and renter's insurance (if any).

IIC. Total monthly expenses. Here, total your nonhousing and housing expenses.

Worksheet 2: Assets and Liabilities

I. **Assets.** In columns 1 and 2, you and any co-borrower write down the cash or market value of the assets listed. Total them up in column 3.

   A. Cash and cash equivalents. List your cash and items easily converted into cash. Deposits include checking accounts, savings accounts, money market accounts and certificates of deposit (even if there is a withdrawal penalty).

   B. Marketable securities. Here you list items like stocks and bonds that are regularly traded and which you can normally turn into cash fairly readily, although not always at the price you'd wish. List the cash surrender value of any life insurance policy. Include items such as a short-term loan you made to a friend under the category "Other."

   C. Total cash and marketable securities. Add up items A and B.

   D. Nonliquid assets. These are items not easily converted into cash.

   1. **Real estate.** List the market value—the amount the property would sell for.

   2. **Retirement funds.** Include public or private pensions and self-directed accounts (IRAs, Keoghs or 401(k) plans). List the amount vested in the plan.

   3. **Business.** If you own a business, list your equity in it (market value less the debts on the business). Many small businesses are difficult to sell, and therefore difficult to value, but do your best.

   4. **Motor vehicles.** List the current market value of any car, truck, RV or motorcycle, even if you're still making payments. Check used car guides for the information.

   5. **Other.** Include nontangible assets such as copyrights, patents and trademarks. Yes, it is hard to value these types of assets, but it can be done, especially if you've been receiving income and it promises to continue. Depending on your field, author, inventor, musician or software writer organizations may be able to help. In the "Other" category, also include the current value of long-term loans you've made to others and any really valuable personal property such as expensive jewelry or electronic gear.

   E. Total nonliquid assets. Total up items D1–5.

   F. Total all assets. Total up items IC and IE.

IIA. **Liabilities—Debts.** In columns 1 and 2, you and any co-borrower write the total balances remaining for your outstanding loans under their respective categories.

   Under "Other," don't include monthly insurance payments or medical (noninsurance) payments, as these go on Worksheet 1, Section IIA, Monthly Expenses—Non-housing. Do include stock pledges, lawyer's and accountant's bills and the like.

IIB. **Total Liabilities.** Total the monthly payments and balances remaining for items 1–7.

III. **Net Worth.** Total of all assets minus total liabilities.

Signing Instructions

There are no signing instructions for the Family Financial Statement. Simply fill it out and use it to help evaluate how much house you can afford.

Form 50: Monthly Carrying Costs Worksheet

Your next step in determining how much house you can afford is to complete Form 50, the Monthly Carrying Costs Worksheet. To use the worksheet, you will need to provide the following information:

   Line 1: Estimated purchase price. How much money you'll need to spend on a house likely to have at least most of the "must have" features listed on your Ideal House Profile (Form 46).

   Line 2: Down payment. Enter the down payment you plan to make. Figure you'll probably need to put down 15% to 20% of the house purchase price, unless you qualify for a government loan or other low down payment loan. If you have a relatively high monthly income and few debts, you may find a lender who will allow you to put down less—but if so, the interest rate and loan fees are almost sure to be higher.

Line 3: Subtract the down payment (line 2) you want to make from your estimated purchase price (line 1). The result is the amount you'll need to borrow.

Line 4: Interest rate. Check mortgage interest tables printed in the Sunday newspaper real estate section and online websites featuring mortgage information. Loan brokers can also be a valuable resource when it comes to determining how much interest you'll need to pay. Use the Mortgage Rates and Terms Worksheet (Form 51) to shop for a mortgage.

Line 5: Principal and mortgage interest payment factor per $1,000 over the length of the loan. You can find this using the amortization chart below.

Line 6: Monthly mortgage payment. Multiply the factor from the amortization chart (line 5) by the loan amount you need to borrow (line 3). For example, if you estimate the house you want to buy will cost $260,000, a 20% down payment of $52,000 leaves you with a $208,000 mortgage loan. Your research shows you can get a 6% interest rate for a fixed-rate loan. The monthly factor per $1,000 for a 30-year loan at a 6% rate is 6. So your monthly mortgage payments will be 208 x 6, or $1,248.

Line 7: Homeowner's insurance. You can get exact quotes in advance from insurance agents. Very roughly, expect to spend $200-$400 per $100,000 of house value, depending on where you live and other factors.

Line 8: Property taxes. These vary tremendously depending on where you live. You'll need to get an estimate from a local tax assessor's office.

Line 9: Now add up your mortgage payment (line 6), insurance (line 7) and taxes (line 8). This is your monthly carrying costs (also called PITI—principal, interest, taxes, insurance).

A lender normally requires a buyer to be able to pay these costs with about 28%–38% of total monthly income, assuming moderate other long-term debts

(ten months or longer) such as child support, car payments and student loans. If you have no other long-term debts, lenders may approve a loan where you'll use up to 36%–38% of your monthly income to pay carrying costs.

Line 10: Long-term debts. These are items such as monthly payments on a car or student loan.

Line 11: Private mortgage insurance (PMI). Your lender may require this if you're making a down payment of less than 20%. PMI is often about .5% of the loan.

Line 12: Homeowners' association fee. You may have to pay this monthly fee if you're looking at a condo or a house in a development.

Line 13: Add lines 9–12 for the sum of your total monthly carrying costs and long-term debts.

Line 14: Lender qualification. Other things being equal (which they rarely are), lenders normally want you to make all monthly payments (mortgage payment, property taxes and homeowner's insurance) with 28%–38% of your monthly income. Whether you qualify at the bottom or top of this range depends on the amount of your down payment, the interest rate on the type of mortgage you want, your credit score and the level of your other long-term debts. Your credit score, a numerical measure that reflects how you've managed credit in the past, is an important consideration for many lenders.

Line 15: Divide line 13 by line 14 to determine the monthly income needed to qualify.

Line 16: Multiply line 15 by 12 to calculate the yearly income to qualify.

Signing Instructions

There are no signing instructions for the Monthly Carrying Costs Worksheet. Simply fill it out and use it to help evaluate how much house you can afford.

Get preapproved. Once you've done the basic calculations and completed your financial statement, you can ask a lender for a preapproval letter, saying that you're able to purchase a loan up to a maximum amount.

Mortgage Principal and Interest Payment Factors (Per $1,000)				
Interest rates (%)	15-year mortgage	20-year mortgage	25-year mortgage	30-year mortgage
5.00	7.91	6.60	5.85	5.37
5.25	8.04	6.74	5.99	5.52
5.50	8.17	6.88	6.14	5.68
5.75	8.30	7.02	6.29	5.84
6.00	8.44	7.16	6.44	6.00
6.25	8.57	7.31	6.60	6.16
6.50	8.71	7.46	6.75	6.32
6.75	8.85	7.60	6.91	6.49
7.00	8.99	7.75	7.07	6.65
7.25	9.13	7.90	7.23	6.82
7.50	9.27	8.06	7.39	6.99
7.75	9.41	8.21	7.55	7.16
8.00	9.56	8.36	7.72	7.34
8.25	9.70	8.52	7.88	7.51
8.50	9.85	8.68	8.05	7.69
8.75	9.99	8.84	8.22	7.87
9.00	10.14	9.00	8.39	8.05
9.25	10.29	9.16	8.56	8.23
9.50	10.44	9.32	8.74	8.41
9.75	10.59	9.49	8.91	8.59
10.00	10.75	9.65	9.09	8.78
10.25	10.90	9.82	9.26	8.96
10.50	11.05	9.98	9.44	9.15
10.75	11.21	10.15	9.62	9.33
11.00	11.37	10.32	9.80	9.52
11.25	11.52	10.49	9.98	9.71
11.50	11.68	10.66	10.16	9.90
11.75	11.84	10.84	10.35	10.09
12.00	12.00	11.01	10.53	10.29
12.25	12.16	11.19	10.72	10.48
12.50	12.33	11.36	10.90	10.67
12.75	12.49	11.54	11.09	10.87
13.00	12.65	11.72	11.28	11.06

Form 51: Mortgage Rates and Terms Worksheet

As with any other consumer product, significant savings can be achieved by carefully shopping for a mortgage. But because of the wide variety of mortgages on the market (fixed, adjustable, hybrid) and the fact that fine-print terms can significantly influence how much you'll really have to pay, it's essential that you carefully compare the total cost of different deals.

You can use the Mortgage Rates and Terms Worksheet to keep track of information you collect on different loans. You can use it whether you'll be working with a loan broker, a person who specializes in matching house buyers and appropriate mortgage lenders, or shopping for a mortgage on your own.

This form is important for three primary reasons:

- Filling it out all but requires that you really understand the fine-print details of every loan you consider.
- Having this information will be an invaluable aid to your memory; days or weeks later you can check what you've been offered.
- Assuming you get information about more than one loan, it will let you efficiently compare features.

Instructions for Completing the Mortgage Rates and Terms Table

Heading

At the top of the table, enter the lender's name (such as Bank of Richmond), the name of the loan agent you met or spoke with, his phone number and the date of your meeting or telephone conversation.

Section 1: General Information

Enter the type of loan: fixed or adjustable; the rate, if it's a fixed mortgage; whether it qualifies for government financing (if that's a need you have); the minimum down payment required; whether private mortgage insurance (PMI) is required and, if so, whether you'll need to set up an impound account; the term (number of years of the loan); whether it's assumable; whether it has a prepayment penalty;

whether it has negative amortization and, if so, whether it lets you (and for how much) lock in at a certain rate. See the table below for a brief description of key mortgage terms. For more information, check the Real Estate section of the Legal Encyclopedia on Nolo's website at http://www.nolo.com.

Section 2: Debt-to-Income Ratios Information

Here you need to indicate the percentage of your income each lender allows for the monthly carrying costs to obtain the mortgage, and for monthly carrying costs plus monthly payments on other long-term debts. Then, based on these debt-to-income ratios, enter the maximum loan each lender will make.

Section 3: Loan Costs

If possible, enter the costs associated with getting the loan—the number of points and their cost, PMI, additional loan fee, credit report, application fee, appraisal fee and other miscellaneous costs. Then total them up. Your estimate will have to be rough, because most lenders won't estimate closing costs until they start processing your loan. Even then, the costs are still estimates. You won't know the actual total of loan costs until you review the final papers you need to close escrow.

Section 4: Time Limits

You want to know how long it will take to process your loan application and, if it's approved, come up with the money (called "funding the loan"), enabling you to close the deal. Enter this information in the fourth section. Also, pay attention to the following items:

- the date each month your payment will be due; the first of the month is standard, although some portfolio lenders set the 15th of the month
- how many "grace" days you have (after which the payment is considered late—15 days is standard), and
- the fee for late mortgage payments.

Section 5: Other Features

If the loan has any special features, such as discounted points if you have a savings account with the bank, indicate them.

Section 6: Fixed Rate Two-Step Loans

If you look at any fixed rate loans that step up to a higher rate after several years, indicate the initial annual percentage rate and for how many years it stays in effect.

Section 7: Fixed Rate Balloon Payment Loans

If you are considering a fixed rate loan for a short period (often three, five or seven years) that ends with one large balloon payment, indicate the interest rate and monthly payment, the term of the loan and the amount of the balloon payment.

Section 8: Adjustable Rate Mortgages (ARMs)

First, enter the adjustable loan criteria—what index it's tied to, the amount of the margin, whether it's convertible and, if so, when.

Next, write down interest rate information—the initial rate, how long it lasts, the interest rate cap, the adjustment period and the life-of-the-loan cap. Be sure you understand whether the interest rate cap is a true periodic cap (caps both what you pay and what you owe) or is a payment cap that lets the amount you owe increase (negative amortization).

Finally, enter the payment information—the initial payment, cap and payment cap period. Also calculate your worst-case scenario: the highest interest rate and monthly payments possible with the adjustable rate loan offered for different time periods.

Section 9: Hybrid Loans

If you are interested in an ARM that has a fixed rate for the first few years and then becomes adjustable, enter the information here. Pay particular attention to how much the interest rate can jump at the first adjustment period.

Signing Instructions

There are no signing instructions for the Mortgage Rates and Terms Worksheet. Simply fill it out and use it to help compare various loan options and packages.

Key Mortgage Terms

Fixed rate mortgage. The interest rate and the amount you pay each month remain the same over the entire mortgage term, which is traditionally between 15 and 30 years. A number of variations are available, including short-term fixed-rate mortgages, five- and seven-year fixed rate loans with balloon payments at the end and two-step mortgages with a lower than normal fixed rate for the first few years, which later step up to the prevailing market rate after the initial period (often five years).

Adjustable rate mortgage (ARM). The interest rates on these mortgages fluctuate according to interest rates in the economy. Initial interest rates are typically offered at a discounted interest rate lower than for fixed rate mortgages. Over time, when initial discounts are filtered out, ARM rates will fluctuate as general interest rates go up and down. Several types of ARMs are available, including an ARM–fixed rate hybrid mortgage. A margin is the factor or percentage a lender adds to the index rate to arrive at the interest rate you pay over the market rate. All ARMs have caps, which come in various forms. A life-of-the-loan or overall cap is the maximum (such as five or six percentage points) your interest rate can go up or down over the term of your mortgage. A periodic cap limits the amount your interest rate can go up or down at each adjustment period, such as going up 2% annually, with your payments increasing accordingly.

Negative amortization. Fortunately, many high-quality mortgages don't use this consumer unfriendly (not to mention confusing) system. Sometimes called "deferred interest" or "interest advances," this negative amortization takes away many of the advantages provided by periodic caps on ARMs. That's because with negative amortization, if interest rates rise, your payment cap only works to limit the amount your monthly payment can go up (not the total you owe, which is not capped). The extra money over the cap is simply added onto the mortgage total you owe, often with the result that you'll owe larger payments in the future or a large balloon payment at the end of the mortgage.

PMI and impound account. Lenders may require private mortgage insurance (PMI) if you're making a down payment of less than 20%. Some PMI policies require that you set up an impound account, where you deposit up to a year's payments of PMI when the house purchase closes. In addition, you make monthly payments into the impound account for property taxes and homeowner's insurance, which in turn are paid by the lender or company that services the loan.

Assumable. A loan which a creditworthy buyer can take over (assume) from a seller.

Prepayment penalty. A charge for paying off your mortgage early. Most high-quality commercial mortgages don't charge a prepayment penalty.

Rate lock-in. A lender's guarantee to make a loan at a particular interest rate, even if the market changes within a specific time period, such as three to six weeks.

Debt-to-income ratios. The ratio of your monthly mortgage payments (including insurance and property taxes) plus long-term debts to your income; also called lender qualification.

Monthly carrying costs. The sum of your monthly payments for your mortgage, homeowner's insurance and property taxes.

Points and loan costs. The fees associated with getting a mortgage, which usually add up to 2%-5% of the cost of the mortgage. Points make up the largest part of lender fees, with one point equaling 1% of the loan principal. Often, loans charging more points have a slightly lower interest rate. If you will own a house for many years, paying relatively high points to get a lower fixed rate of interest is usually a good idea—you have years in which to enjoy the lower interest payments and amortize the cost of the points. But the reverse is also true—if you will move in three to five years or less, try to pay as few points as possible even if you pay a little more interest.

Time limits. How long it takes to process your loan application, including the time required to run a credit check, appraise the property, get your loan approved and come up with the money ("fund the loan").

Form 52: Moving Checklist

Congratulations! If you are looking at this form, chances are you found a good house, closed escrow and are getting ready to move in. Use the Moving Checklist to help you plan your move.

Signing Instructions

There are no signing instructions for the Moving Checklist. Simply fill it out and use it to keep track of moving tasks. ■

Buying or Selling a Car, Dog or Other Personal Property

This chapter contains forms for use when you sell used personal property, such as a car, boat, appliance, furniture or computer. It also includes a bill of sale for a dog. These simple bills of sale are designed to be used to record the terms of sale of all types of property (with the exception of real estate and securities, which are closely regulated by law).

A bill of sale is a written document which at a minimum includes:

- the names of the seller(s) and buyer(s) (there may be two sellers—for example, if the goods are co-owned as joint property by a husband and wife)
- a statement that a sale has taken place
- a description of the item(s) sold
- a statement of the amount paid, and
- the signature of the person selling the property and the date of the signing.

In addition, bills of sale often include:

- a promise by the seller that she owns or otherwise has the right to sell the item, and details on any liens or encumbrances giving someone else ownership in the goods being sold
- a written warranty or guarantee that the item is in good condition and will be repaired or replaced if it fails within a certain period
- an "as is" statement making it clear that no warranty is included (this will help protect the seller against any later claims by the buyer that the item purchased didn't measure up to the seller's representation or the buyer's expectations)
- terms of delivery
- disclosures of any major defects known to the seller, and
- a statement that the item has been inspected by an expert and that the expert's report is attached.

Use a well-drafted bill of sale to head off future legal trouble. When used cars, boats and other items of property are sold without a written bill of sale, the chances of future legal problems—maybe even a court battle—go way up. Far better to define in

advance all key terms of the sale, including, most important, the condition of the goods being sold, and whether the sale includes any seller's warranty (for example, 30 days on parts and labor) or is made "as is."

Form 53: Motor Vehicle Bill of Sale

Use this bill of sale when you buy or sell a vehicle that must be registered with your state's motor vehicles department. This typically includes cars, trucks, motorcycles, recreational vehicles and motor homes. It does not include stationary non-registered mobile homes that are designed to be used semi-permanently at a fixed location such as a mobile home park. Such homes are commonly treated as real property—just as if they were houses—and as such are covered by special transfer, financing and recording rules not discussed here. The category of motor vehicle also doesn't include off-road farm machinery—for that use Form 56 (General Bill of Sale)—unless it can be registered in your state as a motor vehicle.

Describe the vehicle in detail on the bill of sale, including the vehicle identification number or VIN (this is typically found on the driver's side of the dashboard, close to the windshield), and indicate the price paid. (Your state motor vehicles department wants the price to compute the sales tax.) List any personal property included in the sale such as a bicycle rack.

Double-check ownership interest in vehicle. A buyer who doesn't know and thoroughly trust the seller is advised to check with the motor vehicles department where the vehicle is registered to be sure that no one else claims an ownership interest (lien) in the vehicle, as would be the case if the seller hadn't yet repaid a purchase loan.

Clauses 4 and 5, aimed at providing the buyer full disclosure regarding any mechanical problems with the vehicle, give the seller his best chance to avoid future legal problems. If the vehicle is inspected by a mechanic who prepares a written report which is given to the buyer, and the seller conscientiously lists all known defects, it's highly unlikely that an unsatisfied buyer can later get a judge to agree that the seller was guilty of misrepresentation.

Clause 6 is a general disclaimer of the implied warranty of merchantability and other implied warranties. An implied warranty is a guarantee about the quality of goods or services purchased that is not written down or explicitly spoken. We include a disclaimer of implied warranties to help protect the seller against later claims by the buyer that the vehicle didn't measure up to the seller's representations or the buyer's expectations. You can substitute a short warranty covering parts or labor or both for this disclaimer.

Be sure to contact your state motor vehicles department for any special requirements when selling a motor vehicle, such as successfully qualifying for a smog certificate. If these exist, include them in Clause 8.

Signing Instructions

The buyer(s) and seller(s) must sign the Motor Vehicle Bill of Sale for it to be valid. Print out two copies of the form (or enough for each person signing the form to have their own copy). Each person should sign and date all copies of the form and keep a signed document for their own record.

Form 54: Boat Bill of Sale

This form is similar in content to the Motor Vehicle Bill of Sale (Form 53), but it covers boats of all kinds. The form contains questions concerning details of the boat, as well as any engines, electronics and other equipment that are to be sold in this transaction.

Carefully read the discussion that accompanies Form 53, Motor Vehicle Bill of Sale, especially the advice about arranging for an inspection by a third party and the wisdom of the seller bending over

backwards to list (disclose) all defects, so a buyer has no grounds to later claim that the condition of the boat was misrepresented.

This bill of sale includes a number of entries unique to boat sales. But because there are so many sizes and types of boats, you must fill in the details key to your sale, such as a thorough list of all personal property items included in the sale or the maintenance history of the boat. The Introduction, Section B, explains how to prepare attachments of this sort.

Signing Instructions

The buyer(s) and seller(s) must sign the Boat Bill of Sale for it to be valid. Print out two copies of the form (or enough for each person signing the form to have their own copy). Each person should sign and date all copies of the form and keep a signed document for their own record.

Form 55: Computer System Bill of Sale

This bill of sale should be used for computers, computer peripherals and software, especially where a whole system is being sold. If only one or two components are being sold, Form 56, the General Bill of Sale, which is a bit simpler, should be adequate. Before using this form, review the material that precedes the Motor Vehicle Bill of Sale (Form 53), which discusses a number of the key clauses in this agreement.

Signing Instructions

The buyer(s) and seller(s) must sign the Computer System Bill of Sale for it to be valid. Print out two copies of the form (or enough for each person signing the form to have their own copy). Each person should sign and date all copies of the form and keep a signed document for their own record.

Form 56: General Bill of Sale

Form 56, the General Bill of Sale, should be used for the sale of personal property, such as jewelry, art works, sports equipment, rare books, furniture, collections, appliances, tools, photographic equipment and electronic items. Do not use this form if you are selling a car or other motor vehicle, boat or computer system (these categories are specifically covered previously in this chapter). Before using this form, read the brief discussion that precedes the Motor Vehicle Bill of Sale (Form 53) which discusses key clauses in a bill of sale.

Signing Instructions

The buyer(s) and seller(s) must sign the General Bill of Sale for it to be valid. Print out two copies of the form (or enough for each person signing the form to have their own copy). Each person should sign and date all copies of the form and keep a signed document for their own record.

Form 57: Bill of Sale for Dog

Use this bill of sale when you buy or sell a dog. It spells out exactly what terms the seller is promising, including price, how and when the dog will be turned over to the buyer, and who will pay shipping costs (if any). Form 57 provides basic information on the dog, including birth date, medication information such as vaccination history, health, name of breeder, special training (if any) and registration with the American Kennel Club or other entity. Most of the form is self-explanatory. You can also add any items of special concern—for example, if the seller wants the buyer to promise to have the dog spayed or neutered.

Clause 6 gives the buyer two options if a veterinarian certifies, in writing, that the dog has a disease or a congenital defect that was present when the buyer bought the dog. Within 14 days, the buyer may either return the dog to the seller and be reimbursed for the purchase price and for reasonable veterinary bills already paid, or keep the dog and also receive reimbursement for reasonable veterinary bills, up to the amount of the purchase price.

If you're buying a dog from a pet store: You may have other legal rights in addition to those set out in this bill of sale. Because consumers have had so many problems with dogs bought in pet stores, many states impose special requirements on pet retailers, which don't apply to breeders who raise and sell dogs themselves. You may be entitled to a disclosure sheet, stating where the animal came from (it may have been shipped across the country at a young age), and its health and vaccination history. You may also have a right to return or exchange an unhealthy dog, or get reimbursement for veterinary bills that is different from the right this bill of sale gives you.

Signing Instructions

The buyer(s) and seller(s) must sign this Bill of Sale for Dog for it to be valid. Print out two copies of the form (or enough for each person signing the form to have their own copy). Each person should sign and date all copies of the form and keep a signed document for their own record. ■

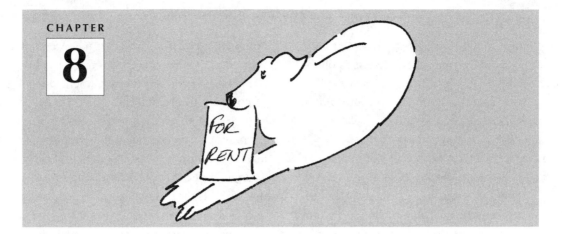

Renting Personal Property and Storing Goods

People frequently rent tools, equipment and other personal property. While this is often done from commercial companies which have their own forms, it is also common to rent objects from a neighbor or friend as an informal way of helping your friend or neighbor with the purchase cost. Many rented items are used to perform a particular task, as would be the case if you rented a rototiller and weight drum to lay sod, or a power saw and sander to do a small remodeling job around your home. In other situations, you might rent property for a recreational purpose—for example, if you're assigned to bring a volleyball net and badminton set to the family reunion.

This chapter includes a form for renting personal property. You can tailor this based on the type of property you're renting, its value and how long you need to rent it for. The chapter also includes a notice to end this type of rental agreement.

In addition to borrowing or renting tools, equipment and other items, people often turn to friends or neighbors to store their personal property, such as furniture, for an extended period of time. This chapter includes a storage contract for use in these situations.

Whether or not a rental or storage fee is paid, it makes sense to write down your understanding of key issues, such as the length of the rental or storage period and who will be responsible if the rented or stored property is damaged. Having a written agreement is especially important if valuable property is to be rented or stored for an extended period. If any problem comes up, having a simple written contract will enhance efforts to arrive at a fair settlement and help preserve relations between the parties.

Form 58: Personal Property Rental Agreement

You can use Form 58 for a short-term rental (30 days or less) of personal (nonreal estate) property. It is primarily geared toward renting relatively inexpensive personal property from a neighbor or friend. Because not much is at stake, this rental agreement doesn't deal with the many potentially complex issues that can arise when expensive property is rented for an extended period. But this personal property rental agreement does a great job of covering the basics, including the names of the parties (Owner and Renter), a description of the property and its condition, the amount of rent (if any), length of the rental period and delivery arrangements. It includes a dispute resolution clause that provides for negotiation, mediation and arbitration as a means for the parties to resolve any disputes that may arise over the agreement. (See Section E of the Introduction for more on dispute resolution procedures.)

Signing Instructions

You must sign this Personal Property Rental Agreement for it to be valid. Print out two copies of the form (or enough for each person who will be signing the form to have their own copy). Each person should sign and date all copies of the form and keep a signed document for their own records.

Form 59: Notice of Termination of Personal Property Rental Agreement

This form can be used by either the owner or the renter to end any personal property rental agreement that is not made for a specific period. You do not need to give a reason (unless this is required by your rental agreement—not the case with Form 58).

⚠ **Do not use this termination notice if you have rented personal property for a specific rental period.** In this case, you cannot terminate the agreement unless both parties agree.

Signing Instructions

There are no specific signing instructions for the Notice of Termination of Personal Property Rental

Agreement. Simply sign the document and give it to the other party. Keep a copy for your records.

Form 60: Storage Contract

It is common to store property with friends and relatives—everything from bikes, beds and books to washing machines, weights and walking sticks. Sometimes, this amounts to nothing more than leaving a few small objects for a short time. On other occasions, however, it means storing a household or garage full of goods for a year or more. In many situations involving friends and family, money isn't charged for storage, although payment certainly can be appropriate when bulky or valuable objects are stored for a considerable period of time. This is especially true when the goods are stored in a place (for example, a garage or spare room) that might otherwise be rented or used.

Form 60 covers the basics of storing personal property, including the names of the parties (we call them Property Owner and Property Custodian); a description of the property being stored and its condition and value; storage location, term and payment; who's responsible for theft of or damage to property during the rental period, and how the custodian will deal with abandoned property never reclaimed by the owner. This storage contract includes a dispute resolution clause that provides for negotiation, mediation and arbitration as a means for the parties to resolve any disputes that may arise over the agreement. (See Section E of the Introduction for more on dispute resolution procedures.)

It is especially important that you carefully identify property and its value and condition. One common cause of disputes concerns a property owner claiming that a valuable item is missing, while the property custodian says it was never present in the first place. The best way to prevent this is to make a thorough list of the items to be stored. In Clause 1, you should identify each item as thoroughly as possible, including (as appropriate) the make, model, year, color and condition. Also, when you specify the value of the property (Clause 8), be sure you're clear as to whether you mean the replacement value or the fair market value of the property, such as a TV set. (You'll be asked to make a choice.) Replacement value is how much it would cost for you to buy another of this item, such as the cost of a new TV set. Fair market value is how much you get for an item, such as a TV set, if you sold it—for example, at a garage sale. Finally, use Clause 9 to spell out any defects or damage in the property being stored (such as a stain on a sofa), and any special terms of the storage. Clause 14 is the place to do this—for example, if you want the Property Custodian to start the car at least once a week while it's in storage.

Signing Instructions

You must sign this Storage Contract for it to be valid. Print out two copies of the form (or enough for each person who will be signing the form to have their own copy). Each person should sign and date all copies of the form and keep a signed document for their own records. ■

CHAPTER

9

Home Repairs and Maintenance

This chapter includes two agreements that cover home maintenance and repairs, and other work you plan to have done at your residence, such as painting or yard work. To assure yourself of a good job, your most important task is to find a contractor that has done excellent work for a number of other people in your community. (Our forms use the term "contractor" for someone who does home repairs or maintenance.) But even with a highly recommended person, serious misunderstandings between a homeowner and contractor can easily arise if the key job specifications, payment details and work schedule haven't been carefully worked out and written down before the work begins. That's the purpose of these forms. These written agreements will help you get the work done right, on time and within your budget.

⚠ **The two forms in this chapter are not suitable for complicated jobs where the contractor will have to replace or install significant materials**—for example, remodeling a kitchen, building a deck, adding a room, putting on a new roof or painting the complete exterior or interior. You'll need a more detailed contract than the ones provided here. A large firm doing major home repairs and remodeling will usually present you with its own contract. The forms in this chapter can help you analyze an agreement proposed by a contractor and make sure the basics are covered.

State Licensing and Registration Requirements for Home Repair Work

Almost all states have licensing requirements for certain categories of highly skilled home improvement and construction work. For example, most states license people who do residential electrical and plumbing work or who build new structures. By contrast, there is less uniformity among the states as to whether licensing is required for contractors who do general repair and remodeling work, such as framing, drywall installation, paneling, deck construction, siding and painting.

License and registration requirements are often tied to the following factors:

- **Size of the project**—for example, a license may be required for work on any job over $5,000.
- **Type of job**—some states require a license for plumbing or electrical work but not for painting.
- **Location of contractor**—most states regulate contracting work of any type that is done by out-of-state contractors.

Most states that require a license for general repair and remodeling tasks require some experience and skills training, and some evidence of financial responsibility or effective customer recourse policy. For details, call your state Consumer Protection Office to find out if your state regulates contractors, and if so, the name and phone number of the agency that does the regulating, such as the State Contractors' Licensing Board. You can find a list of state Consumer Protection Offices on Nolo's website at http://www. nolo.com/encyclopedia/articles/ctim/protection.html. Then contact the agency directly for information. Many state agencies publish and distribute free consumer information on home repair work.

⚠ **Beware of unlicensed contractors.** Even where licenses are required, you can always find someone unlicensed who will do the work, usually promising a "cheap" price. Be wary about accepting these offers when the work requires a license—unlicensed contractors are not bonded and in some states can't be sued. And, of course, an unlicensed contractor is almost sure to work without getting a building permit which may cause problems down the road as discussed below.

Some states require people who do home repair and remodeling work to register with the state. Registration usually does not require any demonstration of experience or training. It is primarily designed to keep track of people offering contractor services so that homeowners can locate them if something goes wrong during or after the job is done.

Local Permits and Approvals for Home Repair Work

In addition to state licensing and registration rules, homeowners must often obtain a permit from a city or county agency for jobs that involve structural alterations, additions (a new room), substantial remodeling (a kitchen or bathroom) or new electrical wiring or plumbing installations. Permits, however, are usually not required for casual carpentry, minor plumbing and electrical repairs or adding a new window or door.

In addition to a local permit, if the house is part of a condominium complex or planned unit development, formal approval of the work by a homeowner's association or "architectural review committee" will be necessary if the work affects the home's exterior appearance. Homeowner association approval is usually necessary for new windows, exterior painting, roofing and room additions.

Either the homeowner or the contractor must be responsible for getting information about the necessary permits. If the job requires a permit or approval, but none is obtained, the homeowner may have to redo all or a portion of the work if a later inspection reveals deficiencies. Also, the value of the home may be adversely affected when it comes to resale if the buyer learns of the non-permit work.

Independent Contractor Versus Employee

Our contracts (Clause 4) assume that the person who will come to your house is an independent contractor, not your employee. As long as the contractor is doing one job or occasional work, this is legal. If the person will work for you regularly (an everyday gardener, for example), the law probably requires that you treat him as an employee, for whom you are legally required to pay income taxes, Social Security and other benefits.

For more information on the difference between an independent contractor and an employee, see IRS Form SS-8, available on the IRS website at http://www.irs.gov, or by phone at 800-424-FORM.

Dispute Resolution Clause

The two forms in this chapter do not include a dispute resolution clause mandating mediation and arbitration to resolve disputes before going to court. If you would like to include a dispute resolution clause in either of these forms, see the Introduction, Section E, which explains how.

Form 61: Home Maintenance Agreement

Form 61 is intended for unskilled labor on a one-time job that isn't expected to last for more than a day or two and doesn't involve the need for a significant amount of materials. Typical jobs that fall into this category are hauling refuse, cleaning a garage or house, washing windows, gardening and other yard work. Such jobs are usually performed by one person who supplies his or her own tools.

This form is easy to complete. Simply spell out the details of the work and the amount, form and schedule of payment.

Signing Instructions

You (the homeowner) and the contractor must sign this Home Maintenance Agreement for it to be valid. Print out two copies of the form and have each party sign and date both copies of the form. Give the contractor one of the signed documents and keep the other for your own records.

Form 62: Home Repairs Agreement

Form 62 covers home repairs done by skilled labor for a job that isn't expected to take more than a few days, such as installing new locks or windows, non-structural carpentry repairs, touch-up painting, masonry work and roofing repairs. Use it to spell out details as to the who (names of the homeowner and contractor); what and how (specific details of the job, such as painting the kitchen or installing new bathroom floor); how much (dollar amount and details of payment) and when (beginning and ending dates) of the work.

Don't pay too much up front—just enough to let the contractor purchase the materials he needs to get started. In addition, it is usually best to agree to make periodic payments which are tied to measurable, easy-to-define goals. Clause 2 is the place to spell out the details of your payment arrangement—for example, if you're paying one lump sum at the end of the work, paying in increments, such as half at the beginning of work and half at the end, paying an hourly rate for work done or some other arrangement.

Simple home repairs probably won't require a contractor's license or permit, but if it does, Clauses 4 and 5 of the Home Repairs Agreement allows you to spell out the details regarding licenses and permits. If you don't need them, follow the instructions in the Introduction, Section B, for deleting unnecessary contract clauses. Clause 6 specifies that the contractor carries his or her own insurance and maintains responsibility for injuries that occur during the course of the work.

Signing Instructions

You (the homeowner) and the contractor must sign this Home Repairs Agreement for it to be valid. Print out two copies of the form and have each party sign and date both copies of the form. Give the contractor one of the signed documents and keep the other for your own records. ■

CHAPTER

10

Handling Personal Finances

You probably don't think too much about monthly budgets, joint accounts or stopping payment on a check unless you are having financial problems. But by being proactive—reviewing your finances in advance and knowing your legal rights—you can often avoid legal and money problems. The forms in this chapter are designed for you to get a handle on your personal finances— budgeting, dealing with debts and debt collectors and reviewing your credit report—whether you're trying to avoid problems or you're in the midst of a crisis.

Detailed information and forms on dealing with debts, planning a budget, rebuilding your credit and other similar topics can be found in *Money Troubles: Legal Strategies to Cope With Your Debts* and *Credit Repair*, both written by Robin Leonard and published by Nolo.

Form 63: Daily Expenses

Creating a budget—comparing your average monthly expenses to your total monthly income—is a first step to putting your financial house in order. Although it's not hard to do, budgeting is a three-step process. Step one is to get a clear picture of how you spend your money. You can do that using Form 63 (Daily Expenses), on which you record everything you spend over the course of a week. Step two is to total up your monthly income using Form 64. The final step is comparing the two. For that you can use Form 65.

Here's how to use Daily Expenses (Form 63):

1. Make nine copies of the Daily Expenses form (if you're using the tear-out form) or print a new copy each week. You will use eight copies of the form to record your expenses for about two months. By using your expense figures for two months, you'll avoid creating a budget based on a week or a month of unusually high or low expenses. If you and another adult (such as a spouse or partner)

share finances, make eight copies each. You will use the ninth copy to record other expenses.

2. Select a Sunday to begin recording your expenses; record that Sunday's date in the blank at the top of one copy of the form.

3. Record every expense you pay for by cash or cash equivalent—check, ATM or debit card or automatic bank withdrawal—on that week's form. Include deposits into savings accounts, certificates of deposit or money market accounts and purchases of investments. Do not record credit card charges. When you make a payment on a credit card bill, however, list the amount of your payment and the items covered by the payment. If you don't pay the entire bill, list the older charges that total the amount paid less that month's finance charge, and attribute the balance to the finance charges.

4. At the end of the week, total your weekly expenses. Put away the completed Daily Expenses form, take out another copy and fill it out according to Step 3. Repeat for eight weeks.

5. At the end of the eight weeks, take out the ninth sheet. Anywhere on it, list seasonal, annual, semi-annual or quarterly expenses you incur each year, but which did not come due during your two-month recording period. Common examples are property taxes, car registration, charitable gifts, magazine subscriptions, tax preparation fees and auto and house insurance payments. Divide the annual cost of these items by 365 to get the "daily expense."

6. Total up all expenses on the nine sheets to get your two months' expenses.

Signing Instructions

There are no signing instructions for this form. Simply fill it out and use it to evaluate your spending patterns and prepare a budget.

Form 64: Monthly Income

Use Form 64 together with Form 63 to help you create a budget. On Form 64, you total up your monthly income. Be sure to include income information for both people if you and another adult share finances.

Part A is for jobs for which you receive a salary or wages. Part B is for self-employment income, including sales commissions. Part C is for investment income and Part D is for other sources of income, such as bonus pay, alimony or child support, pension or retirement income and public assistance.

When you are done listing all sources of income, add them all up for your total monthly income.

Don't include your income that is automatically reinvested. As you list your income, you may be inclined to include your interest and dividends that are automatically reinvested, such as retirement plan income and stock dividends, to get a true sense of your income. But the purpose of creating a budget is to keep track of your actual expenses and the income you have available to pay those expenses. By listing income you don't actually receive, you will be left with the impression that you have more income to cover your expenses each month than you actually receive.

Signing Instructions

There are no signing instructions for the Monthly Income form. Simply fill it out and use it to prepare a monthly budget.

Form 65: Monthly Budget

After you've kept track of your expenses (Form 63) and income (Form 64) for a couple of months, you're ready to create a budget using Form 65. Follow these steps:

1. Using your total actual expenses, project your monthly expenses for the categories relevant to you on Form 65 (Monthly Budget). To find your projected monthly expenses, divide the total of your actual two months' expenses by two. Be sure to include the daily equivalent of any quarterly, semi-annual or annual expenses that you noted on your ninth sheet of Form 63 (Daily Expenses).

2. Enter your projected monthly expenses into the projected (Proj.) column on Form 65. Remember, this is just an estimate based on two months of recordkeeping. Enter the total at the end of the form, near the bottom of the column.

3. Enter your projected monthly income (bottom line of Form 64) below your total projected expenses on Form 65.

4. Figure out the difference. If your expenses exceed your income, you will have to cut your projected expenses or increase your income.

5. During each month, write down your actual expenses in each category. Do this as accurately as possible—remember, creating a budget is really designed to help you adopt a sound spending plan, not to fill in the "correct" numbers. Check your actual monthly expenditures periodically to help you keep an eye on how you're doing. Are you keeping close to your projected figures? If you are not, you will need to change the projected amount for those categories.

When a large payment comes due. While you have included one-twelfth of your quarterly, semi-annual and annual expenses in each month's projection, those expenses and other unanticipated ones don't arise every month. Ideally, your budget provides for a cushion each month—that is, your income exceeds your expenses—so you'll be able to handle the large payments when they come due by using that month's cushion or the savings you've built up from the excess each month. If you don't have the cash on hand to pay the large payment, you will have to cut back in other expense categories.

Signing Instructions

There are no signing instructions for this Monthly Budget form. Simply fill it out and use it to balance your income and expenses.

Form 66: Statement of Assets and Liabilities

Subtracting what you owe (liabilities) from what you own (assets) reveals your net worth. A net worth statement can help you and any lender analyze your eligibility for a loan.

To find your net worth, use Form 66, Statement of Assets and Liabilities. Fill in as much information as you can. Don't worry about listing every asset or debt, as the information on this form changes daily as your assets change value and the balances on your debts rise or fall. You can estimate the date of purchase, or write N/A in this column if you don't know.

What values should you use for your assets? As best you can, you will want to include an asset's current market value—the amount you could get if you sold the item on the open market. This means you are not looking at what you could get in a forced sale—such as a house repossession or foreclosure, or if you had to sell all your personal belongings at a garage sale. Instead, you're looking at what your home could bring in under normal selling conditions, how much you could get for your car by selling it through the paper or to a dealer and how much your household goods are worth, considering they generally depreciate about 20% a year.

For a related form, specifically geared toward determining eligibility for a home loan, see Form 49, the Family Financial Statement, in Chapter 6.

Signing Instructions

There are no signing instructions for this Statement of Assets and Liabilities. Simply fill this form out and update it from time to time. Use it to determine your net worth which will be useful should you apply for a loan.

Form 67: Assignment of Rights

You can use this form to transfer property or money that you are entitled to receive (for example, under a contract or promissory note) to another person. This is called assigning your right to receive the property or money. In legal terms, you are the Assignor, the person transferring your right to property or money to another person, the Assignee. For example, if Bette signed a promissory note owing you money and you owe Roger money, you might assign your right to Bette's money to Roger. Or, you might assign your right to receive income from a book contract to your teenage son so that the money would be taxed in his bracket, not yours.

This Assignment of Rights form allows you to name one or two assignors and one or two assignees. There may be situations in which two people have the right to receive money or property and jointly transfer that right, or in which two people are granted the right to receive money or property. This typically, but not exclusively, arises when a husband and wife jointly have the right to money or property or are jointly granted such a right. The Chapter 5 discussion of promissory notes explains the community property system.

Often the assignment covers a set period, especially when you assign the right to receive payments. Form 67 (Clauses 3 and 4) allows you to specify the beginning and ending dates of the assignment; if you don't have an exact end date in mind, you can simply say that the assignment will end when a specific event occurs or you revoke the assignment.

Here are some questions to ask when considering an assignment:

- **If you are assigning rights based on a previously existing contract, does the contract allow the assignment?** Be sure to carefully read the contract and make sure you can assign your rights under it. For example, leases typically prohibit a tenant's assignment of the lease to another person without the landlord's consent.

- **Are there tax implications of the assignment?** If you assign money to another person and receive something of equal value in return, there should be no tax implications. If, however, you assign your right to receive money to another person as a gift and the IRS learns of the assignment, the IRS will treat the assignment as a taxable transaction. For most assignments, this won't be a problem because you can make a tax-free gift of up to $10,000 per individual per year.
- **Does the assignment substantially change the obligations of the person with whom you signed a contract?** If the contractual obligations will become more onerous, you may not be allowed to make the assignment. For example, if you have signed a contract with Happy House-Keepers to clean your house once a week for $75, you may not assign this obligation to a neighbor whose house would require a lot more time and effort to clean.

Signing Instructions

You must sign the Assignment of Rights form for it to be valid. Print out two copies of the form (or enough for each person who will be signing the form to have their own copy). Each person (Assignor and Assignee) should sign and date all copies of the form and keep a signed document for their own records.

Form 68: Notice to Terminate Joint Account

If you are separating from or divorcing a spouse or partner, you will want to immediately close any joint credit cards or accounts. This involves notifying all creditors of your request to close joint accounts so that no new charges can be made. You should send this notice to every credit card issuer, including banks, department stores and other retailers, with whom you and your spouse or partner hold a joint account. Send it to the customer service address on the back of a billing statement. You must complete a separate Notice to Terminate Joint Account for each credit card account you want to close. Be sure you enter the full names of the joint account holders exactly as they appear on the account.

The only way to make sure that an account is truly closed is to insist, as this notice does, that the creditor do a "hard close," so that no new charges can be made. (You can close your account even if you haven't paid off the balance. In that case, the account will remain active for the purpose of paying off the balance only.) This notice states that if a "hard close" is not done, you will not be responsible for any charges made on the account. While such a letter may not fully protect you, it is better than doing nothing, and you put the burden on the creditor.

Signing Instructions

Print out a copy of the Notice to Terminate Joint Account form and sign it in the space provided. Make two copies of the signed form and mail the original and one of the copies to the creditor you wish to notify of the joint account termination. Include with it a stamped self-addressed envelope. The creditor will sign the copy and return it to you in the self-addressed envelope as a receipt.

Send the form by certified mail, receipt requested, and keep a copy of the form for your records. You may later need it as proof that you properly notified the creditor of your intent to close the joint account.

Don't overlook home equity lines of credit. You and your ex may have applied for a home equity line of credit a while ago and forgotten about it. Equity credit lines which supply a checkbook can be used just like a joint checking account. Whoever has the checkbook has access to the money. Unless you have the checkbook, be sure to pay a visit to your banker. Request that the account be closed or frozen. Even if you have the checkbook, request that the account be closed so that your ex can't request more checks. By leaving an equity line of credit open, you risk losing your home.

Form 69: Notice to Stop Payment of Check

It's not unusual to write a check, hand it over or mail it to the recipient and then change your mind and want to stop payment. For example, you might not notice that delivered goods were defective until after the delivery person was paid and left. Many other situations give rise to the need to put a stop payment on a check.

The first thing to do is call your bank, savings and loan, credit union or other financial institution where your account is located to make an oral request to stop payment. Ask how much the charge is, if any, for this service. Then immediately send or, better yet, drop by a written confirmation of your stop payment notice, Form 69. Include any required charge with your notice,

In many situations, the stop payment notice lasts only six months or a year, and if you fear the person to whom you wrote the check will try to cash it much later, you may need to renew your stop payment notice. Banks, savings and loans, credit unions and other financial institutions have the option of rejecting checks they deem too old, often six months or older, but usually don't exercise this right. In fact, most people who work in a bank or other financial institution never look at the date of the check. They simply post it to the account. If the money is there to cover it, the check is paid.

Signing Instructions

Print out three copies of the Notice to Stop Payment of Check form. Sign the copies and mail or give two of them to the appropriate bank or financial institution along with a stamped, self-addressed envelope. As requested in this form, the financial institution should then sign and return one of the copies, acknowledging receipt of your letter. Keep a copy for your records.

Form 70: Request for Credit Report

If you want to repair your credit, establish credit or apply for a loan, your first step is to get a copy of your credit report. This is a file maintained by a credit reporting company that sells information to banks, lenders, landlords and others who routinely evaluate customers' creditworthiness. Credit reports contain personal information about you, including your current and past use of credit cards; loans (home, car, student and the like); any defaults on bills such as utility payments or doctor's bills; public records, such as lawsuits, and inquiries by creditors for a copy of your report.

You can get your credit report by mailing a written request for a copy to one of the three major national credit bureaus:

- Equifax, P.O. Box 740256, Atlanta, GA 30374-0256; 800-997-2493; http://www.equifax.com.
- Experian, National Consumers Assistance Center, P.O. Box 9600, Allen, TX 75013; 888-397-3742; http://www.experian.com.
- Trans Union, P.O. Box 1000, Chester, PA 19022; 800-888-4213; http://www.transunion.com/creditreport.

You can also get a copy of your credit report via the credit bureaus' websites or you can request one by phone.

The cost of a credit report is usually less than $10 (and free in some cases, listed below), but check first for the exact amount. When requesting your credit report, you'll need to provide your date of birth, Social Security number and a copy of your driver's license or other document showing your full name and address.

You are entitled to a free copy of your credit report if:

- You've been denied credit because of information in your credit file. You must request your free copy within 60 days of being denied credit, and provide a copy of the "credit denied" letter.
- You are unemployed and planning to apply for a job within 60 days following your request for your credit report. You'll need to show documentation verifying your unemployment

(such as a recent unemployment check or lay-off notice).

- You receive public assistance. You'll need to provide a copy of your most recent public assistance check as verification.
- You believe your credit file contains errors due to someone's fraud, such as using your credit card, name or Social Security number.
- In some states, you haven't requested a copy in the last year. You can get a free copy of your credit report once a year if you live in Colorado, Georgia, Maryland, Massachusetts, New Jersey or Vermont. You'll need to show proof of your residence such as a copy of your driver's license or other document showing your full name and address.

Signing Instructions

Sign your Request for Credit Report and mail it certified mail, return receipt requested, to the credit bureau. Keep a copy of the letter for your files. Include payment and any supporting documentation required, as noted above.

Form 71: Challenge Incorrect Credit Report Entry

Under the federal Fair Credit Reporting Act, you have the right to dispute all incorrect, out-of-date or misleading information in your credit file, such as an incorrect name, employer account or tax history, a lawsuit older than seven years or one you weren't involved in or a bankruptcy older than ten years. If you have carefully reviewed your credit report and identified information you want changed or removed, complete the "request for reinvestigation" form which was enclosed with your credit report. If the credit bureau did not enclose such a form, use Form 71 to spell out the information you want corrected or deleted from your credit report. Enclose copies of any documents you have that support your claim. Once the credit bureau receives your request, it

must investigate the items you dispute and contact you within 30 days. For more information, see *Credit Repair*, by Robin Leonard (Nolo).

Signing Instructions

Sign your Challenge Incorrect Credit Report Entry and mail it certified mail, return receipt requested, to the credit bureau that prepared the report you are disputing. Include copies of any documents supporting your claim. Keep a copy of the letter for your files.

Form 72: Dispute Credit Card Charge

If you use a credit or charge card but don't receive the product you purchased or you received a defective item, you can legally refuse to pay if you meet certain criteria:

- **Dispute concerning a purchase made with a credit card issued by the seller such as department store or gas station.** You can legally refuse to pay if you first attempt in good faith to resolve the dispute with the merchant, who refuses to replace, repair or otherwise correct the problem.
- **Dispute concerning a purchase made with a credit card, such as Visa or MasterCard, not issued by the seller.** You can legally refuse to pay if you first attempt in good faith to resolve the dispute with the merchant, who refuses to replace, repair or otherwise correct the problem. But, you can only withhold payment if the purchase was for more than $50 and was made within the state in which you live or was within 100 miles of your home.

If you are entitled to withhold payment, complete and mail Form 72 to the credit card company at the billing address and explain why you aren't paying. Do this promptly: The credit card issuer must receive your letter within 60 days of the statement date on your bill. Explain how you tried to resolve the problem with the merchant. Attach a copy of the credit card bill with the disputed item, along with any additional documentation of your attempt to resolve the dispute, such as a letter you sent to a merchant regarding a defective item.

For more information on credit card problems, check the Federal Trade Commission website at www.ftc.gov.

⚠️ **Do not use this form if the problem is unauthorized use of your credit card**—for example, charges made by someone who stole your card. In this situation, promptly report your loss to the credit card issuer to limit your liability for unauthorized charges.

Signing Instructions

Sign your Dispute Credit Card Charge letter and mail it to the credit card issuer, along with copies of any documents supporting your claim. Keep a copy of the letter for your files.

Form 73: Demand Collection Agency Cease Contact

If you owe money and your debt has been passed along to a collection agency, you will no doubt be contacted by a collector working for the agency. Many people don't understand that they have the legal right under federal law (the Fair Debt Collection Practices Act, 15 U.S.C. § 1692 and following) to tell a bill collector who works for a collection agency to leave them alone. (This does not apply to in-house collectors—for example, at a bank, department store or hospital.) To pursue your rights, you must put your demand in writing (that's the purpose of Form 73) and send it to the collection agency. By law, all collectors from the agency must then cease all phone calls, letters and other communications with you, unless they are contacting you to notify you that:

- collection efforts against you have ended, or
- the collection agency or the creditor will invoke a specific remedy against you, such as suing you.

Signing Instructions

Sign your Demand Collection Agency Cease Contact letter and mail it to the collection agency, along with copies of any documents supporting your demand. Keep a copy of the letter for your files. ■

Dealing With Junk Mail and Telemarketing Calls

The telephone is—depending on one's mood—a boon or a scourge of modern life. One of its undeniably bad aspects is its wide use by telemarketers. Fortunately, there are two federal laws—the Telephone Consumer Protection Act (47 U.S.C. § 227) and the Telemarketing and Consumer Fraud and Abuse Prevention Act (15 U.S.C. § 6101) —that put some limits on how telemarketers must act. Most states also have laws to curb abusive telemarketing. Some provisions are part of an effort to curb telemarketing fraud; others are aimed at reducing annoyance to consumers. For example, before you pay (usually by credit card) for something purchased from a telemarketer, the seller must accurately state the total cost, quantity of goods or services and all other important conditions and restrictions. A seller must also explain its refund policy or state that it doesn't allow a refund, exchange or cancellation.

Even more common than telemarketing fraud are legitimate, but incredibly annoying phone calls that we most often get at dinnertime. It may be some consolation that federal law at least prohibits telemarketers from making these calls before 8 a.m. and after 9 p.m. (local time) unless they have your permission to call. Telemarketers also must put you on a "do not call list" if you so request. And that's where the forms in this chapter come in—we show you how to tell a company to stop calling you and what to do if it doesn't.

Sometimes, your mailbox can become just as irritating as your telephone. For most of us, catalogues, credit card offers and all kinds of other junk mail take up more space than our first-class mail. Again, fortunately some federal laws (for example, amendments to the Fair Credit Reporting Act which restrict credit bureaus' use of your name for marketing purposes) can help you get off various mailing lists. In this chapter, we provide you with the easy-to-use forms to accomplish this.

The Privacy Rights Clearinghouse is a nonprofit consumer organization with extensive information and advice on consumer rights regarding junk mail, telemarketing and related privacy issues. For more information, see their website at http://www.privacyrights.org. or call 619-298-3396.

Form 74: Notice to Remove Name From List

It's quite possible that you want to receive some catalogues, promotional mailings or telemarketing phone calls, but not others. To get yourself onto only the lists you want to be on requires a two step-approach. First, send Form 74 to all companies that collect names in order to sell them to direct marketers and telemarketers, telling them to remove your name. Provide them with all spellings of your name, and the names of any other household members on the mailing label. If you're receiving junk mail for previous occupants at your address, provide their names, too. Then, send Form 75 to only those businesses whose materials or phone calls you want to receive.

Dozens of companies gather names and addresses to sell to direct marketers and telemarketers. While some lists are larger than others, you will get yourself off of most lists if you send Form 74, Notice to Remove Name from List, to the major credit bureaus:

- Experian, Opt Out, P.O. Box 919, Allen, TX 75013; http://www.experian.com.
- Equifax, Options, P.O. Box 740123, Atlanta, GA 30374; http://www.equifax.com.
- Trans Union, Name Removal Option, P.O. Box 97328, Jackson, MS 39288; http://www.transunion.com.

One phone call to 888-5OPTOUT will get you off the lists of all three of these credit bureaus.

The three credit bureaus listed above give you the choice of opting out for two years or permanently. If you opt out, you will no longer appear on direct marketing lists offered by the credit bureaus, but you will continue to receive mailings based on lists from other sources.

Other places to send Form 74 include:

- Mail Preference Service, Direct Marketing Association, P.O. Box 9008, Farmingdale, NY 11735; 212-768-7277. This Service is a good step towards getting rid of junk mail, but it's not a cure-all. Only members of the Direct Marketing Association get the "do not write" list. And these members don't have to comply if they don't want to. The Direct Marketing Association will keep your name in its files for five years. After that time, you should send another letter.

- Telephone Preference Service, Direct Marketing Association, P.O. Box 9014, Farmingdale, NY 11735.
- R.L. Polk & Company, Attn: Name Deletion File, 26955 Northwestern Highway, South Field, MI 48034; 800-873-7655.
- Donnelly Marketing, Inc., Data Base Operations, 1235 North Avenue, Nevada, IA 50201-1419; 888-633-4402.
- National Demographics and Lifestyles, Customer Service Department, 1621 18th St., #300, Denver, CO 80202. Most warranty cards—also called product registration cards—are sent to this company, not to the manufacturer. The cards are used to gather names for mailing lists and to inform customers about product recalls. Often, the cards have nothing to do with whether you get the benefit of the warranty. Usually, you're covered even if you don't send in the warranty card. Check with the manufacturer to find out whether this is the case. Send Form 74 to this company to get your name removed from their list.

Another way to reduce your junk mail is to contact the customer service departments of the companies that send you catalogs you don't want or other unwanted mail and ask to be taken off their mailing list. After you call, send Form 74.

Signing Instructions

Sign and date your Notice to Remove Name From List, and mail it to some or all of the companies listed above that sell lists of names to direct marketers and telemarketers. Keep a copy of the notice for your files.

An excellent resource for getting off of direct marketing and telemarketing lists is *Stop Junk Mail Forever (Telemarketing and Spamming, Too)*, by Marc Eisenson, Nancy Castleman, Marcy Ross and the "Stop Junk Mail-Man" (Good Advice Press, http://www.goodadvicepress.com/sjmf.htm).

Form 75: Notice to Add or Retain Name but Not Sell or Trade It

After sending Form 74 to get your name off the lists of all businesses that sell lists of names to direct marketers and telemarketers, use Form 75 to get onto (or keep yourself on) the lists maintained by businesses whose mailings and/or phone calls you do want to receive. This notice states that you do not want your name sold, traded or shared with any other company or business. Also, you can specify whether or not you want to accept telemarketing phone calls from the company.

Signing Instructions

Sign and date your Notice to Add or Retain Name and mail it to the companies whose mailings and/or phone calls you do want to receive. Keep a copy of the notice for your files.

Form 76: Telemarketing Phone Call Log

A federal law, the Telephone Consumer Protection Act, requires every telemarketer to keep a list of consumers who say that they do not want to be called again. The law has some real teeth: If you tell a telemarketer not to call you, but you get another call within 12 months, you can sue for up to $500. If the court finds that the telemarketer willfully or knowingly violated the law, the court can award you up to $1,500. Most states' small claims courts allow claims of at least $2,000, so you can sue on your own, without hiring a lawyer.

Some states also have telemarketing laws. Often, those laws are even stricter than federal law. Contact your State Consumer Protection Office to find out more about your state's telemarketing laws (see "How to Complain to Government Agencies," below, for information on contacting these agencies).

Use Form 76 to keep a log of telemarketing phone calls. You will need to note the date, the time of the call, the company, the telemarketer's name (probably a fake, but write it down anyway), the product being sold and the fact that you stated "put me on a 'do not call' list." You will need this evidence to prove that you received more than one call from the same telemarketing company.

If you follow up with a letter, such as Form 77, asking to be put on the "do not call" list, note this on the call log, too.

Signing Instructions

There are no signing instructions for the Telemarketing Phone Call Log. Simply fill it out every time you get a call from a telemarketer.

Form 77: Notice to Put Name on "Do Not Call" List

Proving that a telemarketer willfully violated the law by calling you more than once may be difficult. One way you can generate evidence of a company's willful act is to *always* end your phone call by stating "Put me on your 'do not call' list," and follow up with a letter stating the same. Include all of your telephone numbers in the letter. You can use Form 77 for this purpose. You will need to find out the mailing address of the company in order to send your letter. Here are a few suggestions:

- Ask the telemarketer who calls you for the address. Telemarketers are required by law to give you this information. Despite the law, many telemarketers will claim they don't know the address or can't tell you. If that happens, contact your State Consumer Protection Office

(see "How to Complain to Government Agencies," below).

- If it's a local company, or you know the city in which the company is located, see if you can find the address online or in your phone book; if you find a phone number, but not the address, call and ask for the mailing address.
- Consult *Hoover's Handbook of American Business: Profiles of Major U.S. Companies*. Your local library should have a copy, or you can visit the website at http://www.hoovers.com. The site contains a lot of self-promotional ads and other companies' banners, but you can get the information you need if you keep trying.

Signing Instructions

Sign and date your Notice to Put Name on "Do Not Call" List and mail it to the telemarketer whose calls you don't want. Keep a copy of the notice for your own records. You may need this if you end up suing the telemarketer for excessive calls (as described under Form 78).

Form 78: Demand for Damages for Excessive Calls

You can use Form 78 after you receive a second (or third or fourth) telemarketing call from the same business. It details the history of telemarketing phone calls you have received on behalf of the company and your requests to be put on the "do not call" list. Form 78 spells out your right to monetary compensation for a violation of the federal Telephone Consumer Protection Act as explained in the discussion of the Telemarketing Phone Call Log (Form 76), above. It specifies that you will seek all appropriate remedies in court if you do not get the requested compensation within 30 days. You will need to find out the mailing address of the company in order to send your letter. See the discussion under Form 77 (Notice to Put Name on "Do Not Call" List) for some suggestions on obtaining the address.

Signing Instructions

Sign your Demand for Damages for Excessive Calls letter and mail it to the company responsible for the telemarketing calls. Keep a copy for your files.

State "Do Not Call" Registries

Many states maintain a registry of residential telephone subscribers who do not want to receive calls from telemarketers. In order to do business in the state, telemarketers must buy the "do not call" list and are prohibited from calling anyone on the list. Violators are subject to fines. Some state registries are free, others charge a small fee to put your name on the list. Also, all registries exempt some categories of callers. For example, many states allow charities, companies seeking payment of debts and those calling on behalf of political candidates to continue to call you. If an organization is exempt from your state's "do not call" law, you can still follow the procedure outlined above to get on that organization's "do not call" list (see instructions for Forms 76 and 77).

If you are listed on your state's "do not call" registry and get a telephone call from a telemarketer, report the call to the appropriate state agency. Most states provide complaint forms online.

Below is a list of how to contact registries in some states. If your state is not on the list, don't assume that there isn't a registry in your state. Check with your local Consumer Protection Office or State Attorneys General (see "How to Complain to Government Agencies," for information on contacting these agencies).

- Alabama. 877-727-8200; http://www.psc.state.al.us
- Alaska. Register with your local telephone service carrier
- Arkansas. 877-866-8225; http://www.donotcall.org
- Connecticut. 800-842-2649; http://www.state.ct.us/dcp
- Florida. 800-435-7352; http://www.800helpfla.com (choose "online forms")
- Georgia. 877-426-6225; http://www.ganocall.com
- Idaho. 800-432-3545 outside Boise, 208-334-2424 in Boise; http://www.state.id.us/ag
- Missouri. 866-662-2551; http://www.ago.state.mo.us
- New York. 800-697-1220; http://www.consumer.state.ny.us
- Oregon. 877-700-6622; http:// www.ornocall.com
- Tennessee. 877-872-7030; http://www.state.tn.us/tra

How to Complain to Government Agencies

In addition to taking all of the steps suggested in this chapter, it is also a good idea to complain to government enforcement agencies about abusive phone calls and letters. You can simply send a copy of the written notice, such as Form 78, Demand for Damages for Excessive Calls, to one or more of the following agencies:

- **State Attorneys General.** You can find contact information for your State Attorney General's Office from the National Association of Attorneys General at http://www.naag.org. This is also a good resource to find out more about your state telemarketing laws.
- **State Consumer Protection Office.** Nolo's Legal Encyclopedia lists each state's consumer protection office at http://www.nolo.com/encyclopedia/articles/ctim/protection.html.
- **Federal Trade Commission.** Division of Enforcement, 6th & Pennsylvania Ave., NW, Washington, DC 20580; 877-382-4357; http://www.ftc.gov.
- **Federal Communications Commission.** 445 12th St., SW, Washington, DC 20554; 888-225-5322 (voice); 888-835-5322 (TTY); http://www.fcc.gov.

Hiring Child Care, Elder Care or Household Help

Many people hire others to work regularly in their homes—for example, to take care of their children during the workday, care for elderly parents or clean their houses. These relationships are often set up informally, with no written agreement. But informal arrangements can be fraught with problems. If you don't have a written agreement clearly defining responsibilities and benefits, you and your help are all too likely to have different expectations about the job. This can lead to serious disputes—even to either or both of you bitterly backing out of the arrangement. Far better to draft a clear written understanding of what the job entails.

The agreements in this chapter are for hiring child and elder care providers and other household workers who are employees, not independent contractors. When you hire an employee, you set the hours, responsibilities and pay rate of the worker. Legally, most babysitters and household workers who work for you on a regular basis are considered employees for whom you are required to pay taxes, Social Security and other benefits described below. In contrast, independent contractors typically own their own businesses and work for you only occasionally.

This chapter also includes a Child Care Instructions form you can use both for a full-time child care provider or an occasional babysitter.

For information on hiring independent contractors, see *Hiring Independent Contractors: The Employer's Legal Guide*, by Stephen Fishman (Nolo).

Do not use this form if you hire a child or elder care worker or housecleaner through a placement agency that sets and collects the worker's fee from you, pays the worker and controls the terms of the work. If you use an agency, the agency will have its own form for you to complete. People you hire through an agency are not your employees—they are the employees of their agencies.

Legal Obligations for Employees

Assuming your child or elder care worker or housecleaner is your employee, you have enhanced legal obligations to her. You also become responsible for a certain amount of paperwork and recordkeeping. You do not have to put this information in your child or elder care or housekeeping agreement, but you need to be aware of these responsibilities.

Social Security and Income Taxes. If you pay a child or elder care worker $1,300 or more in a calendar year, you must make Social Security (FICA) payments on those wages and withhold the employee's share of FICA. You do not have to deduct income taxes from wages paid to an employee for working in your home unless she requests it and you agree to do so. You make these payments by attaching Schedule H, Household Employment Taxes, to your annual Form 1040.

Unemployment Compensation. If you pay a household employee $1,000 or more in a three-month period, you must pay quarterly taxes under the Federal Unemployment Tax Act (FUTA), using IRS Form 940 or 940-EZ. As with FICA, you pay this amount by attaching Schedule H, Household Employment Taxes, to your annual Form 1040.

Workers' Compensation. Your state may require you to provide workers' compensation insurance against job-related injuries or illnesses suffered by your employees. Check with your state department of labor or employment.

Minimum Wage and Overtime. The federal minimum hourly wage is $5.15. Your child or elder care worker may be entitled to minimum wage, depending upon their particular hours and earnings. If your state minimum wage is higher, you will need to pay the state wage. In addition, under federal law, most domestic workers (other than live-in workers) qualify for overtime pay. Workers must be paid overtime at a rate of one-and-a-half times the regular rate for all hours worked beyond a 40-hour workweek. You can check the U.S. Department of Labor website at http://www.dol.gov/dol/esa/public/minwage/america.htm, for current information about federal and state minimum wage laws.

New Hire Reporting Form. Within a short time after you hire someone—20 days or less, depending on your state's rules—you must file a New Hire Reporting Form with a designated state agency. The information on the form becomes part of the National Directory of New Hires, used primarily to locate parents in order to collect child support. Contact your state department of labor or employment to get the forms and information on where to return them. You can find the phone number for your state's department of labor in the government listings of your phone book, or you can find contact information online. Visit FindLaw at http://www.findlaw.com/11stategov/index.html. Once there, look on your state's home page for the state labor department or commission.

Federal ID Number. If you hire a household employee, you must obtain a federal employer identification number (EIN), required by the IRS of all employers for tax filing and reporting purposes. The form you need is IRS Form SS-4, *Application for Employer Identification Number.*

IRS Resources

The IRS has a number of publications and forms that might help you. Call the IRS at 800-424-FORM or visit its website at http://www.irs.gov to download these forms and publications. Start with Publication 926, *Household Employers' Tax Guide,* which describes the major tax responsibilities of employers. You may also want to look at:

- Form SS-8, which contains IRS definitions of independent contractor and employee
- Form SS-4, *Application for Employer Identification Number,* and
- Form 942, *Employer's Quarterly Tax Return for Household Employees,* for use in reporting Social Security taxes and any federal income tax withheld.

Reality Check

⚠ Many families don't follow the law by paying either required taxes or Social Security for household workers, some of whom are undocumented aliens. This chapter is not intended to preach about the law, but to alert you to the laws that affect your relationships with child and elder care and housekeeping workers. No question, if you fail to pay Social Security and meet your other legal obligations as an employer, there may be several negative consequences:

- You may be assessed substantial financial penalties. For example, if your full-time elder care provider files for Social Security five years from now and can prove prior earnings, but no Social Security has been paid, the IRS could back-bill you at high interest rates.
- If you don't meet a state requirement to provide workers' compensation insurance, and your child care worker is injured while on the job and can't work for a few months, you may be in hot water if she files for workers' compensation. You will probably be held liable for the worker's medical costs and a portion of her lost wages, as well as be fined for not having the insurance in the first place.
- You will not be able to take a child care tax credit on your federal income taxes. The credit is based on your work-related expenses and income.

Form 79: Child Care Agreement

A child care provider who takes care of your children in your house, either part-time or full-time, may live out (often called a care giver or babysitter) or live in (an au pair or nanny). The responsibilities of the position may vary widely, from performing a wide range of housekeeping services to only taking care of the children.

Use Form 79 to spell out your agreement regarding the child care worker's responsibilities, hours, benefits, amount and schedule of payment and other important aspects of the job. The best approach is to be as detailed as possible.

Start by filling in your name, address, phone numbers and other contact information for yourself (and a second parent if he or she will be signing the Child Care Agreement) and your child care provider. List your children's names and birth dates.

Here's some advice on filling in various sections of the Child Care Agreement:

Location and Schedule of Care (Clause 4). Provide the address where child care will be provided (typically your home) and the days and hours of care, such as 8 a.m. to 6 p.m. weekdays. Live-in nannies or au pairs often work some weeknights and weekends.

Beginning Date (Clause 5) and Training or Probation Period (Clause 6). Specify the date employment will begin and the length of any training or probation period, such as the first 15 or 30 days of child care. This is the time to make sure that the relationship will work for everyone involved. A training period helps your child care provider get to know your home and neighborhood and the exact way you want things done. If there will be no training or probation period, you can skip this question.

Responsibilities (Clause 7). The responsibilities of the child care position may vary widely depending on many factors, including the number and age of your children; whether or not the child care worker lives in or out, is full- or part-time; your family situation and needs; and the skills and background of the child care provider. In some households, particularly with infants and toddlers, the babysitter or au pair takes care of only the children—that is, no housework, except for doing the children's laundry. In other families, especially with older children, the employee may function more as a housekeeper, cook and chauffeur. You should specify the child care worker's responsibilities in as much detail as possible, including cooking, bathing and personal care for your children, social and recreational activities (such as arranging the children's play dates), transportation (driving kids to and from school or practices), shopping and errands for the family, housecleaning, ironing and laundry.

EXAMPLE: Here's an example of responsibilities for a live-in au pair taking care of an infant (Kate) and preschooler (Tom):

The child care provider's primary responsibility is to provide loving care of Kate and Tom. This includes playing with and reading to them, taking them to the park as weather permits, making sure they have naps as needed, and preparing their meals and snacks. The care provider will bathe Kate and Tom every other day, more frequently if necessary. Other responsibilities include driving Tom to "Baby Gym" twice a week, doing the children's laundry and keeping their rooms tidy.

Wage or Salary (Clause 8). You should specify exactly how the child care provider will be paid, such as an hourly rate or weekly salary. How much you pay depends on many factors, including the number and ages of your children; the type of care provided and responsibilities; the number of hours, time of day and regularity of the schedule; the experience and training of the employee; benefits such as room and board; and the going rate in your community. Before you fill in this section, be sure you understand your legal obligations when hiring an employee, such as minimum wage rules, as described above.

Payment Schedule (Clause 9). You may want to pay your child care provider weekly (say, on Friday), twice per month (such as on the 15th and on the last day of the month) or once per month.

Benefits (Clause 10). In addition to payment, you may offer the child care provider any benefits you wish, such as paid vacations and holidays, health insurance or sick leave.

Termination Policy (Clause 11). If things don't work out, the Child Care Agreement provides a termination policy that allows either the parents or the child care provider the right to terminate the agreement at any time, for any reason and without notice.

Additional Provisions (Clause 12). Describe any additional terms of this agreement, such as schedule for salary reviews, a no-smoking policy or a requirement that the child care provider take a first aid course.

Modifications (Clause 13). This agreement provides that any changes to it must be made in writing and signed by all parties to the agreement. This protects both the parents and the child care provider against misunderstandings over major issues that were agreed to verbally.

Signing Instructions

To make the Child Care Agreement valid, the parent(s) and the child care provider must sign it. (If you and your children's other parent are living in the same home and raising your kids together, it's best if both of you sign this document.) Print out two copies of the form. You, your children's other parent (if he or she is signing the form) and the caregiver must sign and date the form where indicated. Give one of the signed originals to the child care provider and keep the other for your records.

Shared In-Home Care

Some families pool their resources and share an in-home child care provider. These arrangements are ideal for neighbors or co-workers with children who are close in age. Just as a written agreement between a family and a child care worker can clarify expectations and prevent conflicts, written understanding between the two families who are sharing a child care provider can accomplish the same objectives. If you share in-home care with another family, be sure you both agree on the key issues before drafting your contract with the child care worker, including location of the care, splitting expenses, termination procedures and supervision. The other parents should make their own child care agreement for their own children.

Form 80:   Child Care Instructions

Use this form to provide important information for babysitters and child care providers, such as phone numbers of doctors; instructions about meals and naps, and other details of your child's care, including any allergies or healt care conditions your child has.

The "temporary contact" section of the Child Care Instructions form (Clause 3) is the place to provide information about where you can be reached while you are away from the kids—for example, if you are going out for dinner and to the movies on a Saturday night. Clause 3 will change most frequently. If you do not want to update your Child Care Instructions every time you go out, you can skip this section and give the information to your babysitter on a separate piece of paper.

Form 80 has space for you to fill in the names, addresses and phone numbers of people that your babysitter or child care provider can contact if they can't reach you in an emergency. We suggest that you list at least two to three friends, relatives or neighbors who live nearby and are well known to your children and family. The form will print out with a reminder to call 911 in case of emergency. If you wish to list another emergency number for the police, fire department or poison control, you may do so.

Finally, the Child Care Instructions form has space to provide additional important information a babysitter or child care provider needs to know about your family or home, such as the location of first aid supplies, the phone number of a local taxi service or the fact that you have a "no smoking" rule in the house.

Use a separate form to authorize medical care. While these Child Care Instructions provide important medical information about your child, such as any medications or allergies, this form does not authorize your babysitter or child care provider to arrange medical care for your child. For that, you will need to use the Authorization for Minor's Medical Treatment (Form 2).

Signing Instructions

There is no need to sign the Child Care Instructions. Simply print it out after reading it carefully to make sure all information is complete and correct. Give the babysitter or child care provider a copy and keep one posted in a prominent place, such as on your refrigerator. Be sure to update your Child Care Instructions from time to time.

Form 81: Elder Care Agreement

Many older people remain at home or live with relatives rather than enter a residential facility for extended recovery or long-term care. Often this requires hiring someone (an elder care provider) to help with their personal and medical care, cooking, housekeeping and other services. An elder care provider (sometimes called a home health aide) can either live out or live in, work full- or part-time. The responsibilities of this position may vary widely, from performing a wide range of housekeeping services to attending to the personal and healthcare needs of the older adult (or adults, in case the elder care worker is taking care of two people, such as both of your parents). Responsibilities may range from dispensing medicine to helping bathing to driving to doctor's appointments or social functions.

Use Form 81 to spell out your written agreement regarding the elder care worker's responsibilities, hours, benefits, amount and schedule of payment and other important aspects of the job. The best approach is to be as detailed as possible. Follow the directions for the Child Care Agreement (Form 79, above) when completing this form.

Signing Instructions

To make the Elder Care Agreement valid, the employer(s) and the elder care provider must sign

it. Start by printing out two copies of the form. You (the employer) and the caregiver must sign and date the form where indicated. Give one of the signed originals to the elder care provider and keep the other for your records.

Form 82: Housekeeping Services Agreement

If you hire the same person every week to clean your house, a written contract can be a valuable way to clearly define the worker's responsibilities and benefits. If your housecleaner will be your employee, use this form to spell out the housecleaner's hours, benefits, amount and schedule of payment, termination policy and other aspects of the job. Your agreement should cover regular weekly cleaning tasks (Clause 5)—for example, cleaning the bathroom and mopping the kitchen floor—as well as occasional projects, such as washing blinds. Be sure to spell out non-cleaning responsibilities (Clause 6) as well, such as cooking, laundry, ironing, shopping, gardening and yard work. The best approach is to be as detailed as possible. Follow the directions for the Child Care Agreement (Form 79, above) when completing this form.

Signing Instructions

To make the Housekeeping Services Agreement valid, the employer(s) and the housekeeper must sign it. Finalizing your housekeeping services agreement is easy. Start by printing out two copies of the form. You (the employer) and the housekeeper must sign and date the form where indicated. Give one of the signed originals to the housekeeper and keep the other for your records. ■

Living Together

A contract is no more than an agreement to do (or not to do) something. It contains promises made by one person in exchange for another's actions. Marriage is a contractual relationship, even though the "terms" of the contract are rarely stated explicitly, or even necessarily known by the marrying couple. Saying "I do" commits a couple to a well-established set of state laws and rules governing, among other things, the couple's property rights should one spouse die or the couple split up. (Prenuptial agreements are a way people who plan to marry can modify the contract imposed on married people by state law.)

Unmarried couples—gay and straight—on the other hand, do not automatically agree to any similar state-imposed contractual agreement when they begin living together. Nor does simply living together for a certain period of time entitle you to a property settlement (or inheritance) should you split up (or one of you die) as it would if you were married.

Fortunately, when it comes to financial and property concerns, unmarried couples do have the right to create whatever kind of living together contract they want. Sometimes these agreements are made in anticipation of ending a relationship. But more often, the purpose is to communicate the couple's needs and expectations as to money and property—at either the start of the relationship or when the couple makes a major purchase.

This chapter includes some basic property-ownership agreement forms for unmarried couples. It also includes a basic name change form.

Nolo's *Living Together: A Legal Guide for Unmarried Couples*, by Ralph Warner, Toni Ihara and Frederick Hertz, and *A Legal Guide for Lesbian and Gay Couples*, by Denis Clifford, Robin Leonard and Frederick Hertz, cover the main legal issues affecting unmarried couples in areas of property and money, estate planning, children, house ownership, medical decisions and separation.

Form 83: Agreement to Keep Property Separate

Especially in the first year or two after they get together, unmarried couples usually keep all or most of their money and property separate—with the occasional exception of a joint account to pay household bills or an agreement to jointly purchase one or more items.

You may at first think a decision to keep your property ownership separate is so simple there is no need for a written agreement. Think again. Because most states recognize oral contracts between unmarried couples, the lack of a written agreement can be an invitation for one partner to later claim the existence of an oral property-sharing agreement. This is just what commonly occurs in the so-called "palimony cases" that regularly hit the headlines.

To avoid the possibility of future misunderstandings concerning property ownership, use the Agreement to Keep Property Separate to confirm that each of you plans to keep your property and income separate absent a specific written agreement—for example, to purchase a sofa bed together. Form 83 keeps all of your property separate, including property you brought into the relationship as well as property you purchased or received by gift or inheritance while living together.

Here are a few things to keep in mind when you're using this form:

- Clause 2 states that you will attach a separate list of major items you own to the agreement and includes Attachments A and B of this form for this purpose. You will want to be very specific—at least, list items worth $25 or more.

- Clause 4 specifies that if you register under a domestic partnership program that makes you responsible for each other's basic living expenses, that you agree to only the minimal level of reciprocal financial responsibility. Without this type of disclaimer, registering as domestic partners may imply that you intend to share ownership of property. Of course, if you do not register as domestic partners, you can simply delete this sentence of Clause 4.

• Clause 5 provides that you will share expenses for household items and services equally. If you have a different arrangement, or want to spell out how you will split expenses on non-household items, such as insurance or car repairs, you can edit Clause 5 accordingly.

• Clause 6 refers to a joint ownership agreement which you may prepare from time to time—for example, if you purchase a television or computer together. (You can use Form 84 for this purpose.)

• Clause 9 provides for mediation if a dispute arises out of this agreement. The Introduction, Section E, discusses mediation and dispute resolution procedures.

Signing Instructions

You and your partner must sign this Agreement to Keep Property Separate for it to be valid. Print out two copies of the form, so you'll each have your own copy. Each person should sign and date both copies of the agreement and keep a signed document for their own records. Keep your agreement in a safe place along with other important documents, such as insurance and financial papers, lease, copies of wills and the like.

This form contains a space for the acknowledgment of a notary public. To have a form notarized, you must go to the notary before signing it. (See the Introduction, Section D1, for general advice on having a form notarized.) Notarization will add a measure of legal credibility, but it is not legally required.

Form 84: Agreement for a Joint Purchase

Many couples make purchases item by item, understanding that whoever makes the purchase owns the property. George buys the kitchen table and chairs, and Edna buys the lamp and stereo. If they split up, each keeps the property he or she bought. In this situation, George and Edna would use the Agreement to Keep Property Separate (Form 83). Purchases also can be pooled. Edna and George can jointly own everything bought during the relationship, and divide it all 50-50 if they separate. In this case, the Agreement to Share Property (Form 85) would be appropriate.

While these types of consistent approaches to property ownership may simplify things, they are required by neither law nor logic. Edna and George could choose a combination of the two methods. Some items may be separately owned, some pooled 50-50, and some shared in proportion to how much money each contributed toward the purchase price or how much labor each put into upkeep.

Many unmarried couples opt for a basic keeping-things-separate approach, at least when they first get together. Despite this, however, an unmarried couple will often want to own one or more major items together, as would be the case if they pool income to buy a new bed and an expensive sound system. Clause 6 in the Agreement to Keep Property Separate (Form 83) allows you to easily do this.

Whatever type of property is purchased, it is important that your joint ownership agreement be written down, This is especially true if you have previously signed an agreement (such as Form 83) to keep the bulk of your property separate. Form 84 allows you to record your joint ownership agreement quickly and easily. Simply fill in the details of your joint purchase, including the item or property bought, the percentage of ownership (such as 50-50 or 60-40) each of you has and how you will deal with the property should you split up. For example, you may specify that one person automatically has the right (of first refusal) to buy out the other's share. You may agree to do a simple coin toss or come up with your own approach depending upon the particular property.

Signing Instructions

You and your partner must sign this Agreement for a Joint Purchase for it to be valid. Print out two copies of the form, so you'll each have your own copy. Each person should sign and date both copies of the agreement and keep a signed document for their own records. Keep your agreement in a safe place along with other important documents, such as insurance and financial papers, lease, copies of wills and the like.

⚠ **Don't use the Agreement for a Joint Purchase if you're buying a car or house together.** Check with your state's motor vehicles department for rules regarding the language that should be used to establish joint ownership of a motor vehicle. Also, houses and other real property will have their own specialized rules for ownership and taking title.

Form 85: Agreement to Share Property

Especially if you have been together several years or more and have begun to jointly purchase property (a new car or bed, for example), you may want to do what a fair number of unmarried couples do— abandon your agreement to keep property separate, and instead treat property either of you purchases as jointly owned. If this is your understanding, write it down. Use Form 85 to establish that all newly acquired property—except that given to or inherited by one partner, or that which is clearly specified in writing as separate property, is to be jointly owned by both, and equally divided should you separate.

Note that Clause 3 states that you will attach a list of the property each of you owned prior to the date of your agreement, as well as a list of jointly owned property and includes Attachments A, B and C for this purpose. You may be as detailed as you want in preparing these separate property lists, but at least include major items (valued at $25 or more).

Clause 9 provides for mediation if a dispute arises out of this agreement. The Introduction, Section E, discusses mediation and dispute resolution procedures.

Signing Instructions

You and your partner must sign this Agreement to Share Property for it to be valid. Print out two copies

of the form, so you'll each have your own copy. Each person should sign and date both copies of the agreement and keep a signed document for their own records. Keep your agreement in a safe place along with other important documents, such as insurance and financial papers, lease, copies of wills and the like.

📄 **This form contains a space for the acknowledgment of a notary public.** To have a form notarized, you must go to the notary before signing it. (See the Introduction, Section D1, for general advice on having a form notarized.) Notarization will add a measure of legal credibility, but it is not legally required.

⚠ **Giving or receiving property for the purpose of evading creditors is illegal.** A contract agreeing to keep all property separate will protect you from your partner's creditors and avoid any suggestion of impropriety.

Form 86: Declaration of Legal Name Change

Unmarried partners occasionally prefer to use the same last name, or a hyphenated version of both last names. But doing this means that one or both partners must change their existing name.

One way to change your name is by court order. This is usually fairly simple—you fill out and file at the courthouse a short petition, publish legal notice of your intention to change your name in a local legal newspaper and attend a routine court hearing. This is the foolproof way to change your name; many states won't issue a new driver's license without a court-ordered name change. Once you obtain the court order changing your name, you must still change your records, identity cards and documents. All you need to do is show the various bureaucrats the judge's order.

A simpler way to change your name may be available, if your state does not require the court petition method (where you go to court and obtain a judge's order). Instead, you can simply use your new name consistently (this is called the usage method), in all aspects of your business, personal and social life. Many agencies and organizations have a specific form to request a name change. Others will accept an official-looking form declaring your name. That's the purpose of Form 86, the Declaration of Legal Name Change, which officially states that you have changed to a new name. Use it to change your personal records, identity cards and documents. Getting official agencies such as the Department of Motor Vehicles and Social Security Administration to accept your name change is particularly important to getting your new name accepted. Once you follow those agencies' procedures and actually get official documents in your new name, it will be easy to switch over other accounts and documents. (Keep in mind, however, that, getting a passport or driver's license number with your new name can be a particular hassle, depending on where you live.)

Check your state's rules regarding name changes. Always check first to see if a particular agency, such as the Department of Motor Vehicles, requires a court order to process a name change. Many states, including California, won't issue a driver's license without a court-ordered name change. In California, *How to Change Your Name*, by David Loeb and David Brown (Nolo), will help you do the job quickly and efficiently. Also, keep in mind that parents wishing to

change a minor's name must use the court petition method.

Illegal reasons to change your name. You cannot change your name to defraud creditors, for any illegal purpose, to benefit economically by the use of another person's name or to invade someone's privacy (don't name yourself Madonna or George Bush). Otherwise you can change your name for any reason and assume any name you wish.

Signing Instructions

You must sign this Declaration of Legal Name Change form for it to be valid. Print out enough copies for every agency and organization you wish to notify of your name change. Get each form notarized before you use one. Keep a signed and notarized copy for your own records.

This form contains a space for the acknowledgment of a notary public. Having your form notarized will add a measure of legal credibility to the form, especially important if you will be presenting this form to government agencies (assuming your state does not require the court petition method for all name changes). If you want to have your form notarized, you must go to the notary before you sign it. See the Introduction, Section D1, for details on having a form notarized. ■

CHAPTER

14

Settling Legal Disputes

Becoming involved in any legal dispute can be harrowing. Many people lose sleep, time and money trying to right their wrongs, even informally. Then, take it to the next step—the prospect of going to court and facing an unpredictable court trial can scare even the bravest person. That's why it's so easy to appreciate the traditional Mexican curse that says, "May you have a lawsuit in which you know you are right."

Fortunately, most legal disputes are resolved long before anyone sees the inside of a courtroom—one person demands a settlement, the other person counters and the negotiations continue from there. If settlement still proves illusive, it's common to turn for assistance to a mediator who will attempt to help the parties come to an agreement. (The Introduction, Section E, discusses mediation and other means of resolving disputes.)

Whether the parties arrive at their own compromise settlement or do so with the help of a neutral third party, this chapter presents useful tools you can use to try and settle your dispute. And if you do settle, it also provides several releases you or the other party should sign so neither of you risks being hauled into court after you write or receive the check you believe settles the matter.

Additional information and sample forms for settling disputes can be found in *Everybody's Guide to Small Claims Court*, by Ralph Warner, and *How to Mediate Your Dispute*, by Peter Lovenheim. Sample forms for settling a claim with an insurance company can be found in *How to Win Your Personal Injury Claim*, by Joseph Matthews. For a detailed discussion of representing yourself in court, see *Represent Yourself in Court*, by Paul Bergman and Sarah Berman-Barrett. All titles are published by Nolo.

Form 87: Demand Letter

Assuming your dispute has escalated to the point where you and the other party can no longer civilly discuss a compromise, your next step in trying to resolve it is to send a demand letter clearly stating what you want. That's the purpose of Form 87. Studies show that in as many as one-third of all disputes, your demand letter will serve as a catalyst to arriving at a settlement. It is fair to ask why demand letters work so frequently to resolve disputes that couldn't simply be talked out. The answer seems to be that a written document often acts like a slap in the face to convince the other party you really are serious about going to court if you can't settle the matter. Also, your demand letter gives you a chance to carefully organize the facts of your case. This means if you wind up in mediation, arbitration or court (such as small claims court), you will have already done much of your preparation.

When writing your demand letter, here are some suggestions:

- Be polite. Avoid personally attacking your adversary.
- Concisely review the main facts of the dispute —including who, what, where and when. (See "How to Word a Demand," below.) Even though your adversary knows this information, a judge, mediator or other third party may eventually see your letter.
- Ask for exactly what you want—the return of property, $1,000 or whatever.
- Conclude by stating that if the problem isn't resolved within a set period of time (seven to ten days is often good), you will take further action, such as filing a court case, if necessary.

The demand letter included here indicates that you are willing to try mediation, Mediation, a non-adversarial process involving a neutral person, a mediator, is usually a great way for disputing people to resolve their differences. If you are not willing to try mediation (that is, you plan to sue if your demands aren't met), delete language in the demand letter referring to mediation.

How to Word a Demand

When writing a demand letter, describe in your own words exactly what happened. Specify dates, names of people with whom you dealt and the damages you have suffered. Here's an example:

On September 21, 200x, I took my car to your garage for servicing. Shortly after picking it up the next day, the engine caught fire because of your failure to properly connect the fuel line to the fuel injector. Fortunately, I was able to douse the fire without injury. As a direct result of the engine fire, I paid ABC Garage $1,281 for necessary repair work. I enclose a copy of the invoice. Also, I was without the use of my car for three days and had to rent a car to get to work. I enclose a copy of an invoice showing the rental cost of $145. In total, I was out $1,426.

Signing Instructions

Sign the Demand Letter and send it certified mail (return receipt requested) to the person with whom you're having a dispute. Keep a copy of the letter. You may later need it if you end up filing a lawsuit.

Form 88: Request for Refund or Repair of Goods Under Warranty

Use this form to request compensation when a purchased item such as a VCR or bicycle is defective. Most new products you buy (and even some used ones) come with a warranty that offers protection if the product fails during the warranty period. Here are the basic rules regarding warranties:

- If a product comes with a written warranty from either the seller or the manufacturer, you have the right to rely on it.
- If a seller makes a statement describing a product's feature—for example, "This sleeping bag will keep you warm at 25 degrees below zero"—and because of the statement you make your purchase, the statement is an express warranty that you have a right to rely on.
- For most purchases you automatically have an implied warranty of merchantability, meaning that the item will work for its intended use—for example, a lawnmower will cut grass. If the item doesn't work, you should be able to return it for a refund or replacement.

If a warranty is breached—for example, a TV set with a one-year warranty breaks after two weeks' time—ask the seller for redress. Simply call or visit the store, explain the problem and ask for a refund or replacement of the defective TV set. If the seller refuses, use this form to formally notify the seller and manufacturer of your demand for them to make good under the warranty. Give them a reasonable chance—such as 30 days—to make necessary repairs, replace the defective product or refund the purchase price. Most reputable sellers and manufacturers will. Form 88 states that you may take further action, such as filing a court action, if your request is unmet.

If you are using this form to request warranty coverage, make sure the product warranty covers your situation. Read the warranty to see how long it lasts; who you contact for warranty service (seller or manufacturer); your options if the product fails (refund, replacement or repair); what parts and problems are covered (some warranties cover replacement of parts but not labor, or only cover problems due to faulty material or workmanship); and any conditions (such as registration) or limitations that may apply.

Here's how to prepare a Request for Refund or Repair of Goods form:

Start by filling in the name(s) and address(es) of the seller or manufacturer (depending upon the particular warranty and your complaint). If you have a written manufacturer's warranty, check it for the appropriate address to send requests for warranty coverage; this may be the seller/dealer or the manufacturer. If you are not sure, ask the seller where you purchased the item. This may be a retail store, catalog distributor or website. In many cases, you will need to mail or deliver the product along with your request for warranty coverage to either the seller/dealer or the manufacturer.

If you do not have a written manufacturer's warranty and the dispute is with the seller, send this form to the seller. It shouldn't be too hard for you to determine the name and address of the seller, assuming you made an in-person or catalog purchase. For online purchases, you may have to search the seller's website to locate an address. If you can't find this on the site, look for a phone number to call for the address. If all else fails, ask your local reference librarian for suggestions on how to get the seller's address.

Fill in the item name or description. If possible, include the model number—for example Tasty Toaster Model 9333.

Next, fill in the purchase price, date and place of purchase.

Describe the problem (reason you are demanding redress) and why you are dissatisfied with your purchase. Provide as much detail as possible, including what your written warranty (if any) says; what you were told, by whom when you made the purchase; how you have used the product; what has gone wrong; and what efforts you have made to obtain a new item or refund. For example, if you called the seller, provide details on the date and details of the phone conversation. If you have already sent the seller an informal note about the problem, mention that and attach a copy of the note to this form. If you are enclosing anything such as a copy of the purchase receipt as proof of purchase or a copy of the written warranty, be sure to say so in this section of the form. See "How to Complain About a Defective Product."

Indicate whether or not the item is enclosed. Whether you are seeking redress by mail or in-person, you may need to return the item, such as a broken toaster or punctured tires. This will not always be feasible—for example, in the case of a shattered mirror.

How to Complain About a Defective Product

Here are a couple of examples of how to explain your dissatisfaction with a product you've purchased and why you're seeking redress:

Complaint about manufacturer's warranty. *On May 21, 200x, I purchased a Tasty Toaster (Model 9333) from the Toaster Store, 195 Main Street, Columbus, Ohio. This toaster came with a one-year warranty (copy enclosed). Last week, the toaster coils overheated and the toaster simply does not work. I have owned the toaster only four months, used it only occasionally and have not subjected it to any extraordinary usage.*

Complaint about store's warranty. *On April 16, 200x, I purchased an UpHill Bicycle (model number 12345ht) from CycLeader, 3300 Sharper Avenue, Denver, Colorado. In the presence of my friend, Randy Jacobs, I explained to the store clerk, "Mark," that I planned to use the bicycle for off-road mountain cycling throughout Colorado. The clerk assured me that the tires on this particular UpHill bicycle could "handle any surface." Just last week, less than a month after I purchased the bike, both tires punctured while I was cycling on a much-used mountain bike trail near Greeley. When I asked for a partial refund so as to purchase new tires, the store manager claimed that no one named Mark currently works at CycLeader and claimed that this model UpHill bicycle would never have been sold for off-road use.*

Specify what type of compensation you want. Read your warranty (if any) to find out what kind of redress may be available and to make sure that the warranty covers your situation. Some manufacturer warranties only promise to repair or replace a defective item; others will give you the additional choice of seeking a full or partial refund of your purchase price. If you don't care, or don't have a written warranty, ask for either a refund or a replacement item.

Indicate when you want to receive the requested compensation. We suggest 30 days, after which you will take further action such as filing a lawsuit.

Signing Instructions

Sign the Request for Refund or Repair of Goods and include any relevant material, such as a copy of the written warranty (often part of the owner's manual that came with the item from the manufacturer), advertisement that you relied on when making your purchase, receipt, previous correspondence with the seller or the item itself. If you are addressing this form to the manufacturer, send a copy to the seller, too. You may also want to send a copy of this letter to a state or local consumer agency or the Better Business Bureau. See "How to Complain to Government Agencies" at the end of Form 96 in Chapter 15.

Keep a copy of your form and attached materials for your records. You may need this if you end up filing a small claims court case.

Form 89: Accident Claim Worksheet

Many types of legal disputes involve claims against a person, business or insurance company arising out of an accident where you were injured and/or your property was damaged. This includes both car accidents and "slip and falls." Use Form 89, the Accident Claim Worksheet, to keep track of the names, addresses and phone numbers of parties and witnesses involved and communications with them, dates of various events and conversations, details from insurance companies and other information you will need to process an accident claim. It is for your personal reference and is not intended to become part of your claim.

Get witness statements in writing as soon as possible. Don't count on an eyewitness remembering what she saw, especially given the fact that the witness is likely to be contacted by the other party. Ask the witness to make and sign a note as to what she saw as soon after the accident as possible.

Signing Instructions

There are no signing instructions for the Accident Claim Worksheet. Simply fill it in for use in preparing a claim after an accident.

Use Form 97, Notice of Insurance Claim, to notify the appropriate insurance company of the accident.

Forms 90-94: Releases

A common means of settling minor disputes (such as an argument about an unpaid loan, a minor fender bender or a golf ball crashing through a window) is for one party to pay the other a sum of money in exchange for giving up his legal claim. Another way to settle a claim is for the person in the wrong to do something of benefit for the other. For example, if your neighbor's dog destroys your garden, you might agree to take no further action if your neighbor agrees to replace your most valuable plants and build a fence.

In either situation, you'll want to write out your agreement in the form of a contract commonly called a release. A release usually consists of no more than one party saying, "I'll pay a certain amount or do a certain thing," and the other party saying that, "In exchange, I'll forever give up my legal claim against you."

What Makes a Release Legally Enforceable?

To be legally enforceable, a release must satisfy two contract law requirements:

- **The release must be voluntary.** Each side must enter into the agreement voluntarily. If a party was coerced into signing an agreement because of the other's threats or intimidation, a court may consider it involuntary and therefore unenforceable. Courts are quite leery about tossing out a release for this reason, however. For example, in a dispute involving the repair of a bicycle, one party telling the other "I'll sue for $100,000 tomorrow if you don't agree to this release" is not the kind of threat that will make a release unenforceable. The threat or coercion must be both significant and within the realm of possibility.

- **The agreement must be arrived at fairly.** Judges are usually unwilling to enforce any agreement that is the product of deceit or the result of one side taking undue advantage of the other. For example, if a person is persuaded to sign a release two hours after an accident that left him groggy, or doesn't understand the meaning of the document or the rights he is waiving because he can't speak English, a court will not likely uphold it.

Releases are powerful documents. If you sign one forever giving up a legal claim in exchange for $500, and learn six months later that the extent of your damage is much greater than you realized when you signed the release, you are out of luck unless a court declares the release unenforceable for one of the above reasons.

Questions to Ask Before Signing a Release

In most situations where both sides understand the dispute and the consequences of various settlement options, you can confidently sign a release, knowing that the dispute will be finally laid to rest. But it is always wise for both sides to ask the following questions before they sign on the dotted line:

- Do you both understand the issues that underlie the dispute?
- Do you both fully understand what the release accomplishes?

If the answer to these questions is yes, it's wise to ask another three additional questions, but this time just of yourself:

- Do I understand the alternative to a settlement —the legal result I am likely to obtain (and the time and dollars I am likely to spend to get it) if I go to court rather than accept the release and settle?

- Have I discussed my decision to sign the release with someone who has good business sense and is not emotionally involved with the issue or parties?
- If a lot of money is involved, have I consulted an attorney with practical experience in this field?

If big bucks are at stake and the answer to either of the second two questions is "no," or even a waffling "maybe," do the necessary homework before agreeing to release the other party.

This chapter contains several release forms, including a General Release, Form 90 (to settle a dispute when only one party is alleged to have been injured or suffered damages) and a General Mutual Release, Form 91 (to settle a dispute when both parties claim the other is a fault and that each has suffered injury or damage as a result). We also include specific releases for damage to real estate (Form 92), property damage in an automobile accident (Form 93), personal injury (Form 94) and contract claims (Form 95). Review them all to see which one is most appropriate to your situation.

Note on Legal Terminology

The person with the claim who releases the other is called the *Releasor*. The *Releasee* is the person responsible for the injury or the claim who agrees to pay money or promises to do (or not to do) something of value in exchange for the release. This is called paying *Consideration*. To be binding, all contracts, including releases, require an exchange of consideration. The exchange of consideration (such as payment of a specific sum of money) should ideally occur before the release is signed. If this is not possible or feasible, the release should specify when the payment or consideration will be provided.

Making the Release Binding on Others

If one of the parties dies, you want the release to be binding on his or her heirs. Our release forms include language about successors, assigns and heirs to accomplish this. In addition, in all community property states (and in some non-community property states), one spouse is generally liable for the debts of the other spouse, and is entitled to recover monies owed to the other—even if the first spouse had nothing to do with the event leading up to the liability. For this reason, our release forms are binding on spouses and require the spouse's signature that signifies his or her consent to the deal. The Chapter 5 discussion of promissory notes explains the community property system.

Signing Instructions for Release Forms

You must sign the Release for it to be valid. Print out two copies of the form. All parties to the release, including spouses (if any) should sign and date both copies of the document in the appropriate spaces. Print the name(s) of the spouse(s) in the blank line provided; if one or both of the parties is not married, write "N/A" on the blank line. Give one of the signed documents to the other party and keep one for your own records.

Form 90: General Release

A General Release is appropriate for settling personal disputes over a contract, debt or minor personal injury when only one party is alleged to have been injured or suffered damage. (This form is not appropriate, however, if both parties claim the other is at fault and that each has suffered damage or injury as a result. This requires a mutual release, in which case you would use Form 91.)

You can't release what you don't own. If you've assigned your rights to someone else, that person becomes the Releasor, not you. Paragraph 4 of the General Release form represents your promise that you own the right that is the subject of the release.

Form 91: General Mutual Release

Form 91 is appropriate for settling disputes—for example, over debt or minor personal injury—where both parties claim the other is at fault and that each has suffered damage or injury as a result. Here the main point is often to trade legal releases —in which case, the value or consideration is both sides' mutual relinquishment of their legal rights (for example, to file a lawsuit) involved in the dispute (Clause 3 of this form). It is not unusual, however, for the person who has suffered the more serious loss (or who was less at fault) to receive additional consideration (Clause 4 of this form). This may be a cash payment or other benefit—for example, free use of a spa facility owned by one of the parties.

If the dispute concerns an oral or written contract, use Form 95, Mutual Release of Contract Claims.

Form 92: Release for Damage to Real Estate

Form 92 is appropriate for settling disputes between landowners that arise when one owner's property is damaged by another's action or inaction. Common examples include one person's tree overhanging another's yard or pool, or an uphill neighbor digging a ditch to divert rain runoff onto a downhill neighbor's property. And, of course, walls, fences, view-blocking trees and noise can all lead to serious disagreements between neighbors.

Before you settle a neighbor dispute, it will help for you to understand the legal issues—for example, if a tree grows on the border, which neighbor owns it? For answers to this and similar questions, see *Neighbor Law*, by Cora Jordan (Nolo).

Form 93: Release for Property Damage in Auto Accident

Use Form 94 to settle claims over minor property damage from an auto accident. Do not use it if personal injuries are involved. In that case, use Form 94, Release for Personal Injury.

Form 94: Release for Personal Injury

Use Form 94 when one party has suffered a relatively minor personal injury because of another's actions.

⚠ **Releases involving personal injuries should only be signed when the parties are sure that the scope of the injury is fully known**—for example, an injury has completely healed and your doctor has examined you, clearly established the scope of your injury and unequivocally stated you have fully recovered and that there will be no further problem. It is almost never wise to sign soon after an injury—you never know what problems may develop later.

Here are a few examples of language describing an injury for use in Clause 2:

- Cat scratches sustained on both arms after she was attacked by Releasee's cat, Roscoe.
- Cuts he sustained from a shattered window when a baseball hit by Releasee's son broke a window in Releasor's house.

📖 For detailed advice on filing a personal injury claim, see *How to Win Your Personal Injury Claim*, by Joseph Matthews (Nolo).

Form 95: Mutual Release of Contract Claims

This final release can be used to settle a disagreement that arises from the breach of a written or oral contract. Unlike the General Release (Form 90) or the General Mutual Release (Form 91), this release is only useful to deal with contract disputes.

What If One of the Parties to a Release Doesn't Follow Through?

If either of the people signing the release doesn't pay the money or do the promised deed, the other has a choice. He or she can take the appropriate legal steps concerning the original dispute, as if the two of you never contemplated a release. Or, either person could go to court and ask a judge to enforce the release (after all, it's a contract). A judge will consider whether the release was voluntary and the agreement arrived at fairly.

Especially if the other person has not paid money (as opposed to not doing something), consider going to small claims court and asking the judge to enforce the release. You'll want to make sure that the amount involved is less than the jurisdictional limit for the court, or you may be content to trim the amount down to the limit.

■

CHAPTER

15

Miscellaneous Forms for Personal Use

The forms in this chapter are designed to help with various consumer issues, including writing a complaint letter to a government agency, asking your school to evaluate your child's eligibility for special education services and requesting a copy of your (or a family member's) birth certificate.

Form 96: Complaint Letter

Every state and the federal government prohibit unfair or deceptive trade acts or practices. This means that a seller can't deceive, abuse, mislead, defraud or otherwise cheat you. If you think you've been cheated by someone selling a service or product, and you have been unable to resolve the problem directly, let the appropriate federal, state and local government offices know. Although law enforcement in the area of consumer fraud is not uniformly great, many hardworking investigators do their jobs superbly. The more agencies you notify, the more likely someone will take notice of your complaint and act on it—especially if more than one consumer has registered a complaint about the same company.

Your first step is to draft a complaint letter, using this form. Be as detailed as possible regarding your complaint, including the name and title of the person you dealt with and the dates and details of the service or product problem and any follow-up communication. Keep your language neutral and state the facts of the situation. See "How to Word a Complaint" for sample language.

To back up your complaint, attach copies (never the originals) of all purchase receipts, contracts, warranties, advertisements and other written documents relating to your complaint. Finally, your letter will be more persuasive if you suggest a solution, such as a refund, or at least a reply from the person investigating your complaint.

How to Word a Complaint

Here's an example of language to include in a complaint letter:

I wish to complain about a business located in your state called Celebrity Cards. About three months ago, I received a package of cards from this company unsolicited. I received a second package two months ago. Last month I received a bill from the company for $50 plus shipping and handling. I never ordered these cards and wrote to the company to say so. (A copy of my letter is attached.) I also stated that I considered the unsolicited items sent to my home to be a gift. Just this week, I received a second bill and a threat to send this debt to a collection agency and report it to a credit bureau.

Next, compile a list of agencies and their addresses where you will send your complaint letter. Start by checking http://www.consumer.gov, a website with consumer information offered by the federal government. This will help you identify the appropriate federal agency to send your complaint, depending on the nature of your problem. For example, a complaint about a mail order company or an online auction would go to the Federal Trade Commission (http://www.ftc.gov) which handles fraudulent, deceptive and unfair business practices. See "How to Complain to Government Agencies," below, for lists of resources.

Be sure to send a copy of your letter to the company you are complaining about.

How to Complain to Government Agencies

Depending on the problem, you can send a copy of your complaint letter to one or more of the following agencies. You can also contact your local district attorney's consumer fraud division regarding local consumer protection services available.

- **State Attorneys General.** You can find contact information for your State Attorney General's Office from the National Association of Attorneys General at http://www.naag.org.
- **State Consumer Protection Office.** Your state consumer protection office can also provide advice, including the name of the appropriate licensing board that handles consumer complaints (for example, if your complaint concerns a licensed professional such as a contractor or lawyer). Nolo's Legal Encyclopedia lists each state's consumer protection office at http://www.nolo.com/encyclopedia/articles/ctim/protection.html.
- **Federal Trade Commission.** Division of Enforcement, 6th & Pennsylvania Ave., NW, Washington, DC 20580; 877-382-4357; http://www.ftc.gov.
- **Federal Communications Commission.** 445 12th St., SW, Washington, DC 20554; 888-225-5322 (voice); 888-835-5322 (TTY); http://www.fcc.gov.

Signing Instructions

There are no specific signing instructions for this Complaint Letter. Simply sign the form and send it to the appropriate government agencies with a copy to the company you're complaining about. Be sure to include copies of any relevant material such as previous correspondence with the seller. Keep a copy of your complaint letter and attached materials for your records. You may need this if you end up filing a small claims court case or taking other legal action.

If your complaint concerns a defective product under warranty, use Form 88, Request for Refund or Repair of Goods Under Warranty.

Form 97: Notice of Insurance Claim

If you're planning to make a claim against an insurance company—you were in a car accident, a victim of a slip and fall or animal bite or something similar—you can use Form 97 to notify the appropriate company or companies. Depending on the circumstances, send your letter to the insurance company of the individual or business you believe was at fault. If you were in a car accident, send your insurance claim notice to the insurance company of the owner and driver of the vehicle involved in the accident. If you were in a slip and fall, such as at a store, send your notice to the insurance company of the owner of the building where the accident occurred and of the store where you had the slip and fall. You will need to get the name and address of the insurance company from the appropriate party—for example, you will need to ask the person driving the car involved in the accident for the name and policy number of his or her insurance company.

In addition, if you are covered by your own auto, homeowner's, business or other policy, be sure to notify your own insurer. You can begin by contacting your agent or broker by phone, but it's nevertheless a good idea to mail or fax in a written claim as well, keeping a copy for yourself.

Your insurance claim notice (Form 97) should be a simple letter giving only basic information and asking for a written response. It should not discuss fault or responsibility, or the details of your injuries. Make sure your notice includes the following:

- Your name, address and phone number.
- The date, approximate time of day and general location of the accident or incident.
- The type of accident (such as motor vehicle or animal bite) and an indication of whether you were injured or suffered property damage in the accident.

- If a vehicle was involved: details on the driver's car (such as make, model, license plate number) and driver's license number.

If you completed the Accident Claim Worksheet (Form 89), you should already have this information at hand.

Form 97 includes a request that the insurance company confirm by return letter whom it represents, liability coverage of the insured and whether the company is aware of anyone else who might be responsible for the accident. If the insurance company does not feel you provided sufficient information, it may send you its own form to complete.

Signing Instructions

There are no specific signing instructions for the Notice of Insurance Claim form. Simply sign the form and send it to the other party's company with a copy to your own insurance company. Keep a copy of your insurance claim notice for your records. You may need this if you end up filing a small claims court case or taking other legal action.

Form 98: Notice to Cancel Certain Contracts

Under the Federal Trade Commission (FTC) "Cooling-Off Rule," consumers have the right to cancel certain types of consumer contracts if done quickly—specifically, within three days of signing. This right-to-cancel law applies to door-to-door sales contracts for more than $25, and contracts for more than $25 made anywhere other than the seller's normal place of business—for instance, at a sales presentation at a friend's house, hotel or restaurant, outdoor exhibit, computer show or trade show. (Real estate, insurance, public car auctions and craft fairs are exempted from coverage.)

The Cooling-Off Rule applies only to goods or services primarily intended for personal, family or household purposes. It does not apply to sales made as part of a request for a seller to do home repairs or maintenance (but purchases made beyond the maintenance or repair request are covered).

To take advantage of this right to cancel, you have until midnight of the third business day following the day you signed the contract to cancel the contract either in person or by mail. If you were not given notice of this right and a cancellation form when you sign the contract, simply use this form.

After canceling, the seller must refund your money within ten days. Then, the seller must either pick up the items purchased or reimburse you within 20 days for your expense of mailing the goods back to the seller (many states give the seller 40 days). If the seller doesn't come for the goods or make an arrangement for you to mail them back, you can keep them.

For more information on the federal Cooling-Off Rule, see www.ftc.gov or call 877-FTC-HELP.

Consumer Rights to Cancel Other Types of Contracts

Federal law (the Truth in Lending Act) lets you cancel a home improvement loan, second mortgage or other loan where you pledge your home as security (except for a first mortgage or first deed of trust). Again, you have until midnight of the first business day after you signed the contract to cancel it. Contact the FTC for more information on the Truth in Lending Act. In addition, contact your state office of consumer protection regarding state laws that allow consumers to cancel contracts for other types of goods and services (such as a health club membership) within a few days of signing. Nolo's online Legal Encyclopedia includes a list of state consumer protection offices at http://www.nolo.com/encyclopedia/articles/ctim/protection.html.

Signing Instructions

To cancel a contract under the FTC Cooling-Off Rule, sign and date one copy of the Notice to Cancel Certain Contracts. Mail it to the seller or the address given for cancellation (if different from the place of purchase). Keep a copy of the notice for your own file. Be sure your envelope is postmarked before midnight of the third business day after the contract date. (Note: Saturday is considered a business date, while Sundays and federal holidays are not.) It is a good idea to send this form by certified mail so you can get a return receipt. You may need this later as proof that you properly canceled the contract.

Form 99:   Cancel Membership or Subscription Notice

Use Form 99 to provide written confirmation that you wish to cancel membership in a club or organization or that you wish to cancel your a subscription to a magazine, newspaper or other periodical.

Look in the front of the publication for the department and address that handles subscriptions. Check mailings from membership groups for similar information. If there is not a separate membership or subscription department, send your Cancel Membership or Subscription Notice to the publication's or organization's main address.

Fill in the requested information, specifically how your name, address and identifying information is listed on mailing labels on the magazine or on printed materials you receive from a membership organization. If there is a business name or second name listed on the subscription or membership materials, fill in both names.

State the date you want to cancel the particular subscription or membership, such as "effective May 1, 200x." If you want, you may specify the reason you are canceling a magazine subscription or other periodical, or no longer want to receive mailings from a membership organization. You may also request a refund for the remainder of the subscription or membership period if you think it is appropriate.

EXAMPLE 1: I want to cancel my subscription to *Beef Roundup* because I have recently become a vegetarian.

EXAMPLE 2: I want to cancel my subscription to *Beef Roundup* because I am offended by your recent series on the lifestyles of vegetarians. Please refund the value of my remaining issues.

Signing Instructions

Sign the Cancel Membership or Subscription Notice in the space provided. Make a copy of the form and mail the original to the publisher or organization of the periodical or membership you wish to cancel. If applicable, attach a copy of the mailing label or payment invoice to your notice. Keep a copy of the form for your records.

Form 100:   Request to Begin Special Education Process

This form should be used by anyone who believes their child is in need of special help from their school district and would benefit from an evaluation (assessment) of the child's performance, an analysis of any possible learning disabilities and recommendations as to needed educational services and programs.

A federal law—the Individuals with Disabilities Act (IDEA)—gives parents and guardians the right to request evaluations (assessments) of their children for physical or psychological disabilities that may affect their ability to learn. Upon your request, the school must present you with an assessment plan, listing all testing to be done on your child. Assessments usually include objective tests of your child's abilities in all areas of suspected disability (for example, academic performance and emotional status). In addition to formal tests, assessments often include subjective information, such as teacher reports, relating to your child's educational status.

The IDEA requires that the school provide special services (an Individualized Education Program, or

IEP) to a child found to have disabilities affecting their learning. "Special education" is the broad term used to describe the educational system for children between the ages of three and 22 with disabilities, such as mental retardation; autism; a specific learning disability; hearing, speech, language, orthopedic or visual impairment; or serious emotional disturbance.

An assessment must be completed before your child's eligibility for special education is determined and an initial IEP program developed. This letter starts the formal process, by requesting an initial assessment of your child's eligibility for special education, an assessment plan and general information on the IEP process.

This letter also asks the school district to make available a copy of your child's school file, including all tests, report cards, disciplinary records and teacher notes about your child, so you can learn everything they already know about your child at school. This information is crucial as you assess the seriousness of your child's difficulties and the need for special education services. You have a legal right to inspect and review any educational record relating to your child. If your child has not yet been found eligible for services under the IDEA, you have the right to a copy of his school file under the Family Educational Rights and Privacy Act (FERPA) (20 U.S.C. §1232 (g)). State laws also may provide you the right to your child's file. Rules vary in different states, but you should be entitled to obtain the file without unnecessary delay. You may also be charged for the copies as long as the fee "does not effectively prevent you from exercising your right to inspect and review the records" (34 C.F.R. §300.566).

Simply by sending this letter, the school district is required by federal law to inform you of the regulations, guidelines and procedures for applying for special education services and to begin the process of evaluation (assessment).

Send this Request to Begin Special Education Process to the special administrator at your child's school. Ask your child's teacher or the school principal for this person's name and address. Be sure to include a brief summary of your child's difficulties at school, such as developmental delays in language or problems reading, that you have noticed or have been pointed out to you by teachers, doctors, friends or anyone who has spent time with your child.

For a comprehensive and thorough guide to special education laws and services, see *The Complete IEP Guide*, by Lawrence Siegel (Nolo).

Describing Your Child's Special Needs

It is very common for parents to recognize that their child has problems with school and simply not know what to do. It may be that your child's difficulties can be isolated and addressed very specifically, or the problems may be more serious. Following are some examples of difficulties your child may be experiencing in school that you should mention in your letter to the special education administrator. Be as specific as possible, but do not worry about listing everything. Don't get bogged down in things such as special classes or eligibility. Just write down what you have observed about your child's behavior and focus on specific behavior patterns. Keep in mind that this is just the beginning of the process. Trained professionals and assessments will help determine if your intuition is correct.

- academic problems in reading, spelling or math
- delays in developmental areas, such as language or fine motor skills
- difficulties processing or retaining information, such as understanding simple instructions or problems with short- or long-term memory
- social or emotional problems
- trouble sleeping, eating or getting along with family
- sustained difficulties in paying attention or staying focused
- inappropriate or hyperactive behavior, or
- delays in physical milestones or other physiological difficulties, such as hearing loss, sight problems, difficulties with mobility or handwriting problems.

Signing Instructions

There are no specific signing instructions for the Request to Begin Special Education Process. Simply sign the form and keep a copy for your records.

Form 101:   Request for Birth Certificate

A birth certificate is an essential record. You may need a birth certificate when applying for a passport, a Social Security card or a driver's license. You may also need a birth certificate if you seek government benefits. In addition, you may just want to have copies of your family members' birth certificates on file in your home. Use this form to obtain certified copies of a birth certificate.

Where to send the request form. Immediately after a birth, you can order copies of the birth certificate by sending this form to the vital statistics office or county health department in the county where the child was born. Call the office first to find out where to send your request and how much money to enclose. If several months have passed since the birth, you can also obtain copies by writing to your state's vital statistics office. To find out where to write in your state, and how much the copies cost (about $5 to $15 each, depending on the state), go to the website of the National Center for Health Statistics at http://www.cdc.gov/nchs and click on the link "How to Obtain Birth, Death, Marriage and Divorce Certificates."

Information to include in your request. You will need to provide the following information in your birth certificate request:

- The full name at birth of the person whose birth certificate you are requesting, along with the date and place of birth, including the city and county; specifying the hospital where the birth took place is optional, but can be helpful for identification purposes.
- The full name of the father of the person named in the birth certificate, along with the maiden name of the mother.
- Your relationship to the person whose birth certificate you are requesting. If you are a family

member or spouse, specify that relationship (for example, daughter, husband or grand-mother). If you are requesting your own birth certificate, put in "self."

⚠ **Your state may restrict who can request a birth certificate.** Many states restrict access to birth records to those who are related to the person named in the birth certificate and his or her family members. Check with your state's vital records office to find out what restrictions they might have.

Reason for the request. Most states now require you to include the reason why you are requesting the birth certificate. If you are requesting your own birth certificate, you can simply fill in "for my records" as a reason you are requesting it. If you are requesting the record for someone else, you should be as specific as possible, for example: "for passport application," "to apply for driver's license" or "to obtain son's Social Security card."

⚠ **Check state rules.** Many vital records offices restrict the purposes for which they will release records—for example, many offices state that they will not issue records when genealogical research is the reason for the request. Also, many states are changing their laws about releasing birth certificates and other vital records, and they are sometimes adding special requirements—for example, several states now require that the person requesting the record send in a photocopy of his or her driver's license or other photo identification with the request. Before you mail in your request, it is important to check with your state's office about any special requirements you must follow.

Signing Instructions

Your Request for Birth Certificate is easy to finalize. Sign and date the form in the space provided. Mail it to the appropriate agency, along with a check for the amount you specified in your request and a stamped self-addressed envelope (use a business-sized envelope). Keep a copy of the form for your records. ■

CHAPTER

A

Using the Forms CD-ROM

The tear-out forms in Appendix B are included on a CD-ROM in the back of the book. This CD-ROM, which can be used with Windows computers, installs files that can be opened, printed and edited using a word processor or other software. It is *not* a stand-alone software program. Please read this Appendix and the README.TXT file included on the CD-ROM for instructions on using the Forms CD.

Note to Mac users: This CD-ROM and its files should also work on Macintosh computers. Please note, however, that Nolo cannot provide technical support for non-Windows users.

How to View the README File

If you do not know how to view the file README.TXT, insert the Forms CD-ROM into your computer's CD-ROM drive and follow these instructions:

- Windows 9x, 2000 and ME: (1) On your PC's desktop, double-click the My Computer icon; (2) double-click the icon for the CD-ROM drive into which the Forms CD-ROM was inserted; (3) double-click the file README.TXT.
- Macintosh: (1) On your Mac desktop, double-click the icon for the CD-ROM that you inserted; (2) double-click on the file README.TXT.

While the README file is open, print it out by using the Print command in the File menu.

Two different kinds of forms are contained on the CD-ROM:

- Word processing (RTF) forms that you can open, complete, print and save with your word processing program (see Section B, below), and
- Forms (PDF) that can be viewed only with Adobe Acrobat Reader 4.0 or higher. You can install Acrobat Reader from the Forms CD (see Section C below). These forms are designed to

be printed out and filled in by hand or with a typewriter.

See Appendix B for a list of forms, their file names and file formats.

A. Installing the Form Files Onto Your Computer

Before you can do anything with the files on the CD-ROM, you need to install them onto your hard disk. In accordance with U.S. copyright laws, remember that copies of the CD-ROM and its files are for your personal use only.

Insert the Forms CD and do the following:

1. Windows 9x, 2000 and ME Users

Follow the instructions that appear on the screen. (If nothing happens when you insert the Forms CD-ROM, then (1) double-click the My Computer icon; (2) double-click the icon for the CD-ROM drive into which the Forms CD-ROM was inserted; and (3) double-click the file WELCOME.EXE.)

By default, all the files are installed to the \101 Law Forms folder in the \Program Files folder of your computer. A folder called "101 Law Forms" is added to the "Programs" folder of the Start menu.

2. Macintosh Users

Step 1: If the "101 Law Forms CD" window is not open, open it by double-clicking the "101 Law Forms CD" icon.

Step 2: Select the "101 Law Forms" folder icon.

Step 3: Drag and drop the folder icon onto the icon of your hard disk.

B. Using the Word Processing Files to Create Documents

This section concerns the files for forms that can be opened and edited with your word processing program.

All word processing forms come in rich text format. These files have the extension ".RTF." For example, the form for the Temporary Guardianship Authorization for Care of Minor discussed in Chapter 1 is on the file FORM01.RTF. All forms, their file names and file formats are listed in Appendix B.

RTF files can be read by most recent word processing programs including all versions of MS Word for Windows and Macintosh, WordPad for Windows, and recent versions of WordPerfect for Windows and Macintosh.

To use a form from the CD to create your documents you must: (1) open a file in your word processor or text editor; (2) edit the form by filling in the required information; (3) print it out; and (4) rename and save your revised file.

The following are general instructions on how to do this. However, each word processor uses different commands to open, format, save and print documents. Please read your word processor's manual for specific instructions on performing these tasks.

Do not call Nolo's technical support if you have questions on how to use your word processor.

Step 1: Opening a File

There are three ways to open the word processing files included on the CD-ROM after you have installed them onto your computer.

- Windows users can open a file by selecting its "shortcut" as follows: (1) Click the Windows "Start" button; (2) open the "Programs" folder; (3) open the "101 Law Forms" subfolder; (4) open the appropriate chapter's subfolder; and (5) click on the shortcut to the form you want to work with.
- Both Windows and Macintosh users can open a file directly by double-clicking on it. Use My Computer or Windows Explorer (Windows 9x, 2000 or ME) or the Finder (Macintosh) to go to the folder you installed or copied the CD-ROM's files to. Then, double-click on the specific file you want to open.

- You can also open a file from within your word processor. To do this, you must first start your word processor. Then, go to the File menu and choose the Open command. This opens a dialog box where you will tell the program (1) the type of file you want to open (*.RTF); and (2) the location and name of the file (you will need to navigate through the directory tree to get to the folder on your hard disk where the CD's files have been installed). If these directions are unclear you will need to look through the manual for your word processing program—Nolo's technical support department will *not* be able to help you with the use of your word processing program.

Where Are the Files Installed?

Windows Users
- RTF files are installed by default to a folder named \101 Law Forms in the \Program Files folder of your computer.

Macintosh Users
- RTF files are located in the "101 Law Forms" folder.

Step 2: Editing Your Document

Fill in the appropriate information according to the instructions and sample agreements in the book. Underlines are used to indicate where you need to enter your information, frequently followed by instructions in brackets. *Be sure to delete the underlines and instructions from your edited document.* If you do not know how to use your word processor to edit a document, you will need to look through the manual for your word processing program—Nolo's technical support department will *not* be able to help you with the use of your word processing program.

Editing Forms That Have Optional or Alternative Text

Some of the forms have check boxes before text. The check boxes indicate:

- Optional text, where you choose whether to include or exclude the given text.
- Alternative text, where you select one alternative to include and exclude the other alternatives.

If you are using the tear-out forms in Appendix B, you simply mark the appropriate box to make your choice.

If you are using the Forms CD, however, we recommend that instead of marking the check boxes, you do the following:

Optional text

If you **don't want** to include optional text, just delete it from your document.

If you **do want** to include optional text, just leave it in your document.

In either case, delete the check box itself as well as the italicized instructions that the text is optional.

Alternative text

First delete all the alternatives that you do not want to include.

Then delete the remaining check boxes, as well as the italicized instructions that you need to select one of the alternatives provided.

Step 3: Printing Out the Document

Use your word processor's or text editor's "Print" command to print out your document. If you do not know how to use your word processor to print a document, you will need to look through the manual for your word processing program—Nolo's technical support department will *not* be able to help you with the use of your word processing program.

Step 4: Saving Your Document

After filling in the form, use the "Save As" command to save and rename the file. Because all the files are "read-only" you will not be able to use the "Save" command. This is for your protection. *If you save the file without renaming it, the underlines that indicate where you need to enter your information will be lost and you will not be able to create a new document with this file without recopying the original file from the CD-ROM.*

If you do not know how to use your word processor to save a document, you will need to look through the manual for your word processing program—Nolo's technical support department will *not* be able to help you with the use of your word processing program.

C. Using PDF Files to Print Out Forms

Electronic copies of useful forms are included on the CD-ROM in Adobe Acrobat PDF format. You must have the Adobe Acrobat Reader installed on your computer (see below) to use these forms. All forms, their file names and file formats are listed in Appendix B.

These forms cannot be filled out using your computer. To create your document using these files, you must: (1) open the file; (2) print it out; and (3) complete it by hand or typewriter.

Installing Acrobat Reader

To install the Adobe Acrobat Reader, insert the CD into your computer's CD-ROM drive and follow these instructions:

- Windows 9x, 2000 and ME: Follow the instructions that appear on screen. (If nothing happens when you insert the Forms CD-ROM, then (1) double-click the My Computer icon; .(2) double-click the icon for the CD-ROM drive into which the Forms CD-ROM was inserted; and (3) double click the file WELCOME.EXE.)
- Macintosh: (1) If the "101 Law Forms CD" window is not open, open it by double-clicking the "101 Law Forms CD" icon; and (2) double-click on the "Acrobat Reader Installer" icon.

If you do not know how to use Adobe Acrobat to view and print the files, you will need to consult the online documentation that comes with the Acrobat Reader program.

Do *not* call Nolo technical support if you have questions on how to use Acrobat Reader.

the folder you created and copied the CD-ROM's files to. Then, double-click on the specific file you want to open.

- You can also open a PDF file from within Acrobat Reader. To do this, you must first start Reader. Then, go to the File menu and choose the Open command. This opens a dialog box where you will tell the program the location and name of the file (you will need to navigate through the directory tree to get to the folder on your hard disk where the CD's files have been installed). If these directions are unclear you will need to look through the manual for your word processing program—Nolo's technical support department will *not* be able to help you with the use of your word processing program.

Where Are the PDF Files Installed?

- Windows Users: PDF files are installed by default to a folder named \101 Law Forms in the \Program Files folder of your computer.
- Macintosh Users: PDF files are located in the "101 Law Forms" folder.

Step 1: Opening PDF Files

PDF files, like the word processing files, can be opened one of three ways.

- Windows users can open a file by selecting its "shortcut" as follows: (1) Click the Windows "Start" button; (2) open the "Programs" folder; (3) open the "101 Law Forms" subfolder; (4) open the appropriate chapter's subfolder; and (5) click on the shortcut to the form you want to work with.
- Both Windows and Macintosh users can open a file directly by double-clicking on it. Use My Computer or Windows Explorer (Windows 9x, 2000 or ME) or the Finder (Macintosh) to go to

Step 2: Printing PDF files

Choose Print from the Acrobat Reader File menu. This will open the Print dialog box. In the "Print Range" section of the Print dialog box, select the appropriate print range, then click OK.

Step 3: Filling in PDF files

The PDF files cannot be filled out using your computer. To create your document using one of these files, you must first print it out (see Step 2, above), and then complete it by hand or typewriter. ■

Tear-Out Forms

Temporary Guardianship Authorization for Care of Minor

Child

Name: _____

Permanent address: _____

Phone: _____ Birthdate: _____

Child's School or Day Care

(Leave this section blank if your child is not in school or any type of child care program.)

School or Child Care Program: _____ Grade (if in school): _____

Address: _____

Phone: _____

Other Child Care Program (such as after-school program): _____

Address: _____

Phone: _____

Child's Doctor, Dentist and Insurance

Doctor (or HMO): _____

Address: _____

Name of Medical Insurer/Health Plan: _____

Policy No.: _____ Phone: _____

Dentist: _____

Address: _____

Name of Dental Insurer/Dental Plan: _____

Policy No.: _____ Phone: _____

Parents (or Legal Guardians)

Parent 1

Name: _____

Address: _____

_____

Home phone: _____ Work phone: _____

Cell phone or pager: _____ Email: _____

Parent 2

Name: _____

Address: _____

_____

Home phone: _____ Work phone: _____

Cell phone or pager: _____ Email: _____

Temporary Guardian

Name: _____

Address: _____

_____

Home phone: _____ Work phone: _____

Cell phone or pager: _____ Email: _____

Relationship to minor: _____

Emergency Contact

In case of emergency, if the guardian cannot be reached, please contact: _____

_____

Home phone: _____ Work phone: _____

Cell phone or pager: _____ Email: _____

Authorization and Consent of Parent(s) or Legal Guardian(s)

If there is more than one parent, the use of the singular incorporates the plural.

1. I affirm that the minor child named above is my child and that I have legal custody of that child.

2. I give my full authorization and consent for my child to live with and travel with the temporary guardian, and for the temporary guardian to establish a place of residence for my child.

3. I give the temporary guardian permission to act in my place and make decisions pertaining to my child's educational, recreational and religious activities.

4. I give the temporary guardian permission to authorize medical and dental care for my child, including but not limited to medical examinations, x-rays, tests, anesthesia, surgical operations, hospital care or other treatments that in the temporary guardian's sole opinion are needed or useful for my child. Such medical treatment shall be provided only upon the advice of and supervision by a physician, surgeon, dentist or other medical practitioner licensed to practice in the United States.

5. This authorization shall cover the period from _____, _____, to
   _____, _____ .

6. While the temporary guardian cares for my child, the costs of my child's upkeep, living expenses, medical and dental expenses shall be paid as follows: _____
   _____
   _____
   _____ .

I declare under penalty of perjury under the laws of the state of _____
that the foregoing is true and correct.

_____   _____
Parent 1's signature   Date

_____   _____
Parent 2's signature   Date

Consent of Temporary Guardian

I solemnly affirm that I will assume full responsibility for the minor who will live with me during the period designated above. I agree to make necessary decisions and to provide consent for the minor as set forth in the above Authorization and Consent of Parent(s). I also agree to the terms of the costs of the minor's upkeep, living expenses, medical and dental expenses as set forth in the above Authorization and Consent of Parent(s).

I declare under penalty of perjury under the laws of the state of _____
that the foregoing is true and correct.

_____   _____
Temporary guardian's signature   Date

[Notary Seal]

Authorization for Minor's Medical Treatment

Child

Name: _____

Birthdate: _____ Age: _____ Grade in school: _____

Doctor (or HMO): _____

Address: _____

Name of Medical Insurer/Health Plan: _____

Policy No.: _____ Phone: _____

Allergies (medications): _____

Allergies (other): _____

Conditions for which child is currently receiving treatment: _____

_____

_____

Other important medical information: _____

_____

_____

Dentist: _____

Address: _____

Name of Dental Insurer/Dental Plan: _____

Policy No.: _____ Phone: _____

Parents (or Legal Guardians)

Parent 1

Name: _____

Address: _____

_____

Home phone: _____ Work phone: _____

Cell phone or pager: _____ Email: _____

Additional contact information: _____

Parent 2

Name: _____

Address: _____

_____

Home phone: _____ Work phone: _____

Cell phone or pager: _____ Email: _____

Additional contact information: _____

Other Adult to Notify in Case Parent(s) Cannot Be Reached

Name: _____

Address: _____

_____

Home phone: _____ Work phone: _____

Cell phone or pager: _____ Email: _____

Authorization and Consent of Parent(s) or Legal Guardian(s)

I affirm that I have legal custody of the minor child indicated above. I give my authorization and consent

for *[name of supervising adult]*, who is a(n) _____

_____

[title and name of organization, if appropriate] to authorize necessary medical or dental care for my child.
Such medical treatment shall be provided upon the advice of and supervision by any physician, surgeon,
dentist or other medical practitioner licensed to practice in the United States.

_____   _____

Parent 1's signature   Date

_____   _____

Parent 2's signature   Date

[Notary Seal]

Authorization for Foreign Travel With Minor

To Whom It May Concern:

This letter concerns my child, _____

[name of child], a United States citizen and a minor born on _____ , _____ ,

[child's date of birth], who carries a United States passport with the number _____ .

I affirm that I have legal custody of my child, and that there are no pending divorce or child custody proceedings that involve my child. I give my full authorization and consent for my child to travel outside of the United States with _____

[name of adult with whom child will travel], who is the _____ [state adult's relationship with child] of my child. The purpose of the travel is _____

_____

[specify vacation, touring, to visit relatives, to accompany adult on business trip or other reason].

I have approved the following travel plans:

Dates of travel	Destinations/Accommodations
_____	_____
_____	_____
_____	_____
_____	_____
_____	_____
_____	_____

Furthermore, I hereby authorize _____

[name of adult with whom child will travel] to modify the travel plans specified above as he/she deems necessary.

I declare under penalty of perjury under the laws of the state of _____ that the foregoing is true and correct.

Parent 1's signature _____ Date: _____

Printed name: _____

Address: _____

_____

Home phone: _____ Work phone: _____

Cell phone or pager: _____ Email: _____

Parent 2's signature _____ Date: _____

Printed name: _____

Address: _____

_____

Home phone: _____ Work phone: _____

Cell phone or pager: _____ Email: _____

[Notary Seal]

_____

Pet Care Agreement

Pet Owner

Name: _____

Home address: _____

_____

Home phone: _____ Work phone: _____

Cell phone or pager: _____ Email: _____

Temporary address while pet is in Caregiver's care: _____

Phone: _____ Cell phone or pager: _____ Email: _____

[if more than one temporary address, attach itinerary]

Caregiver

Name: _____

Home address: _____

_____

Home phone: _____ Work phone: _____

Cell phone or pager: _____ Email: _____

1. Pet(s)

Caregiver will take care of these pet(s): _____

_____

_____

[list name, species, breed, age and, if necessary, any distinguishing characteristics]

2. Dates of Care

Caregiver will care for the animal(s) from _____ *[beginning date]*

☐ until_____ *[ending date].* OR

☐ until Owner notifies Caregiver otherwise.

3. Reimbursement and Compensation

Owner will reimburse Caregiver for reasonable out-of-pocket expenses, including veterinary bills, incurred while caring for the animal(s). Owner will also compensate Caregiver as follows *[Select none, one or both]*:

☐ payment of $ _____

☐ other: _____

4. Care Instructions

Caregiver will exercise reasonable care to protect the animal(s) from sickness, injury and theft, and will follow these instructions:

Food

Type of food: _____

Amount: _____ Frequency: _____

Special instructions: _____

_____

_____

Medication

1. Name: _____ Dosage: _____

   Special instructions: _____

2. Name: _____ Dosage: _____

   Special instructions: _____

Exercise

Frequency and type: _____

Special instructions: _____

Grooming

Frequency and type: _____

Special instructions: _____

Veterinary Care

Name: _____

Address: _____

Phone: _____ Veterinary insurance company and policy#: _____

Special instructions: _____

5. Emergency Contact

If Caregiver becomes unable to care for the pet(s), Caregiver will contact _____

_____ _____ [name] at _____ [phone

number] to try to make substitute arrangements for their care.

If arrangements cannot be made, Caregiver will turn the pet(s) over to _____

_____ _____ [name] at _____ _ [phone

number] and promptly notify Owner.

6. Disputes

If any dispute arises under this agreement, the parties agree to select a mutually agreeable third party to help them mediate it, and to share equally any costs of mediation.

7. Additional Terms

_____

_____

_____

8. Entire Agreement

This agreement contains the entire agreement between Owner and Caregiver. Any modifications must be in writing.

Signatures

_____

Pet Owner's name

_____   _____

Signature   Date

_____

Caregiver's name

_____   _____

Signature   Date

Authorization to Drive a Motor Vehicle

Vehicle Owner (Owner)

Name: _____

Address: _____

_____

Home phone: _____ Work phone: _____

Cell phone or pager: _____ Email: _____

Vehicle

Make, model and year of vehicle: _____

Vehicle license plate number: _____

State of registration: _____ Vehicle registration number: _____

Insurance company: _____

Insurance policy number: _____

Person Authorized to Drive (Borrower)

Name: _____

Address: _____

_____

Home phone: _____ Work phone: _____

Cell phone or pager: _____ Email: _____

Driver's license number: _____

Motor vehicle insurance company (if any): _____

Insurance policy number (if any): _____

Authorization and Consent of Vehicle Owner

I am the lawful owner of the vehicle indicated above. I give my authorization and consent for Borrower to use this vehicle as follows:

Dates of use: _____

Area in which vehicle may be used: _____

Any restrictions or conditions on use: _____

I declare under penalty of perjury under the laws of the state of _____

that the foregoing is true and correct.

_____   _____

Owner's signature   Date

RECORDING REQUESTED BY AND
WHEN RECORDED MAIL TO

_____

_____

_____

Power of Attorney for Finances (Full Power)

WARNING TO PERSON EXECUTING THIS DOCUMENT

THIS IS AN IMPORTANT LEGAL DOCUMENT. IT CREATES A POWER OF ATTORNEY FOR FINANCES. BEFORE EXECUTING THIS DOCUMENT, YOU SHOULD KNOW THESE IMPORTANT FACTS:

THIS DOCUMENT MAY PROVIDE THE PERSON YOU DESIGNATE AS YOUR ATTORNEY-IN-FACT WITH BROAD LEGAL POWERS, INCLUDING THE POWERS TO MANAGE, DISPOSE, SELL AND CONVEY YOUR REAL AND PERSONAL PROPERTY AND TO BORROW MONEY USING YOUR PROPERTY AS SECURITY FOR THE LOAN.

THESE POWERS WILL EXIST UNTIL YOU REVOKE OR TERMINATE THIS POWER OF ATTORNEY. YOU HAVE THE RIGHT TO REVOKE OR TERMINATE THIS POWER OF ATTORNEY AT ANY TIME.

THIS DOCUMENT DOES NOT AUTHORIZE ANYONE TO MAKE MEDICAL OR OTHER HEALTHCARE DECISIONS FOR YOU.

IF THERE IS ANYTHING ABOUT THIS FORM THAT YOU DO NOT UNDERSTAND, YOU SHOULD ASK A LAWYER TO EXPLAIN IT TO YOU.

1. Principal and Attorney-in-Fact

I, _____ *[your name]*,

of _____ *[your city and state]*,

appoint _____

[name of your attorney-in-fact] as my attorney-in-fact to act for me in any lawful way with respect to the powers delegated in Part 5 below. If that person (or all of those persons, if I name more than one) is unable or unwilling to serve as attorney-in-fact, I appoint the following alternates, to serve alone in the order named:

First Alternate

Name: _____

Address: _____

_____

Second Alternate

Name: _____

Address: _____

_____

2. Authorization of Attorneys-in-Fact

If I have named more than one attorney-in-fact, they are authorized to act:

☐ jointly.

☐ independently.

3. Delegation of Authority

☐ My attorney-in-fact may delegate, in writing, any authority granted under this power of attorney to a person he or she selects. Any such delegation shall state the period during which it is valid and specify the extent of the delegation.

☐ My attorney-in-fact may not delegate any authority granted under this power of attorney.

4. Effective Dates

This power of attorney is not durable. It shall begin on _____ , _____, and shall continue until terminated in writing, or until _____ , whichever comes first.

5. Powers of the Attorney-in-Fact

I grant my attorney-in-fact power to act on my behalf in the following matters, as indicated by my initials next to each granted power or on line (14), granting all the listed powers. Powers that are struck through are not granted.

INITIALS

_____ (1) Real estate transactions.

_____ (2) Tangible personal property transactions.

_____ (3) Stock and bond, commodity and option transactions.

_____ (4) Banking and other financial institution transactions.

_____ (5) Business operating transactions.

_____ (6) Insurance and annuity transactions.

_____ (7) Estate, trust and other beneficiary transactions.

_____ (8) Living trust transactions.

_____ (9) Legal actions.

_____ (10) Personal and family care.

_____ (11) Government benefits.

_____ (12) Retirement plan transactions.

_____ (13) Tax matters.

_____ (14) ALL POWERS (1 THROUGH 13) LISTED ABOVE.

These powers are defined in Part 13, below.

6. Special Instructions to the Attorney-in-Fact

_____

_____

_____

_____

_____

_____

_____

_____

_____

_____

7. Compensation and Reimbursement of the Attorney-in-Fact

☐ My attorney-in-fact shall not be compensated for services, but shall be entitled to reimbursement, from my assets, for reasonable expenses. Reasonable expenses include but are not limited to reasonable fees for information or advice from accountants, lawyers or investment experts relating to my attorney-in-fact's responsibilities under this power of attorney.

☐ My attorney-in-fact shall be entitled to reimbursement for reasonable expenses and reasonable compensation for services. What constitutes reasonable compensation shall be determined exclusively by my attorney-in-fact. If more than one attorney-in-fact is named in this document, each shall have the exclusive right to determine what constitutes reasonable compensation for his or her own duties.

☐ My attorney-in-fact shall be entitled to reimbursement for reasonable expenses and compensation for services in the amount of $ _____ . If more than one attorney-in-fact is named in this document, each shall be entitled to receive this amount.

8. Personal Benefit to the Attorney-in-Fact

☐ My attorney-in-fact may buy any assets of mine or engage in any transaction he or she deems in good faith to be in my interest, no matter what the interest or benefit to my attorney-in-fact.

☐ My attorney-in-fact may buy any assets of mine or engage in any transaction he or she seems in good faith to be in my interest, no matter what the interest or benefit to my attorney-in-fact. However, if an alternate attorney-in-fact is serving under this document, he or she may not benefit personally from any transaction engaged in on my behalf.

☐ My attorney-in-fact may not benefit personally from any transaction engaged in on my behalf.

9. Commingling by the Attorney-in-Fact

☐ My attorney-in-fact may commingle any of my funds with any funds of his or hers.

☐ My attorney-in-fact may commingle any of my funds with his or hers. However, if an alternate attorney-in-fact is serving under this document, the alternate attorney-in-fact may not commingle any of my funds with any funds of his or hers.

☐ My attorney-in-fact may not commingle any of my funds with any funds of his or hers.

10. Liability of the Attorney-in-Fact

My attorney-in-fact shall not incur any liability to me, my estate, my heirs, successors or assigns for acting or refraining from acting under this document, except for willful misconduct or gross negligence. My attorney-in-fact is not required to make my assets produce income, increase the value of my estate, diversify my investments or enter into transactions authorized by this document, as long as my attorney-in-fact believes his or her actions are in my best interests or in the interests of my estate and of those interested in my estate. A successor attorney-in-fact shall not be liable for acts of a prior attorney-in-fact.

11. Reliance on This Power of Attorney

Any third party who receives a copy of this document may rely on and act under it. Revocation of the power of attorney is not effective as to a third party until the third party has actual knowledge of the revocation. I agree to indemnify the third party for any claims that arise against the third party because of reliance on this power of attorney.

12. Severability

If any provision of this document is ruled unenforceable, the remaining provisions shall stay in effect.

13. Definition of Powers Granted to the Attorney-in-Fact

The powers granted in Part 5 of this document authorize my attorney-in-fact to do the following:

(1) Real estate transactions

Act for me in any manner to deal with all or any part of any interest in real property that I own at the time of execution of this document or later acquire, under such terms, conditions and covenants as my attorney-in-fact deems proper. My attorney-in-fact's powers include but are not limited to the power to:

(a) Accept as a gift, or as security for a loan, reject, demand, buy, lease, receive or otherwise acquire ownership or possession of any estate or interest in real property.

(b) Sell, exchange, convey with or without covenants, quitclaim, release, surrender, mortgage, encumber, partition or consent to the partitioning of, grant options concerning, lease, sublet or otherwise dispose of any interest in real property.

(c) Maintain, repair, improve, insure, rent, lease, and pay or contest taxes or assessments on any estate or interest in real property I own or claim to own.

(d) Prosecute, defend, intervene in, submit to arbitration, settle and propose or accept a compromise with respect to any claim in favor of or against me based on or involving any real estate transaction.

(2) Tangible personal property transactions

Act for me in any manner to deal with all or any part of any interest in personal property that I own at the time of execution of this document or later acquire, under such terms as my attorney-in-fact deems proper. My attorney-in-fact's powers include but are not limited to the power to lease, buy, exchange, accept as a gift or as security for a loan, acquire, possess, maintain, repair, improve, insure, rent, convey, mortgage, pledge and pay or contest taxes and assessments on any tangible personal property.

(3) Stock and bond, commodity, option and other securities transactions

Do any act which I can do through an agent, with respect to any interest in a bond, share, other instrument of similar character or commodity. My attorney-in-fact's powers include but are not limited to the power to:

(a) Accept as a gift or as security for a loan, reject, demand, buy, receive or otherwise acquire ownership or possession of any bond, share, instrument of similar character, commodity interest or any investment with respect thereto, together with the interest, dividends, proceeds or other distributions connected with it.

(b) Sell (including short sales), exchange, transfer, release, surrender, pledge, trade in or otherwise dispose of any bond, share, instrument of similar character or commodity interest.

(c) Demand, receive and obtain any money or other thing of value to which I am or may become or may claim to be entitled as the proceeds of any interest in a bond, share, other instrument of similar character or commodity interest.

(d) Agree and contract, in any manner, with any broker or other person and on any terms, for the accomplishment of any purpose listed in this section.

(e) Execute, acknowledge, seal and deliver any instrument my attorney-in-fact thinks useful to accomplish a purpose listed in this section, or any report or certificate required by law or regulation.

(4) Banking and other financial institution transactions

Do any act that I can do through an agent in connection with any banking transaction that might affect my financial or other interests. My attorney-in-fact's powers include but are not limited to the power to:

(a) Continue, modify and terminate any deposit account or other banking arrangement, or open either in the name of the agent alone or my name alone or in both our names jointly, a deposit account of any type in any financial institution, rent a safe deposit box or vault space, have access to a safe deposit box or vault to which I would have access and make other contracts with the institution.

(b) Make, sign and deliver checks or drafts, and withdraw my funds or property from any financial institution by check, order or otherwise.

(c) Prepare financial statements concerning my assets and liabilities or income and expenses and deliver them to any financial institution, and receive statements, notices or other documents from any financial institution.

(d) Borrow money from a financial institution on terms my attorney-in-fact deems acceptable, give security out of my assets, and pay, renew or extend the time of payment of any note given by or on my behalf.

(5) Business operating transactions

Do any act that I can do through an agent in connection with any business operated by me that my attorney-in-fact deems desirable. My attorney-in-fact's powers include but are not limited to the power to:

(a) Perform any duty and exercise any right, privilege or option which I have or claim to have under any contract of partnership, enforce the terms of any partnership agreement, and defend, submit to arbitration or settle any legal proceeding to which I am a party because of membership in a partnership.

(b) Exercise in person or by proxy and enforce any right, privilege or option which I have as the holder of any bond, share or instrument of similar character and defend, submit to arbitration or settle a legal proceeding to which I am a party because of any such bond, share or instrument of similar character.

(c) With respect to a business owned solely by me, continue, modify, extend or terminate any contract on my behalf; demand and receive all money that is due or claimed by me and use such funds in the operation of the business; engage in banking transactions my attorney-in-fact deems desirable; determine the location of the operation, the nature of the business it undertakes, its name, methods of manufacturing, selling, marketing, financing and accounting, form of organization and insurance and method of hiring and paying employees and independent contractors.

(d) Execute, acknowledge, seal and deliver any instrument of any kind that my attorney-in-fact thinks useful to accomplish any purpose listed in this section.

(e) Pay, compromise or contest business taxes or assessments.

(f) Demand and receive money or other things of value to which I am or claim to be entitled as the proceeds of any business operation, and conserve, invest, disburse or use anything so received for purposes listed in this section.

(6) Insurance and annuity transactions

Do any act that I can do through an agent, in connection with any insurance or annuity policy, that my attorney-in-fact deems desirable. My attorney-in-fact's powers include but are not limited to the power to:

(a) Continue, pay the premium on, modify, rescind or terminate any annuity or policy of life, accident, health, disability or liability insurance procured by me or on my behalf before the execution of this power of attorney. My attorney-in-fact cannot name himself or herself as beneficiary of a renewal, extension or substitute for such a policy unless he or she was already the beneficiary before I signed the power of attorney.

(b) Procure new, different or additional contracts of health, disability, accident or liability insurance on my life; modify, rescind or terminate any such contract and designate the beneficiary of any such contract.

(c) Sell, assign, borrow on, pledge or surrender and receive the cash surrender value of any policy.

(7) Estate, trust and other beneficiary transactions

Act for me in all matters that affect a trust, probate estate, guardianship, conservatorship, escrow, custodianship or other fund from which I am, may become or claim to be entitled, as a beneficiary, to a share or payment. My attorney-in-fact's authority includes the power to disclaim any assets from which I am, may become or claim to be entitled, as a beneficiary, to a share or payment.

(8) Living trust transactions

Transfer ownership of any property over which he or she has authority under this document to the trustee of a revocable trust I have created as settlor. Such property may include real estate, stocks, bonds, accounts with financial institutions, insurance policies or other property.

(9) Legal actions

Act for me in all matters that affect claims in favor of or against me and proceedings in any court or administrative body. My attorney-in-fact's powers include but are not limited to the power to:

(a) Hire an attorney to assert any claim or defense before any court, administrative board or other tribunal.

(b) Submit to arbitration or mediation or settle any claim in favor of or against me or any litigation to which I am a party, pay any judgment or settlement and receive any money or other things of value paid in settlement.

(10) Personal and family care

Do all acts necessary to maintain my customary standard of living, and that of my spouse and children and other persons customarily supported by or legally entitled to be supported by me. My attorney-in-fact's powers include but are not limited to the power to:

(a) Pay for medical, dental and surgical care, living quarters, usual vacations and travel expenses, shelter, clothing, food, appropriate education and other living costs.

(b) Continue arrangements with respect to automobiles or other means of transportation; charge accounts; discharge of any services or duties assumed by me to any parent, relative or friend; and contributions or payments incidental to membership or affiliation in any church, club, society or other organization.

(11) Government benefits

Act for me in all matters that affect my right to government benefits, including Social Security, Medicare, Medicaid or other governmental programs or civil or military service. My attorney-in-fact's powers include but are not limited to the power to:

(a) Prepare, execute, file, prosecute, defend, submit to arbitration or settle a claim on my behalf to benefits or assistance, financial or otherwise.

(b) Receive the proceeds of such a claim and conserve, invest, disburse or use them on my behalf.

(12) Retirement plan transactions

Act for me in all matters that affect my retirement plans. My attorney-in-fact's powers include but are not limited to the power to select payment options under any retirement plan in which I participate, make contributions to those plans, exercise investment options, receive payment from a plan, roll over plan benefits into other retirement plans, designate beneficiaries under those plans and change existing beneficiary designations.

(13) Tax matters

Act for me in all matters that affect my local, state and federal taxes. My attorney-in-fact's powers include but are not limited to the power to:

(a) Prepare, sign and file federal, state, local and foreign income, gift, payroll, Federal Insurance Contributions Act returns and other tax returns; claims for refunds; requests for extension of time; petitions; any power of attorney required by the Internal Revenue Service or other taxing authority and other documents.

(b) Pay taxes due, collect refunds, post bonds, receive confidential information, exercise any election available to me and contest deficiencies determined by a taxing authority.

I understand the importance of the powers I delegate to my attorney-in-fact in this document. I recognize that the document gives my attorney-in-fact broad powers over my assets.

Signed: This _____ day of _____ , _____

State of: _____ County of: _____

Signature: _____ , Principal

Social Security Number: _____

Witnesses

On the date written above, the principal declared to me that this instrument is his or her financial power of attorney, and that he or she willingly executed it as a free and voluntary act. The principal signed this instrument in my presence.

Witness 1

_____

Signature

_____

Name

_____

Address

Witness 2

_____

Signature

_____

Name

_____

Address

Certificate of Acknowledgment of Notary Public

State of _____

County of _____ } ss

On _____, _____, before me, _____,

a notary public in and for said state personally appeared _____,

personally known to me (or proved on the basis of satisfactory evidence) to be the person whose name is

WITNESS my hand and official seal.

_____

Notary Public for the State of _____

My commission expires _____

[NOTARY SEAL]

Attorney-in-Fact Acknowledgment

By accepting or acting under the appointment, the attorney-in-fact assumes the fiduciary and other legal responsibilities and liabilities of an agent.

Name of Attorney-in-Fact: _____

Signature of Attorney-in-Fact: _____

Preparation Statement

This document was prepared by:

_____

Name

_____

Address

RECORDING REQUESTED BY AND
WHEN RECORDED MAIL TO

_____

_____

_____

Power of Attorney for Finances (Limited Power)

I, _____ *[your name]*,

of _____ *[your city and state]*,

appoint _____

[name of your attorney-in-fact] to act in my place for the purposes of:

_____

_____

_____

_____

This power of attorney takes effect on _____ ,

and shall continue until terminated in writing, or until _____ ,

whichever comes first.

I grant my attorney-in-fact full authority to act in any manner both proper and necessary to the exercise of the foregoing powers, and I ratify every act that my attorney-in-fact may lawfully perform in exercising those powers.

I agree that any third party who receives a copy of this document may act under it. Revocation of the power of attorney is not effective as to a third party until the third party has actual knowledge of the revocation. I agree to indemnify the third party for any claims that arise against the third party because of reliance on this power of attorney.

Signed: This _____ day of _____ ,

State of: _____ County of: _____

Signature: _____ , Principal

Social Security Number: _____

Witnesses

On the date written above, the Principal declared to me that this instrument is his or her financial power of attorney, and that he or she willingly executed it as a free and voluntary act. The Principal signed this instrument in my presence.

Witness 1

_____

Signature

_____

Name

_____

Address

Witness 2

_____
Signature

_____
Name

_____
Address

Certificate of Acknowledgment of Notary Public

State of _____

County of _____ } ss

On _____, _____, before me, _____,
a notary public in and for said state personally appeared _____,
personally known to me (or proved on the basis of satisfactory evidence) to be the person whose name is
subscribed to the within instrument, and acknowledged to me that he or she executed the same in his or
her authorized capacity and that by his or her signature on the instrument, the person, or the entity upon
behalf of which the person acted, executed the instrument.

WITNESS my hand and official seal.

_____

Notary Public for the State of _____

My commission expires _____

[NOTARY SEAL]

Attorney-in-Fact Acknowledgment

By accepting or acting under the appointment, the attorney-in-fact assumes the fiduciary and other legal
responsibilities and liabilities of an agent.

Name of Attorney-in-Fact: _____

Signature of Attorney-in-Fact: _____

Preparation Statement

This document was prepared by:

Name: _____

Address: _____

_____

Notice of Revocation of Power of Attorney

I, _____ [your name],

of _____ [your city and state],

revoke the power of attorney dated _____ , empowering

_____ [name of your

attorney-in-fact] to act as my attorney-in-fact. I revoke and withdraw all power and authority granted under that power of attorney.

[if applicable]: That power of attorney was recorded on _____ ,

in Book _____ , at Page _____ , of the Official Records, County of _____ ,

State of _____ .

Signed: This _____ day of _____ ,

State of: _____ County of: _____

Signature: _____ , Principal

Social Security Number: _____

Certificate of Acknowledgment of Notary Public

State of _____

County of _____ } ss

On _____ , _____ , before me, _____ ,

a notary public in and for said state personally appeared _____ ,

personally known to me (or proved on the basis of satisfactory evidence) to be the person whose name is subscribed to the within instrument, and acknowledged to me that he or she executed the same in his or her authorized capacity and that by his or her signature on the instrument, the person, or the entity upon behalf of which the person acted, executed the instrument.

WITNESS my hand and official seal.

_____

Notary Public for the State of _____

My commission expires _____

[NOTARY SEAL]

Property Worksheet

Property	Name of Any Existing Beneficiary

Real Estate *(list each piece of real estate by address)*

_____   _____
_____   _____
_____   _____
_____   _____

Cash and Other Liquid Assets

cash

_____   _____
_____   _____
_____   _____

checking accounts

_____   _____
_____   _____
_____   _____

savings and money market accounts

_____   _____
_____   _____
_____   _____

certificates of deposit

_____   _____
_____   _____
_____   _____

precious metals

_____   _____
_____   _____
_____   _____

Securities (not in retirement accounts)

mutual funds

_____   _____
_____   _____
_____   _____

listed and unlisted stocks

_____   _____
_____   _____
_____   _____
_____   _____
_____   _____

Property   **Name of Any Existing Beneficiary**

Securities (continued)

government, corporate and municipal bonds

_____   _____

_____   _____

_____   _____

annuities

_____   _____

_____   _____

_____   _____

Retirement Plan Assets (IRAs, Keoghs, Roth IRAs, 401(k) and 403(b) plans)

_____   _____

_____   _____

_____   _____

Vehicles

automobiles, trucks and recreational vehicles

_____   _____

_____   _____

_____   _____

planes, boats and other vehicles

_____   _____

_____   _____

Other Personal Property

household goods

_____   _____

_____   _____

_____

valuable clothing, jewelry and furs

_____   _____

_____   _____

_____   _____

collectibles, including artworks and antiques

_____   _____

_____   _____

_____   _____

tools and equipment

_____   _____

_____   _____

_____   _____

_____

Property   **Name of Any Existing Beneficiary**

Other Personal Property (continued)

livestock or other valuable animals

_____   _____

_____   _____

money owed you (personal loans, etc.)

_____   _____

_____   _____

_____   _____

death benefits

_____   _____

_____   _____

_____   _____

_____   _____

life insurance (other than term insurance)

_____   _____

_____   _____

miscellaneous (any personal property not listed above)

_____   _____

_____   _____

_____   _____

_____   _____

Business Personal Property

business ownerships (partnerships, sole proprietorships, limited partnerships, limited liability companies, corporations)

_____   _____

_____   _____

_____   _____

patents, copyrights, trademarks (including the right to receive royalties)

_____   _____

_____   _____

miscellaneous receivables (mortgages, deeds of trust or promissory notes held by you; any rents due from income property owned by you; and payments due for professional or personal services or property sold by you that have not been fully paid by the purchaser)

_____   _____

_____   _____

_____   _____

_____

Beneficiary Worksheet

Specific Gifts

**Beneficiary
already
named**

☐   **Item:** _____

     Beneficiary(ies): _____

     Address(es): _____

     Alternate Beneficiary(ies): _____

     Address(es): _____

☐   **Item:** _____

     Beneficiary(ies): _____

     Address(es): _____

     Alternate Beneficiary(ies): _____

     Address(es): _____

☐   **Item:** _____

     Beneficiary(ies): _____

     Address(es): _____

     Alternate Beneficiary(ies): _____

     Address(es): _____

☐   **Item:** _____

     Beneficiary(ies): _____

     Address(es): _____

     Alternate Beneficiary(ies): _____

     Address(es): _____

☐   **Item:** _____

     Beneficiary(ies): _____

     Address(es): _____

     Alternate Beneficiary(ies): _____

     Address(es): _____

☐   **Item:** _____

     Beneficiary(ies): _____

     Address(es): _____

     Alternate Beneficiary(ies): _____

     Address(es): _____

☐   **Item:** _____

     Beneficiary(ies): _____

     Address(es): _____

     Alternate Beneficiary(ies): _____

     Address(es): _____

☐ **Item:** _____

Beneficiary(ies): _____

Address(es): _____

Alternate Beneficiary(ies): _____

Address(es): _____

☐ **Item:** _____

Beneficiary(ies): _____

Address(es): _____

Alternate Beneficiary(ies): _____

Address(es): _____

☐ **Item:** _____

Beneficiary(ies): _____

Address(es): _____

Alternate Beneficiary(ies): _____

Address(es): _____

Debts Forgiven

Amount Forgiven: _____ Date of loan: _____

Debtor: _____

Amount Forgiven: _____ Date of loan: _____

Debtor: _____

Amount Forgiven: _____ Date of loan: _____

Debtor: _____

Amount Forgiven: _____ Date of loan: _____

Debtor: _____

Residuary Beneficiary or Beneficiaries

Residuary beneficiary(ies) and percentage each one receives:

_____ _____%

_____ _____%

_____ _____%

_____ _____%

_____ _____%

_____ _____%

First Alternate Residuary Beneficiary or Beneficiaries

Residuary beneficiary(ies) and percentage each one receives:

_____ _____%

_____ _____%

_____ _____%

_____ _____%

_____ _____%

_____ _____%

⚠️ ***Do not just fill in and sign this form.*** *To be legally valid, your will must be printed out (using the CD-ROM that comes with this book) or typed, eliminating all items that don't apply to you. You cannot just fill in the blanks of this form and try to use the completed form as your will.*

Will for Adult With No Child(ren)

Will of _____

I, _____ ,

a resident of _____ *[county]*, State of _____ ,

declare that this is my will.

1. **Revocation.** I revoke all wills that I have previously made.

2. **Marital Status.** I am ☐ married ☐ single.

3. **Specific Gifts.** I make the following specific gifts:

I leave _____

_____

_____

to _____

or, if he/she/they do/does not survive me, to _____

_____ .

I leave _____

_____

_____

to _____

or, if he/she/they do/does not survive me, to _____

_____ .

I leave _____

_____

_____

to _____

or, if he/she/they do/does not survive me, to _____

_____ .

I leave _____

_____

_____

to _____

or, if he/she/they do/does not survive me, to _____

_____ .

[repeat as needed]

4. **Residuary Estate.** I leave my residuary estate, that is, the rest of my property not otherwise specifically and validly disposed of by this will or in any other manner, to _____

_____

or, if   he/she/they   do/does not survive me, to _____

_____ .

5. **Beneficiary Provisions.** The following terms and conditions apply to the beneficiary clauses of this will.

   A. **45-Day Survivorship Period.** As used in this will, the phrase "survive me" means to be alive or in existence as an organization on the 45th day after my death. Any beneficiary, except any alternate residuary beneficiary, must survive me to take property under this will.

   B. **Shared Gifts.** If I leave property to be shared by two or more beneficiaries, it shall be shared equally by them unless this will provides otherwise.

   If any beneficiary of a shared specific gift left in a single paragraph of the Specific Gifts clause, above, does not survive me, the gift shall be given to the surviving beneficiaries in equal shares.

   If any beneficiary of a shared residuary gift does not survive me, the residue shall be given to the surviving residuary beneficiaries in equal shares.

   C. **Encumbrances.** All property that I leave by this will shall pass subject to any encumbrances or liens on the property.

6. **Executor.** I name _____

   as executor, to serve without bond. If *he/she* does not qualify, or ceases to serve, I name

   _____

   as executor, also to serve without bond.

   I direct that my executor take all actions legally permissible to probate this will, including filing a petition in the appropriate court for the independent administration of my estate.

   I grant to my executor the following powers, to be exercised as the executor deems to be in the best interests of my estate:

   A. To retain property, without liability for loss or depreciation resulting from such retention.

   B. To sell, lease or exchange property and to receive or administer the proceeds as a part of my estate.

   C. To vote stock, convert bonds, notes, stocks or other securities belonging to my estate into other securities, and to exercise all other rights and privileges of a person owning similar property.

   D. To deal with and settle claims in favor of or against my estate.

   E. To continue, maintain, operate or participate in any business which is a part of my estate, and to incorporate, dissolve or otherwise change the form of organization of the business.

   F. To pay all debts and taxes that may be assessed against my estate, as provided under state law.

   G. To do all other acts, which in the executor's judgment may be necessary or appropriate for the proper and advantageous management, investment and distribution of my estate.

These powers, authority and discretion are in addition to the powers, authority and discretion vested in an executor by operation of law, and may be exercised as often as deemed necessary, without approval by any court in any jurisdiction.

Signature

I subscribe my name to this will this _____ day of _____ , _____ , at
_____ *[county]*, State of _____ .

I declare that it is my will, that I sign it willingly, that I execute it as my free and voluntary act for the purposes expressed and that I am of the age of majority or otherwise legally empowered to make a will and under no constraint or undue influence.

Signature: _____

Witnesses

On this _____ day of _____ , _____ , the testator,
_____ , _____

declared to us, the undersigned, that this instrument was ☐ his ☐ her will and requested us to act as witnesses to it. The testator signed this will in our presence, all of us being present at the same time. We now, at the testator's request, in the testator's presence and in the presence of each other, subscribe our names as witnesses and each declare that we are of sound mind and of proper age to witness a will. We further declare that we understand this to be the testator's will, and that to the best of our knowledge the testator is of the age of majority, or is otherwise legally empowered to make a will and appears to be of sound mind and under no constraint or undue influence.

We declare under penalty of perjury that the foregoing is true and correct, this _____ day of
_____ , _____ , at _____ *[county]*,
State of _____ .

Witness 1

Signature: _____

Typed or printed name: _____

Residing at: _____

City, state, zip: _____

Witness 2

Signature: _____

Typed or printed name: _____

Residing at: _____

City, state, zip: _____

Witness 3

Signature: _____

Typed or printed name: _____

Residing at: _____

City, state, zip: _____

⚠️ ***Do not just fill in and sign this form.*** *To be legally valid, your will must be printed out (using the CD-ROM that comes with this book) or typed, eliminating all items that don't apply to you. You cannot just fill in the blanks of this form and use the completed form as your will.*

Will for Adult With Child(ren)

Will of _____

I, _____ ,

a resident of _____ *[county]*, State of _____ ,

declare that this is my will.

1. **Revocation.** I revoke all wills that I have previously made.

2. **Marital Status.** I am ☐ married ☐ single.

3. **Children.** I have the following natural and legally adopted child(ren):

   Name   Date of Birth

   _____   _____

   _____   _____

   _____   _____

   _____   _____

   _____   _____

   _____   _____

   _____   _____

   [repeat as needed]

   If I do not leave property to one or more of the children whom I have identified above, my failure to do so is intentional.

4. **Specific Gifts.** I make the following specific gifts:

   I leave _____

   _____

   _____

   to _____

   or, if he/she/they do/does not survive me, to _____

   _____ .

   I leave _____

   _____

   _____

   to _____

   or, if he/she/they do/does not survive me, to _____

   _____ .

   I leave _____

   _____

to _____

or, if he/she/they do/does not survive me, to _____

_____ .

I leave _____

_____

_____

to _____

or, if he/she/they do/does not survive me, to _____

_____ .

[repeat as needed]

5. **Residuary Estate.** I leave my residuary estate, that is, the rest of my property not otherwise specifically and validly disposed of by this will or in any other manner, to _____

_____

or, if he/she/they do/does not survive me, to _____

_____ .

6. **Beneficiary Provisions.** The following terms and conditions apply to the beneficiary clauses of this will.

   A. **45-Day Survivorship Period.** As used in this will, the phrase "survive me" means to be alive or in existence as an organization on the 45th day after my death. Any beneficiary, except any alternate residuary beneficiary, must survive me to take property under this will.

   B. **Shared Gifts.** If I leave property to be shared by two or more beneficiaries, it shall be shared equally by them unless this will provides otherwise.

   If any beneficiary of a shared specific gift left in a single paragraph of the Specific Gifts clause, above, does not survive me, the gift shall be given to the surviving beneficiaries in equal shares.

   If any beneficiary of a shared residuary gift does not survive me, the residue shall be given to the surviving residuary beneficiaries in equal shares.

   C. **Encumbrances.** All property that I leave by this will shall pass subject to any encumbrances or liens on the property.

7. **Executor.** I name _____

as executor, to serve without bond. If *he/she* does not qualify, or ceases to serve, I name

_____

as executor, also to serve without bond.

   I direct that my executor take all actions legally permissible to probate this will, including filing a petition in the appropriate court for the independent administration of my estate.

   I grant to my executor the following powers, to be exercised as the executor deems to be in the best interests of my estate:

   1. To retain property, without liability for loss or depreciation resulting from such retention.

   2. To sell, lease or exchange property and to receive or administer the proceeds as a part of my estate.

3. To vote stock, convert bonds, notes, stocks or other securities belonging to my estate into other securities, and to exercise all other rights and privileges of a person owning similar property.

4. To deal with and settle claims in favor of or against my estate.

5. To continue, maintain, operate or participate in any business which is a part of my estate, and to incorporate, dissolve or otherwise change the form of organization of the business.

6. To pay all debts and taxes that may be assessed against my estate, as provided under state law.

7. To do all other acts, which in the executor's judgment may be necessary or appropriate for the proper and advantageous management, investment and distribution of my estate.

8. **Personal Guardian.** If at my death any of my children are minors, and a personal guardian is needed, I nominate _____

to be appointed personal guardian of my minor children. If ☐ he ☐ she cannot serve as personal guardian, I nominate _____

to be appointed personal guardian.

I direct that no bond be required of any personal guardian.

9. **Property Guardian.** If at my death any of my children are minors, and a property guardian is needed, I appoint _____

as the property guardian of my minor children. If ☐ he ☐ she cannot serve as property guardian, I appoint _____

as property guardian.

I direct that no bond be required of any property guardian.

10. **Gifts Under the Uniform Transfers to Minors Act.** All property left by this will to _____

_____ [name of minor]

shall be given to _____ [name of custodian]

as custodian for _____ [name of minor]

under the Uniform Transfers to Minors Act of _____ [your state].

If _____ [name of custodian]

cannot serve as custodian, _____

[name of successor custodian] shall serve as custodian. If _____

[your state] allows testators to choose the age at which the custodianship ends, I choose the oldest age allowed by my state's Uniform Transfers to Minors Act.

[repeat as needed]

Signature

I subscribe my name to this will this _____ day of _____ , _____ , at _____ [county], State of _____ .

I declare that it is my will, that I sign it willingly, that I execute it as my free and voluntary act for the purposes expressed and that I am of the age of majority or otherwise legally empowered to make a will and under no constraint or undue influence.

Signature: _____

Witnesses

On this _____ day of _____ , _____ , the testator,

_____,
_____

declared to us, the undersigned, that this instrument was ☐ his ☐ her will and requested us to act as witnesses to it. The testator signed this will in our presence, all of us being present at the same time. We now, at the testator's request, in the testator's presence and in the presence of each other, subscribe our names as witnesses and each declare that we are of sound mind and of proper age to witness a will. We further declare that we understand this to be the testator's will, and that to the best of our knowledge the testator is of the age of majority, or is otherwise legally empowered to make a will and appears to be of sound mind and under no constraint or undue influence.

We declare under penalty of perjury that the foregoing is true and correct, this _____ day of

_____ , _____ , at _____[county],

State of _____ .

Witness 1

Signature: _____

Typed or printed name: _____

Residing at: _____

City, state, zip: _____

Witness 2

Signature: _____

Typed or printed name: _____

Residing at: _____

City, state, zip: _____

Witness 3

Signature: _____

Typed or printed name: _____

Residing at: _____

City, state, zip: _____

⚠ *Do not just fill in and sign this form.* *To be legally valid, your will must be printed out (using the CD-ROM that comes with this book) or typed, eliminating all items that don't apply to you. You cannot just fill in the blanks of this form and use the completed form as your will.*

Will Codicil

First Codicil to the Will of _____

I, _____,

a resident of _____ [county], State of _____,

declare this to be the first codicil to my will dated _____ , _____.

FIRST: I revoke the provision of Clause _____ of my will that provided:

[include the exact will language you wish to revoke]

_____

_____

_____

_____

_____

SECOND: I add the following provision to Clause _____ of my will:

[add whatever is desired]

_____

_____

_____

_____

_____

THIRD: In all other respects I confirm and republish my will dated _____ , _____.

Dated _____ , _____ .

Signature

I subscribe my name to this codicil this _____ day of _____ , _____.
_____ [county], State of _____.

    I declare under penalty of perjury that I sign and execute this codicil willingly, that I execute it as my free and voluntary act for the purposes expressed and that I am of the age of majority or otherwise legally empowered to make a codicil and under no constraint or undue influence.

Signature: _____

Witnesses

On this _____ day of _____ , _____ ,
_____ *[codicil maker's name]*,
declared to us, the undersigned, that this instrument was the codicil to ☐ his ☐ her will and requested us to act as witnesses to it. The testator signed this codicil in our presence, all of us being present at the same time. We now, at the testator's request, in the testator's presence and in the presence of each other, subscribe our names as witnesses and declare we understand this to be the testator's codicil and that to the best of our knowledge the testator is of the age of majority, or is otherwise legally empowered to make a codicil and is under no constraint or undue influence.

    We declare under penalty of perjury that the foregoing is true and correct, this _____ day of _____ , _____ , at _____*[county]*, State of _____ .

Witness 1

Signature: _____

Typed or printed name: _____

Residing at: _____

City, state, zip: _____

Witness 2

Signature: _____

Typed or printed name: _____

Residing at: _____

City, state, zip: _____

Witness 3

Signature: _____

Typed or printed name: _____

Residing at: _____

City, state, zip: _____

Request for Death Certificate

Date: _____

_____

_____

_____

_____

[insert address of vital statistics office]

Name of deceased: _____

Date of death: _____ Place of death: _____

Place of birth: _____ Social Security number: _____

Please send me _____ certified copy(ies) of the death certificate of the above-named person. I have enclosed a check in the amount of $_____ and a stamped, self-addressed envelope. The reason for my request is to administer the affairs of the deceased's estate.

Thank you for your assistance.

Signature: _____

Printed or typed name: _____

Relationship to deceased: _____

Address: _____

_____

Home phone: _____ Work phone: _____

Notice to Creditor of Death

Date: _____

_____

_____

_____

_____

[insert name and address of creditor]

Name of deceased: _____

Deceased's address: _____

Account number: _____ Date of death: _____

To whom it may concern:

I am the representative of the above-named decedent. Please cancel this account at once.

Please also acknowledge that you received this notice by signing the duplicate of this letter and returning it to me in the enclosed stamped, self-addressed envelope.

If there is any outstanding balance on this account, please promptly forward it to me at the address set out below.

Thank you for your assistance.

Signature: _____

Printed or typed name: _____

Relationship to deceased: _____

Address: _____

_____

Home phone: _____ Work phone: _____

Receipt acknowledged by:

Signature: _____

Printed or typed name: _____

Title: _____

Date of receipt of notice: _____

Notice to Stop Social Security Payments After a Death

Date: _____

Social Security Administration

_____

_____

_____

[insert address where Social Security checks originate]

Name of deceased: _____

Social Security number: _____

Deceased's address: _____

Date of death: _____

To Whom It May Concern:

This letter is to notify you of the death of the above-named decedent. I am the representative of the above-named decedent.

[choose one of the following]

☐ Enclosed is the decedent's Social Security check for *[date]*, which is being returned as required. Please cease sending checks.

☐ The decedent's Social Security benefits were paid by direct deposit. I have notified the decedent's bank to return the funds to Social Security. Please cease depositing checks directly into the decedent's account.

Please acknowledge receipt of this notice by signing a duplicate of this letter and returning it to me in the enclosed stamped, self-addressed envelope.

Thank you for your assistance.

Signature: _____

Printed or typed name: _____

Relationship to deceased: _____

Address: _____

_____

Home phone: _____ Work phone: _____

Receipt acknowledged by:

Signature: _____

Printed or typed name: _____

Title: _____

Date of receipt of notice: _____

General Notice of Death

Date: _____

_____

_____

_____

_____

[insert name and address of organization]

This letter is to notify you that _____ *[name]*

of _____

_____ *[address]*

died on _____ *[date]*. Please let me know if you would like further information.

Signature: _____

Printed or typed name: _____

Relationship to deceased: _____

Address: _____

_____

Notice to Deceased's Homeowner's Insurance Company

Date: _____

_____

_____

_____

_____

[insert insurance company name and address]

Name of deceased: _____

Deceased's address: _____

Deceased's Social Security number: _____ Date of death: _____

Homeowner's insurance policy number: _____

This letter is to notify you that your insured, _____
_____ *[deceased's name]*, has died.

I am the executor of the estate and would like to be added as a named insured to the above-referenced homeowner's insurance policy. Enclosed with this letter you will find a certified death certificate for
_____ *[deceased's name]*.

Please contact me so that we may discuss this matter. I can be reached using the information listed below. Please sign and return the second copy of this letter in the enclosed, stamped and self-addressed envelope.

Thank you for your assistance.

Signature: _____

Printed or typed name: _____

Relationship to deceased: _____

Address: _____

_____ Home phone: _____

Work phone: _____ Email address: _____

Receipt acknowledged by:

Signature: _____

Printed or typed name: _____

Title: _____

Date of receipt of notice: _____

Notice to Deceased's Vehicle Insurance Company

Date: _____

_____

_____

_____

_____

[insert insurance company name and address]

Name of deceased: _____

Deceased's address: _____

Deceased's Social Security number: _____ Date of death: _____

Vehicle insurance policy number: _____

Make, model and year of vehicle: _____

This letter is to notify you that your insured, _____

_____ *[deceased's name]*, has died.

I am the executor of the estate and would like to be added as a named insured to the above-referenced insurance policy. Enclosed with this letter you will find a certified death certificate for _____

_____ *[deceased's name]*

and a state-certified copy of my driving record.

Please contact me so that we may discuss this matter. I can be reached using the information listed below. Please sign and return the second copy of this letter in the enclosed, stamped and self-addressed envelope.

Thank you for your assistance.

Signature: _____

Printed or typed name: _____

Relationship to deceased: _____

Address: _____

_____ Home phone: _____

Work phone: _____ Email address: _____

Receipt acknowledged by:

Signature: _____

Printed or typed name: _____

Title: _____

Date of receipt of notice: _____

Apartment-Finding Service Checklist

Name of company: _____

Address: _____

Phone number: _____ Hours: _____

Date this form is completed: _____

1. Description of listings

Geographical areas covered: _____

Type of rentals: _____

Total number of listings: _____ Number of new listings per day: _____

Frequency of listing updates (as available or once a day): _____

% of listings exclusive to this service: _____

Type of information available for each listing: _____

_____

_____

2. Type of access to listings, cost and duration of service

☐ Phone: _____ ☐ Fax: _____

☐ Email: _____ ☐ Pager: _____

☐ Listing books available in office: _____

3. Free phone available in office for members' use?   ☐ yes   ☐ no

4. Other services and costs

☐ roommate referrals: _____

☐ credit screening: _____

☐ other: _____

5. Percentage of members who find a rental unit through service: _____

6. Refund if rental unit not found through company: _____

7. Length of time in business: _____

8. Other comments: _____

_____

_____

_____

_____

_____

Rental Application

Separate application required from each applicant age 18 or older.

```
┌─────────────────────────────────────────────────────────────┐
│              This section to be completed by landlord         │
│                                                               │
│  Address of property to be rented: _____  │
│                                                               │
│  _____  │
│                                                               │
│  Rental Term: ☐ month-to-month  ☐ lease from _____ to ___│
│  Amounts Due Prior to Occupancy                               │
│      First month's rent ................................ $____ │
│      Security deposit .................................. $____ │
│      Credit check fee .................................. $____ │
│      Other (specify): _____ $____ │
│                         TOTAL .............. $____            │
└─────────────────────────────────────────────────────────────┘
```

Applicant

Full name—include all names you use(d): _____

Home phone: (   )   Work phone: (   )

Email: _____   Social Security number: _____

Driver's license number/state: _____

Vehicle make: _____ Model: _____ Color: _____ Year: _____

License plate number/state: _____

Additional Occupants

List everyone, including children, who will live with you:

Full name   Relationship to applicant

_____

_____

_____

_____

Rental History

Current address: _____

Dates lived at address: _____ Reason for leaving: _____

Landlord/manager: _____ Landlord/manager's phone: (   )

Previous address: _____

Dates lived at address: _____ Reason for leaving: _____

Landlord/manager: _____ Landlord/manager's phone: (   )

Previous address: _____

Dates lived at address: _____ Reason for leaving: _____

Landlord/manager: _____ Landlord/manager's phone: (___)

Employment History

Name and address of current employer: _____

_____ Phone: (___)

Name of supervisor: _____ Supervisor's phone: (___)

Dates employed at this job: _____ Position or title: _____

Name and address of previous employer: _____

_____ Phone: (___)

Name of supervisor: _____ Supervisor's phone: (___)

Dates employed at this job: _____ Position or title: _____

Income

1. Your gross monthly employment income (before deductions): $ _____

2. Average monthly amounts of other income (specify sources): $ _____

_____

_____

TOTAL: _____ $ _____

Credit and Financial Information

Bank/financial accounts	Account number	Bank/institution	Branch
Savings account:			
Checking account:			
Money market or similar account:			

Credit accounts & loans	Type of account (Auto loan, Visa, etc.)	Account Number	Name of Creditor	Amount Owed	Monthly Payment
Major credit card:					
Major credit card:					
Loan (mortgage, car, student loan, etc.):					
Other major obligation:					

Miscellaneous

Describe the number and type of pets you want to have in the rental property: _____

_____

Describe water-filled furniture you want to have in the rental property: _____

_____

Do you smoke? ☐ yes ☐ no

Have you ever: Filed for bankruptcy? ☐ yes ☐ no   Been sued? ☐ yes ☐ no

Been evicted? ☐ yes ☐ no   Been convicted of a crime? ☐ yes ☐ no

Explain any "yes" listed above: _____

_____

References and Emergency Contact

Personal reference: _____   Relationship: _____

Address: _____

Phone: (____) _____

Personal reference: _____   Relationship: _____

Address: _____

Phone: (____) _____

Contact in emergency: _____   Relationship: _____

Address: _____

Phone: (____) _____

I certify that all the information given above is true and correct and understand that my lease or rental agreement may be terminated if I have made any false or incomplete statement in this application. I authorize verification of the information provided in this application from my credit sources, credit bureaus, current and previous landlords and employers, and personal references.

_____   _____

Applicant   Date

Notes (Landlord/Manager): _____

_____

_____

_____

_____

_____

Fixed-Term Residential Lease

Clause 1. Identification of Landlord and Tenant

This Agreement is entered into between _____ ("Tenant")

and _____ ("Landlord").

Each Tenant is jointly and severally liable for the payment of rent and performance of all other terms of this Agreement.

Clause 2. Identification of Premises

Subject to the terms and conditions in this Agreement, Landlord rents to Tenant, and Tenant rents from Landlord, for residential purposes only, the premises located at _____

_____ ("the premises"),

to_____ _____

_____ .

Re_____

_____ .

Clau

Th_____ ted in Clause 1 of this

A_____ n _____ is prohibited

w_____ each of this Agreement.

Clau

T_____ _____, _____, and end

o_____ _____ .

Clau

R

T_____ , payable in advance on the first

o_____ holiday, in which case rent is

o_____ er unless Landlord designates

o

L

F

☐ _____ .

☐ _____ .

☐ _____ .

☐ _____ .

☐ money order.

☐ cash.

☐ other (specify) _____ .

Handwritten note overlaid:

Clause 1
① David or Jodo Sch...

Clause 2   615 Soquel to
                 A
refrigerator, stove, Blinds

also includes H₂0 + Trash

Clause 3   two weeks

Clause 5:   500⁰⁰

mail to David or Jods
in person   "   "
              "   - "

Prorated first month's rent.

For the period from Tenant's move-in date, _____ , _____ , through
the end of the month, Tenant will pay to Landlord a _____ . This
amount will be paid on or before the date the Tenan_____

Clause 6. Late Charges

If Tenant fails to pay the rent in full before the end _____
Landlord a late charge as follows: _____

_____

Landlord does not waive the right to insist on pa_____

Clause 7. Returned Check and Other Bank Cha___

If any check offered by Tenant to Landlord in _____
Agreement is returned for lack of sufficient fu_____
pay Landlord a returned check charge of $ _____

Clause 8. Security Deposit

On signing this Agreement, Tenant will pa_____
deposit. Tenant may not, without Landlor_____
last month's rent or to any other sum due_____
after Tenant has vacated the premises, re_____
Landlord will return the deposit in full _____
and the dollar amount of, any of the _____
deposit balance.

Other details on security deposi_____

_____

_____

Clause 9. Utilities

Tenant will pay all utility c_____

Clause 10. Assignment a____

Tenant will not suble_____
consent of Landlord_____

Clause 11. Tenant's Maintenan___

Tenant will:

a. keep the premises clean, sanitary and in good _____ tenancy,
   return the premises to Landlord in a condition identical t_____ enant took
   occupancy, except for ordinary wear and tear and any additions o._____ orized by
   Landlord

b. immediately notify Landlord of any defects or dangerous conditions in and about the premises of
   which Tenant becomes aware, and

c. reimburse Landlord, on demand by Landlord, for the cost of any repairs to the premises damaged
   by Tenant or Tenant's guests or business invitees through misuse, accident or neglect.

Handwritten notes:

Rent or portion [rent] + [will be paid]

Late Charges: 2% of Balance
Per day.
Returned Check $25
Security Deposit
$505.00

in 14 days

Clause 9 H₂O + Trash.
and $5 / day until electric
+ gas are in tenants name

Clause 14, Pets?

Tenant has examined the premises, including appliances, fixtures, carpets, drapes and paint, and has found them to be in good, safe and clean condition and repair, except as noted in the Landlord-Tenant Checklist.

Clause 12. Repairs and Alterations by Tenant

a. Except as provided by law or as authorized by the prior written consent of Landlord, Tenant will not make any repairs or alterations to the premises, including nailing holes in the walls or painting the rental unit.

b. Unless authorized by law, Tenant will not, without Landlord's prior written consent, alter, re-key or install any locks to the premises or install or alter any burglar alarm system. Tenant will provide Landlord with a key or keys capable of unlocking all such re-keyed or new locks as well as instructions on how to disarm any altered or new burglar alarm system.

Clause 13. Violating Laws and Causing Disturbances

Tenant and guests or invitees will not use the premises or adjacent areas in such a way as to:

a. violate any law or ordinance, including laws prohibiting the use, possession or sale of illegal drugs

b. commit waste (severe property damage), or

c. create a nuisance by annoying, disturbing, inconveniencing or interfering with the quiet enjoyment and peace and quiet of any other tenant or nearby resident.

Clause 14. Pets

No animal, bird or other pet will be kept on the premises, even temporarily, except properly trained dogs needed by blind, deaf or disabled persons and _____

under the following conditions: _____

_____

_____ .

Clause 15. Landlord's Right to Access

Landlord or Landlord's agents may enter the premises in the event of an emergency, to make repairs or improvements or to show the premises to prospective buyers or tenants. Landlord may also enter the premises to conduct an annual inspection to check for safety or maintenance problems. Except in cases of emergency, Tenant's abandonment of the premises, court order or where it is impractical to do so, Landlord shall give Tenant _____ notice before entering.

Clause 16. Extended Absences by Tenant

Tenant will notify Landlord in advance if Tenant will be away from the premises for _____ or more consecutive days. During such absence, Landlord may enter the premises at times reasonably necessary to maintain the property and inspect for needed repairs.

Clause 17. Possession of the Premises

a. *Tenant's failure to take possession.*

If, after signing this Agreement, Tenant fails to take possession of the premises, Tenant will still be responsible for paying rent and complying with all other terms of this Agreement.

b. *Landlord's failure to deliver possession.*

If Landlord is unable to deliver possession of the premises to Tenant for any reason not within Landlord's control, including but not limited to partial or complete destruction of the premises, Tenant will have the right to terminate this Agreement upon proper notice as required by law. In such event, Landlord's liability to Tenant will be limited to the return of all sums previously paid by Tenant to Landlord.

Clause 18. Tenant Rules and Regulations

Tenant acknowledges receipt of, and has read a copy of, tenant rules and regulations, which are attached to and incorporated into this Agreement by this reference.

Clause 19. Payment of Court Costs and Attorney Fees in a Lawsuit

In any action or legal proceeding to enforce any part of this Agreement, the prevailing party ☐ shall not ☐ shall recover reasonable attorney fees and court costs.

Clause 20. Disclosures

Tenant acknowledges that Landlord has made the following disclosures regarding the premises:

☐ disclosure of information on lead-based paint and/or lead-based paint hazards

☐ other disclosures: _____

_____

Clause 21. Authority to Receive Legal Papers

The Landlord, any person managing the premises and anyone designated by the Landlord are authorized to accept service of process and receive other notices and demands, which may be delivered to:

☐ the Landlord, at the following address: _____

☐ the Manager, at the following address: _____

☐ the following person, at the following address: _____

Clause 22. Additional Provisions

Additional provisions are as follows: _____

_____
_____
_____
_____
_____
_____
_____
_____
_____

Clause 23. Validity of Each Part

If any portion of this Agreement is held to be invalid, its invalidity will not affect the validity or enforceability of any other provision of this Agreement.

Clause 24. Grounds for Termination of Tenancy

The failure of Tenant or their guests or invitees to comply with any term of this Agreement is grounds for termination of the tenancy, with appropriate notice to Tenant and procedures as required by law.

Clause 25. Entire Agreement

This document and any Attachments constitutes the entire Agreement between the parties, and no promises or representations, other than those contained here and those implied by law, have been made by Landlord or Tenant. Any modifications to this Agreement must be in writing signed by Landlord and Tenant.

_____   _____
Landlord/Agent's signature   Date

_____
Title

_____
Address

_____   _____
                                                                                          Phone

_____   _____
Tenant 1's signature   Date

_____
Print name

_____   _____
Tenant 2's signature   Date

_____
Print name

_____   _____
Tenant 3's signature   Date

_____
Print name

Month-to-Month Residential Rental Agreement

Clause 1. Identification of Landlord and Tenant

This Agreement is entered into between _____ ("Tenant")

and _____ ("Landlord").

Each Tenant is jointly and severally liable for the payment of rent and performance of all other terms of this Agreement.

Clause 2. Identification of Premises

Subject to the terms and conditions in this Agreement, Landlord rents to Tenant, and Tenant rents from Landlord, for residential purposes only, the premises located at _____

_____ ("the premises"),

together with the following furnishings and appliances: _____

_____ .

Rental of the premises also includes: _____

_____ .

Clause 3. Limits on Use and Occupancy

The premises are to be used only as a private residence for Tenant(s) listed in Clause 1 of this Agreement and their minor children. Occupancy by guests for more than _____ is prohibited without Landlord's written consent and will be considered a material breach of this Agreement.

Clause 4. Term of the Tenancy

The term of the rental will begin on _____ , _____ , and continue on a month-to-month basis. Landlord may terminate the tenancy or modify the terms of this Agreement by giving the Tenant _____ days written notice. Tenant may terminate the tenancy by giving the Landlord _____ days written notice.

Clause 5. Payment of Rent

Regular monthly rent.

Tenant will pay to Landlord a monthly rent of $ _____ , payable in advance on the first day of each month, except when that day falls on a weekend or a legal holiday, in which case rent is due on the next business day. Rent will be paid in the following manner unless Landlord designates otherwise:

Delivery of payment.

Rent will be paid:

☐ by mail, to _____ .

☐ in person, at _____ .

Form of payment.

Landlord will accept payment in these forms:

☐ personal check made payable to _____ .

☐ cashier's check made payable to _____ .

☐ credit card.

☐ money order.

☐ cash.

☐ other (specify) _____.

Prorated first month's rent.

For the period from Tenant's move-in date, _____, _____ , through

the end of the month, Tenant will pay to Landlord a prorated monthly rent of $ _____.

This amount will be paid on or before the date the Tenant moves in.

Clause 6. Late Charges

If Tenant fails to pay the rent in full before the end of the _____ day after it's due, Tenant will pay

Landlord a late charge as follows: _____

_____.

Landlord does not waive the right to insist on payment of the rent in full on the date it is due.

Clause 7. Returned Check and Other Bank Charges

If any check offered by Tenant to Landlord in payment of rent or any other amount due under this

Agreement is returned for lack of sufficient funds, a "stop payment" or any other reason, Tenant will

pay Landlord a returned check charge of $ _____ .

Clause 8. Security Deposit

On signing this Agreement, Tenant will pay to Landlord the sum of $ _____ as a security

deposit. Tenant may not, without Landlord's prior written consent, apply this security deposit to the

last month's rent or to any other sum due under this Agreement. Within _____

after Tenant has vacated the premises, returned keys and provided Landlord with a forwarding address,

Landlord will return the deposit in full or give Tenant an itemized written statement of the reasons for,

and the dollar amount of, any of the security deposit retained by Landlord, along with a check for any

deposit balance.

Other details on security deposit: _____

_____

_____.

Clause 9. Utilities

Tenant will pay all utility charges, except for the following, which will be paid by Landlord: _____

_____.

Clause 10. Assignment and Subletting

Tenant will not sublet any part of the premises or assign this Agreement without the prior written

consent of Landlord.

Clause 11. Tenant's Maintenance Responsibilities

Tenant will:

a. keep the premises clean, sanitary and in good condition and, upon termination of the tenancy,

   return the premises to Landlord in a condition identical to that which existed when Tenant took

   occupancy, except for ordinary wear and tear and any additions or alterations authorized by

   Landlord

b. immediately notify Landlord of any defects or dangerous conditions in and about the premises of

   which Tenant becomes aware, and

   c. reimburse Landlord, on demand by Landlord, for the cost of any repairs to the premises damaged by Tenant or Tenant's guests or business invitees through misuse, accident or neglect.

Tenant has examined the premises, including appliances, fixtures, carpets, drapes and paint, and has found them to be in good, safe and clean condition and repair, except as noted in the Landlord-Tenant Checklist.

Clause 12. Repairs and Alterations by Tenant

   a. Except as provided by law or as authorized by the prior written consent of Landlord, Tenant will not make any repairs or alterations to the premises, including nailing holes in the walls or painting the rental unit.

   b. Unless authorized by law, Tenant will not, without Landlord's prior written consent, alter, re-key or install any locks to the premises or install or alter any burglar alarm system. Tenant will provide Landlord with a key or keys capable of unlocking all such re-keyed or new locks as well as instructions on how to disarm any altered or new burglar alarm system.

Clause 13. Violating Laws and Causing Disturbances

Tenant and guests or invitees will not use the premises or adjacent areas in such a way as to:

   a. violate any law or ordinance, including laws prohibiting the use, possession or sale of illegal drugs

   b. commit waste (severe property damage), or

   c. create a nuisance by annoying, disturbing, inconveniencing or interfering with the quiet enjoyment and peace and quiet of any other tenant or nearby resident.

Clause 14. Pets

No animal, bird or other pet will be kept on the premises, even temporarily, except properly trained dogs needed by blind, deaf or disabled persons and _____

under the following conditions: _____

_____

_____

_____ .

Clause 15. Landlord's Right to Access

Landlord or Landlord's agents may enter the premises in the event of an emergency, to make repairs or improvements or to show the premises to prospective buyers or tenants. Landlord may also enter the premises to conduct an annual inspection to check for safety or maintenance problems. Except in cases of emergency, Tenant's abandonment of the premises, court order or where it is impractical to do so, Landlord shall give Tenant _____ notice before entering.

Clause 16. Extended Absences by Tenant

Tenant will notify Landlord in advance if Tenant will be away from the premises for _____ or more consecutive days. During such absence, Landlord may enter the premises at times reasonably necessary to maintain the property and inspect for needed repairs.

Clause 17. Possession of the Premises

   a. Tenant's failure to take possession.

If, after signing this Agreement, Tenant fails to take possession of the premises, Tenant will still be responsible for paying rent and complying with all other terms of this Agreement.

b. Landlord's failure to deliver possession.

If Landlord is unable to deliver possession of the premises to Tenant for any reason not within Landlord's control, including but not limited to partial or complete destruction of the premises, Tenant will have the right to terminate this Agreement upon proper notice as required by law. In such event, Landlord's liability to Tenant will be limited to the return of all sums previously paid by Tenant to Landlord.

Clause 18. Tenant Rules and Regulations

Tenant acknowledges receipt of, and has read a copy of, tenant rules and regulations, which are attached to and incorporated into this Agreement by this reference.

Clause 19. Payment of Court Costs and Attorney Fees in a Lawsuit

In any action or legal proceeding to enforce any part of this Agreement, the prevailing party ☐ shall not ☐ shall recover reasonable attorney fees and court costs.

Clause 20. Disclosures

Tenant acknowledges that Landlord has made the following disclosures regarding the premises:

☐ disclosure of information on lead-based paint and/or lead-based paint hazards

☐ other disclosures: _____

_____

Clause 21. Authority to Receive Legal Papers

The Landlord, any person managing the premises and anyone designated by the Landlord are authorized to accept service of process and receive other notices and demands, which may be delivered to:

☐ the Landlord, at the following address: _____

_____.

☐ the Manager, at the following address: _____

                                                                                    .

☐ the following person, at the following address: _____

                                                                                    .

Clause 22. Additional Provisions

Additional provisions are as follows: _____

_____

_____

_____

_____

_____

_____

_____

_____

_____

_____

Clause 23. Validity of Each Part

If any portion of this Agreement is held to be invalid, its invalidity will not affect the validity or enforceability of any other provision of this Agreement.

Clause 24. Grounds for Termination of Tenancy

The failure of Tenant or their guests or invitees to comply with any term of this Agreement is grounds for termination of the tenancy, with appropriate notice to Tenant and procedures as required by law.

Clause 25. Entire Agreement

This document and any Attachments constitutes the entire Agreement between the parties, and no promises or representations, other than those contained here and those implied by law, have been made by Landlord or Tenant. Any modifications to this Agreement must be in writing signed by Landlord and Tenant.

_____   _____
Landlord/Agent's signature   Date

_____
Title

_____
Address

_____   _____
                                                Phone

_____   _____
Tenant 1's signature   Date

_____
Print name

_____   _____
Tenant 2's signature   Date

_____
Print name

_____   _____
Tenant 3's signature   Date

_____
Print name

Landlord-Tenant Agreement to Terminate Lease

Landlord: _____ and

Tenant: _____

agree that the lease they entered into for the time period of _____ , _____ ,

to _____ , _____ , for premises at _____

_____

will terminate on _____ .

Additional conditions for cancellation of lease: _____

_____

_____

_____   _____
Landlord's signature   Date

_____
Print name

_____   _____
Tenant 1's signature   Date

_____
Print name

_____   _____
Tenant 2's signature   Date

_____
Print name

_____   _____
Tenant 3's signature   Date

_____
Print name

Consent to Assignment of Lease

Landlord: _____

Tenant: _____

Assignee: _____

Landlord, Tenant and Assignee agree as follows:

1. Location of Premises

Tenant has leased the premises located at _____

from Landlord.

2. Lease Beginning and Ending Dates

The lease was signed on _____ , _____ .

It will expire on _____ , _____ .

3. Assignment

Tenant is assigning the balance of Tenant's lease to Assignee, beginning on _____ ,

_____ . It will end on _____ , _____ .

4. Tenant's Future Liability

Tenant's financial responsibilities under the terms of the lease are ended by this assignment.
Specifically, Tenant's responsibilities for future rent and future damage are ended.

5. Tenant's Right to Occupy

As of the effective date of the assignment, Tenant permanently gives up the right to occupy the
premises.

6. Binding Nature of Agreement

Assignee is bound by every term and condition in the lease that is the subject of this assignment.

_____   _____

Landlord's signature   Date

_____

Print name

_____   _____

Tenant's signature   Date

_____

Print name

_____   _____

Assignee's signature   Date

_____

Print name

Landlord-Tenant Checklist

GENERAL CONDITION OF RENTAL UNIT AND PREMISES

Street Address   Unit Number   City

	Condition on Arrival	Condition on Departure	Estimated Cost of Repair/Replacement
LIVING ROOM			
Floors & floor coverings			
Drapes & window coverings			
Walls & ceilings			
Light fixtures			
Windows, screens & doors			
Front door & locks			
Fireplace			
Other			
Other			
KITCHEN			
Floors & floor coverings			
Walls & ceilings			
Light fixtures			
Windows, screens & doors			
Cabinets			
Counters			
Stove/oven			
Refrigerator			
Dishwasher			
Garbage disposal			
Sink & plumbing			
Other			
Other			
DINING ROOM			
Floors & floor covering			
Walls & ceilings			
Light fixtures			
Windows, screens & doors			
Other			
Other			
Other			

	Condition on Arrival	Condition on Departure	Estimated Cost of Repair/Replacement
Bathroom 1			
Floors & floor coverings			
Walls & ceilings			
Windows, screens & doors			
Light fixtures			
Bathtub/shower			
Sink & counters			
Toilet			
Other			
Other			
Bathroom 2			
Floors & floor coverings			
Walls & ceilings			
Windows, screens & doors			
Light fixtures			
Bathtub/shower			
Sink & counters			
Toilet			
Other			
Other			
Bedroom 1			
Floors & floor coverings			
Windows, screens & doors			
Walls & ceilings			
Light fixtures			
Other			
Other			
Other			
Bedroom 2			
Floors & floor coverings			
Windows, screens & doors			
Walls & ceilings			
Light fixtures			
Other			
Other			
Other			

	Condition on Arrival	Condition on Departure	Estimated Cost of Repair/Replacement
Bedroom 3			
Floors & floor coverings			
Windows, screens & doors			
Walls & ceilings			
Light fixtures			
Other			
Other			
Other			
Other			
OTHER AREAS			
Furnace/heater			
Air conditioning			
Lawn/ground covering			
Garden			
Patio, terrace, deck, etc.			
Stairs and hallway			
Basement			
Parking Area			
Other			
Other			
Other			
Other			

☐ Tenants acknowledge that all smoke detectors and fire extinguishers were tested in their presence and found to be in working order, and that the testing procedure was explained to them. Tenants agree to test all detectors at least once a month and to report any problems to Landlord/Manager in writing. Tenants agree to replace all smoke detector batteries as necessary.

FURNISHED PROPERTY

	Condition on Arrival	Condition on Departure	Estimated Cost of Repair/Replacement
LIVING ROOM			
Coffee table			
End tables			
Lamps			
Chairs			
Sofa			
Other			
Other			
KITCHEN			
Broiler pan			
Ice trays			
Other			
Other			
DINING AREA			
Chairs			
Stools			
Table			
Other			
Other			
Bathroom 1			
Dresser tables			
Mirrors			
Shower curtain			
Hamper			
Other			
Bathroom 2			
Dresser tables			
Mirrors			
Shower curtain			
Hamper			
Other			
Bedroom 1			
Beds (single)			
Beds (double)			
Chairs			

	Condition on Arrival	Condition on Departure	Estimated Cost of Repair/Replacement
Chests			
Dressing tables			
Lamps			
Mirrors			
Night tables			
Other			
Other			
Bedroom 2			
Beds (single)			
Beds (double)			
Chairs			
Chests			
Dressing tables			
Lamps			
Mirrors			
Night tables			
Other			
Other			
Bedroom 3			
Beds (single)			
Beds (double)			
Chairs			
Chests			
Dressing tables			
Lamps			
Mirrors			
Night tables			
Other			
Other			
OTHER AREAS			
Bookcases			
Desks			
Pictures			
Other			
Other			

Use this space to provide any additional explanation:

_____

_____

_____

_____

_____

_____

_____

_____

_____

_____

_____

_____

_____

Landlord-Tenant Checklist completed on moving in on _____ [date] and approved by:

_____ and _____
Landlord/Manager   Tenant

                                           _____
                                           Tenant

                                           _____
                                           Tenant

Landlord-Tenant Checklist completed on moving out on _____ [date] and approved by:

_____ and _____
Landlord/Manager   Tenant

                                           _____
                                           Tenant

                                           _____
                                           Tenant

Notice of Needed Repairs

To: _____ *[name of landlord or manager]*

At: _____

From: _____ *[tenant]*

At: _____
     [address]

I am writing to inform you of the following problem(s) in my rental unit:

_____

_____

_____

_____

_____

_____

_____

I would very much appreciate it if you would promptly look into the problem(s). Please call me so that I'll know when to expect you or a repair person. You can reach me as follows:

Work (daytime): _____ Home (evenings): _____

Thank you very much for your attention to this problem.

_____   _____
Signature   Date

Tenant's Notice of Intent to Move Out

Date: _____

Landlord/Manager: _____

Street address: _____

City and state: _____

Regarding rental unit address: _____

Dear _____ :

This is to notify you that the undersigned tenant(s) will be moving from the above noted rental unit on

_____, _____, or _____ days from today.

This notice provides you with at least _____ days' written notice, as required in our rental agreement.

_____

Tenant 1's signature

_____

Print name

_____

Tenant 2's signature

_____

Print name

_____

Tenant 3's signature

_____

Print name

Demand for Return of Security Deposit

Date: _____

_____

_____

_____

_____

[insert landlord's name and address]

Dear _____ *[name of landlord]*:

On _____ *[date]*, we vacated the apartment at _____

_____ and gave you our new address and phone number.

As of today, we haven't received our $_____ *[amount of security deposit owed]* security

deposit, nor any accounting from you for that money. We were entitled to receive our deposit on *[date*

when deposit was due]. You are now _____ *[number of days or weeks]* late.

We left our apartment clean and undamaged, paid all of our rent and gave you proper notice of our

intention to move. In these circumstances, it's difficult to understand your oversight in not promptly

returning our money.

Perhaps your check is in the mail. If not, please put it there promptly. Should we fail to hear from you by

_____ *[date]*, we'll take this matter to small claims court. And please understand that

if we are compelled to do this, we shall also sue you for any additional punitive damages allowed by

state law.

Please mail our deposit immediately to the above address. If you have any questions, please contact us at

the number below.

Very truly yours,

_____   _____

Signature of Tenant   Date

_____   _____

Signature of Tenant   Date

_____

Address

_____

_____

_____   _____

Home phone   Work Phone

Loan Comparison Worksheet

Purpose of loan: _____

Amount looking to borrow: $ _____

	Loan 1	Loan 2	Loan 3
General Information			
Lender:	_____	_____	_____
Contact:	_____	_____	_____
Address:	_____	_____	_____
	_____	_____	_____
	_____	_____	_____
Phone:	_____	_____	_____
Loan Terms			
APR:	_____%	_____%	_____%
Interest rate:	_____%	_____%	_____%
Adjustable?	_____	_____	_____
Cap:	_____%	_____%	_____%
Number of months:	_____	_____	_____
Monthly payment:	$_____	$_____	$_____
Total payments (# of mos. X monthly payment):	$_____	$_____	$_____
Other Costs			
Loan application fee:	$_____	$_____	$_____
Credit check:	$_____	$_____	$_____
Credit insurance:	$_____	$_____	$_____
Other:	$_____	$_____	$_____
Other Features			
Collateral required?	_____	_____	_____
If yes, specify:	_____	_____	_____
Balloon payment?	_____	_____	_____
Prepayment penalty?	_____	_____	_____
If yes, amount:	_____	_____	_____
Cosigner required?	_____	_____	_____
Payment due date:	_____	_____	_____
Grace period?	_____	_____	_____
Late fee?	_____	_____	_____
Possible loan discounts:	_____	_____	_____
Account with lender:	_____	_____	_____
Automatic deduction:	_____	_____	_____
On-time payments:	_____	_____	_____

Authorization to Conduct Credit Check

Borrower

Full name—include generations (Jr., Sr., III): _____

Other names used: _____

Street address: _____

City, state and zip code: _____

Date moved into current address: _____

Previous address: _____

City, state and zip code: _____

Dates there: _____

Home phone: _____ Social Security number: _____

Date of birth: _____

Employment History

Name and address of current employer: _____

_____

Name of supervisor: _____ Supervisor's phone: _____

Annual gross income: _____

Credit and Financial Information

Bank/Financial Accounts	Account Number	Bank/Institution	Branch
Bank savings account:			
Bank checking account:			
Bank certificate of deposit:			
Mutual fund account:			
Brokerage account:			
Other:			
Other:			
Other:			

Credit accounts & loans	Type of account (auto loan, Visa, etc.)	Account Number	Name of Creditor	Amount Owed	Monthly Payment
Credit card:					
Credit card:					
Loan (specify type):					
Loan (specify type):					
Loan (specify type):					
Other (specify type):					

I certify that all the information given above is true and correct. I authorize verification of the information provided from my credit sources and employer.

_____   _____

Signature of Borrower   Date

Monthly Payment Record

Name of lender: _____

Original amount borrowed: _____ Date loan made: _____

Month	(A) Beginning balance (or prior month ending balance)	(B) Annual interest rate divided by 12	(C) Interest due (A) x (B)	(D) Amount of payment made	(E) Principal reduction (D)–(C)	(F) New balance (A)–(E)
1						
2						
3						
4						
5						
6						
7						
8						
9						
10						
11						
12						
13						
14						
15						
16						
17						
18						
19						
20						
21						
22						
23						
24						
25						
26						
27						
28						
29						
30						

Promissory Note

Loan repayable in installments with interest

Name of Borrower 1: _____

Name of Borrower 2: _____

Name of Lender: _____

1. For value received, Borrower promises to pay to Lender the amount of $ _____

    on _____ *[due date]* at _____

    _____ *[address where payments are to be sent]* at the

    rate of _____ % per year from the date this note was signed until the date it is *[choose one]:*

    ☐ paid in full *[Borrower will receive credits for prepayments, reducing the total amount of interest to
    be repaid].*

    ☐ due or is paid in full, whichever date occurs last *[Borrower will not receive credits for prepayments].*

2. Borrower agrees that this note shall be paid in installments, which include principal and interest, of not

    less than $ _____ per month, due on the first day of each month, until such time as the

    principal and interest are paid in full.

3. If any installment payment due under this note is not received by Lender within _____ days of its due

    date, the entire amount of unpaid principal shall become immediately due and payable at the option

    of Lender without prior notice to Borrower.

4. In the event Lender prevails in a lawsuit to collect on it, Borrower agrees to pay Lender's attorney fees

    in an amount the court finds to be just and reasonable.

*The term Borrower refers to one or more borrowers. If there is more than one borrower, they agree to be jointly and
severally liable. The term Lender refers to any person who legally holds this note, including a buyer in due course.*

_____   _____

Borrower 1's signature   Date

_____

Print name

_____

Location *[city or county where signed]*

_____

Address

_____   _____

Borrower 2's signature   Date

_____

Print name

_____

Location *[city or county where signed]*

_____

Address

[Notary Seal]

Promissory Note

Loan repayable in installments with interest and balloon payment

Name of Borrower 1: _____

Name of Borrower 2: _____

Name of Lender: _____

1. For value received, Borrower promises to pay to Lender the amount of $ _____

   on _____ *[due date]* at _____

   _____ *[address where payments are to be sent]* at the

   rate of _____ % per year from the date this note was signed until the date it is *[choose one]:*

   ☐ paid in full *[Borrower will receive credits for prepayments, reducing the total amount of interest to be repaid].*

   ☐ due or is paid in full, whichever date occurs last *[Borrower will not receive credits for prepayments].*

2. Borrower agrees that this note shall be paid in installments, which include principal and interest, of not less than $ _____ per month, due on the first day of each month, until such time as the principal and interest are paid in full.

3. Borrower agrees to make one final payment for the entire balance owed on or before_____ *[date balloon payment is due].*

4. If any installment payment due under this note is not received by Lender within _____ days of its due date, the entire amount of unpaid principal shall become immediately due and payable at the option of Lender without prior notice to Borrower.

5. In the event Lender prevails in a lawsuit to collect on it, Borrower agrees to pay Lender's attorney fees in an amount the court finds to be just and reasonable.

The term Borrower refers to one or more borrowers. If there is more than one borrower, they agree to be jointly and severally liable. The term Lender refers to any person who legally holds this note, including a buyer in due course.

_____   _____

Borrower 1's signature   Date

_____

Print name

_____

Location *[city or county where signed]*

_____

Address

_____   _____

Borrower 2's signature   Date

_____

Print name

_____

Location *[city or county where signed]*

_____

Address

[Notary Seal]

_____

Promissory Note

Loan repayable in installments without interest

Name of Borrower 1: _____

Name of Borrower 2: _____

Name of Lender: _____

1. For value received, Borrower promises to pay to Lender the amount of $ _____

   on _____ *[due date]* at _____

   _____ *[address where payments are to be sent]*.

2. Borrower also agrees that this note shall be paid in equal installments of $ _____ per

   month, due on the first day of each month, until the principal is paid in full.

3. If any installment payment due under this note is not received by Lender within _____ days of

   its due date, the entire amount of unpaid principal shall become immediately due and payable at the

   option of Lender without prior notice to Borrower.

4. In the event Lender prevails in a lawsuit to collect on it, Borrower agrees to pay Lender's attorney fees

   in an amount the court finds to be just and reasonable.

The term Borrower refers to one or more borrowers. If there is more than one borrower, they agree to be jointly and severally liable. The term Lender refers to any person who legally holds this note, including a buyer in due course.

_____   _____

Borrower 1's signature   Date

_____

Print name

_____

Location *[city or county where signed]*

_____

Address

_____   _____

Borrower 2's signature   Date

_____

Print name

_____

Location *[city or county where signed]*

_____

Address

[Notary Seal]

Promissory Note

Loan repayable in lump sum with interest

Name of Borrower 1: _____

Name of Borrower 2: _____

Name of Lender: _____

1. For value received, Borrower promises to pay to Lender the amount of $ _____

   on _____ *[due date]* at _____

   _____ *[address where payments are to be sent]*.

2. Simple interest shall be charged on the sum specified in Clause 1 at the rate of _____ % per year

   from the date this note was signed until the date it is *[choose one]*:

   ☐ paid in full (Borrower will receive credits for prepayments, reducing the total amount of interest to
   be repaid).

   ☐ due or is paid in full, whichever date occurs last (Borrower will not receive credits for making
   prepayments).

3. In the event Lender prevails in a lawsuit to collect on it, Borrower agrees to pay Lender's attorney fees
   in an amount the court finds to be just and reasonable.

*The term Borrower refers to one or more borrowers. If there is more than one borrower, they agree to be jointly and
severally liable. The term Lender refers to any person who legally holds this note, including a buyer in due course.*

_____   _____

Borrower 1's signature   Date

_____

Print name

_____

Location *[city or county where signed]*

_____

Address

_____   _____

Borrower 2's signature   Date

_____

Print name

_____

Location *[city or county where signed]*

_____

Address

[Notary Seal]

Promissory Note

Loan repayable in lump sum without interest

Name of Borrower 1: _____

Name of Borrower 2: _____

Name of Lender: _____

1. For value received, Borrower promises to pay to Lender the amount of $ _____

   on _____ *[due date]* at _____

   _____ *[address where payments are to be sent]*.

2. In the event Lender prevails in a lawsuit to collect on it, Borrower agrees to pay Lender's attorney fees
   in an amount the court finds to be just and reasonable.

The term Borrower refers to one or more borrowers. If there is more than one borrower, they agree to be jointly and severally liable. The term Lender refers to any person who legally holds this note, including a buyer in due course.

_____   _____

Borrower 1's signature   Date

_____

Print name

_____

Location *[city or county where signed]*

_____

Address

_____   _____

Borrower 2's signature   Date

_____

Print name

_____

Location *[city or county where signed]*

_____

Address

[Notary Seal]

Cosigner Provision

Name of Cosigner 1: _____

Name of Cosigner 2: _____

Name of Borrower 1: _____

Name of Borrower 2: _____

Name of Lender: _____

1. Borrower has agreed to pay to Lender the amount indicated in the attached Promissory Note under the terms specified in that Note.

2. Cosigner agrees to guarantee this debt; Cosigner wants to accept this responsibility and understands this obligation means the following:

   • If Borrower doesn't pay the debt on time, that fact may become a part of Cosigner's credit record.

   • If Borrower doesn't pay the debt at all, Cosigner will be legally obligated to do so.

   • Cosigner may have to pay late fees or collection costs, which will increase this amount.

   • Lender can collect this debt from Cosigner without first trying to collect from Borrower.

   • Lender can use the same collection methods against Cosigner that can be used against Borrower, including filing a lawsuit against Cosigner, and if the lawsuit is successful, garnishing Cosigner's wages, seizing other personal property of Cosigner and putting a lien against Cosigner's house.

The term Cosigner refers to one or more cosigner. If there is more than one cosigner, they agree to be jointly and severally liable.

_____   _____

Cosigner 1's signature   Date

_____

Print name

_____

Location *[city or county where signed]*

_____

Address

_____   _____

Cosigner 2's signature   Date

_____

Print name

_____

Location *[city or county where signed]*

_____

Address

Security Agreement Provision for Promissory Note

Here are some examples of the kind of language to include in the security agreement provision.

If a house is security, use this language:

Borrower agrees that until such time as the principal and interest owed under this note are paid in full, the note shall be secured by the following mortgage or deed of trust:

Deed of trust to real property commonly known as: _____

_____ *[address or other description]*

owned by: _____ *[name of owner]*

executed on: _____*[date signed]* at: _____

_____ *[place signed]*

and recorded at: _____ *[place recorded]*

in the records of:_____ *[county and state where recorded]*

If a vehicle is security, use this language:

Borrower agrees that until such time as the principal and interest owed under this note are paid in full, the note shall be secured by the following security agreement:

Security agreement signed by: _____ *[name of owner]*

on: _____ *[date signed]* which gives title to: _____

_____ *[date, make, model and VIN of vehicle]*

If other valuable personal property is security, use this language:

Borrower agrees that until such time as the principal and interest owed under this note are paid in full, the note shall be secured by the following security agreement:

Security agreement signed by: _____ *[name of owner]*

on: _____*[date signed]* which gives a security interest in: _____

_____ *[description of the personal*

property used as collateral]

U.C.C. Financing Statement

This Financing Statement is presented for filing under the Uniform Commercial Code as adopted in

_____ *[name of your state]*.

Name of Borrower: _____

Address of Borrower: _____

_____

Name of Lender/Secured party: _____

Address of Lender/Secured party: _____

_____

The term Borrower refers to one or more borrowers. If there is more than one borrower, they agree to be jointly and severally liable. The term Lender refers to any person who legally holds this note, including a buyer in due course.

The property listed as collateral in the security agreement is as follows *[identify or describe]:*

_____

_____

This Financing Statement secures the following debt:

Promissory note dated: _____

Amount of debt: _____

Pay back due date: _____

All other terms and conditions are stated in the promissory note, which is attached.

Borrower's signature: _____

Print name: _____

Date: _____

(For Use of the Filing Officer)

Date of filing: _____ Time of filing: _____

File number and address of filing office: _____

_____

Release of U.C.C. Financing Statement

This Release of Financing Statement is presented for filing under the Uniform Commercial Code as

adopted in _____ *[name of your state]*.

Name of Borrower: _____

Address of Borrower: _____

_____

Name of Lender/Secured party: _____

Address of Lender/Secured party: _____

_____

The term Borrower refers to one or more borrowers. The term Lender refers to any person who legally holds this note, including a buyer in due course.

The property listed as collateral in the security agreement is as follows *[identify or describe]*:

_____

_____

File number of Financing Statement: _____

Date filed: _____

Address of filing office: _____

Borrower's signature: _____

Print name: _____

Date: _____

_____

(For Use of the Filing Officer)

Date of filing: _____ Time of filing: _____

File number and address of filing office: _____

_____

Release of Security Interest

Name of Borrower: _____

Address of Borrower: _____

_____

Name of Lender/Secured party: _____

Address of Lender/Secured party: _____

_____

For valuable consideration, Lender releases Borrower from the following specific security agreement *[identify the security agreement, including the date signed, amount borrowed, collateral named and pay back date]:*

_____

_____

_____

The term Borrower refers to one or more borrowers. The term Lender refers to any person who legally holds this note, including a buyer in due course.

Any claims and obligations not specifically mentioned here are not covered by this Release.

Lender has not assigned any claims or obligations covered by this Release to any other party.

Lender will sign a Release of U.C.C. Financing Statement if such a statement was filed with a public agency.

_____   _____
Lender's signature   Date

_____
Print name

Agreement to Modify Promissory Note

Name of Borrower 1: _____

Name of Borrower 2: _____

Name of Lender: _____

1. This Agreement modifies an original promissory note dated _____ , _____ ,
   under which Borrower promises to pay to Lender the amount of $ _____ at the rate of
   _____% per year from the date this note was signed until _____ , _____ .

2. Lender and Borrower agree to the following modifications *[choose all that apply]*:

   ☐ Borrower has until _____ to pay the note in full.

   ☐ Borrower will make interest-only payments beginning on _____ , _____ ,
   until _____ , _____ , at which time the remaining principal balance
   will be reamortized over the remaining months of the note.

   ☐ Beginning on _____ , _____ , the interest rate will change
   to _____ %. The new monthly payments will be in the amount of $ _____ .

   ☐ Other: _____ .

The term Borrower refers to one or more borrowers. If there is more than one borrower, they agree to be jointly and severally liable. The term Lender refers to any person who legally holds this note, including a buyer in due course.

_____   _____
Borrower 1's signature   Date

_____
Print name

_____
Location *[city or county where signed]*

_____
Address

_____   _____
Borrower 2's signature   Date

_____
Print name

_____
Location *[city or county where signed]*

_____
Address

Overdue Payment Demand

Date: _____

To:

_____

_____

_____

[insert name and address of person borrowing money]

Re: Promissory Note dated _____

Dear _____ :

This is to notify you that I have not received the following payment(s) under our Promissory Note.

Amount:	$ _____	Due date:	_____
Amount:	$ _____	Due date:	_____
Total:	$ _____		

Please let me know at once if there is a problem. If I do not hear from you within 15 days, I will have no choice but to assume that you do not intend to repay me what is due under this Note. I will proceed to enforce my rights under the Promissory Note, including possibly filing a lawsuit, to collect the entire balance.

Sincerely,

_____

Signature of Lender

_____

Print name of Lender

_____

Address

_____

_____   _____

Home phone   Work Phone

Demand to Make Good on Bad Check

Date: _____

To:

_____

_____

_____

[insert name and address of check writer]

Re: Check # _____ Dated _____ , _____

Issuing financial institution: _____

Dear _____ :

Your check was returned to my bank and refused payment for the following reason *[choose one]:*

☐ insufficient funds in the account on which the check was drawn to cover the amount of the check.

☐ the account on which the check was drawn has been closed.

Please let me know at once if there is a problem. If I do not hear from you within 30 days, I will have no choice but to assume that you do not intend to make good on this check. I will proceed to enforce my rights, which may include filing a lawsuit. I will request that the court award me the maximum monetary damages allowed under state law, as well as:

☐ the amount of the check

☐ bad check processing fee charged by my bank

☐ expenses incurred in attempting to collect on the check

Sincerely,

_____

Signature of Check Recipient

_____

Print name of Check Recipient

_____

Address

_____

_____   _____
Home phone   Work Phone

Ideal House Profile

Upper price limit: _____

Maximum down payment: _____

Special financing needs: _____

	Must Have	Hope to Have
Neighborhood or location:		
_____	_____	_____
_____	_____	_____
_____	_____	_____
School needs:		
_____	_____	_____
Desired neighborhood features:		
_____	_____	_____
_____	_____	_____
_____	_____	_____
_____	_____	_____
Length of commute:		
_____	_____	_____
Access to public transportation:		
_____	_____	_____
Size of house:		
_____	_____	_____
Number and type of rooms:		
_____	_____	_____
_____	_____	_____
_____	_____	_____
_____	_____	_____
Condition, age and type of house:		
_____	_____	_____
_____	_____	_____
Type of yard and grounds:		
_____	_____	_____
_____	_____	_____
Other desired features:		
_____	_____	_____
_____	_____	_____
_____	_____	_____
Absolute no ways:		
_____		
_____		
_____		

House Priorities Worksheet

Date visited: _____

Address: _____

Price: $ _____

Contact: _____ Phone #: _____

Must have:

☐ _____

☐ _____

☐ _____

☐ _____

☐ _____

☐ _____

☐ _____

☐ _____

Hope to have:

☐ _____

☐ _____

☐ _____

☐ _____

☐ _____

☐ _____

☐ _____

☐ _____

Absolute no way:

☐ _____

☐ _____

☐ _____

☐ _____

Comments about the particular house:

_____

_____

_____

_____

_____

House Comparison Worksheet

House 1 _____

House 2 _____

House 3 _____

House 4 _____

Must have: 1   2   3   4

_____   ___ ___ ___ ___

_____   ___ ___ ___ ___

_____   ___ ___ ___ ___

_____   ___ ___ ___ ___

_____   ___ ___ ___ ___

_____   ___ ___ ___ ___

_____   ___ ___ ___ ___

_____   ___ ___ ___ ___

_____   ___ ___ ___ ___

_____   ___ ___ ___ ___

_____   ___ ___ ___ ___

_____   ___ ___ ___ ___

Hope to have:

_____   ___ ___ ___ ___

_____   ___ ___ ___ ___

_____   ___ ___ ___ ___

_____   ___ ___ ___ ___

_____   ___ ___ ___ ___

_____   ___ ___ ___ ___

_____   ___ ___ ___ ___

_____   ___ ___ ___ ___

Absolute no ways:

_____   ___ ___ ___ ___

_____   ___ ___ ___ ___

_____   ___ ___ ___ ___

_____   ___ ___ ___ ___

Family Financial Statement

	Borrower	Co-Borrower
Name:	_____	_____
Address:	_____	_____
	_____	_____
Home phone:	_____	_____
Employer:	_____	_____
Employer's address:	_____	_____
Work phone:	_____	_____

Worksheet 1: Income and Expenses

I. INCOME	Borrower ($)	Co-Borrower ($)	Total ($)
A. Monthly gross income			
1. Employment	_____	_____	_____
2. Public benefits	_____	_____	_____
3. Dividends	_____	_____	_____
4. Royalties	_____	_____	_____
5. Interest/investments	_____	_____	_____
6. Other (specify): _____	_____	_____	_____
B. Total monthly gross income	_____	_____	_____

II. MONTHLY EXPENSES	Borrower ($)	Co-Borrower ($)	Total ($)
A. Non-housing			
1. Child care	_____	_____	_____
2. Clothing	_____	_____	_____
3. Food	_____	_____	_____
4. Insurance	_____	_____	_____
a. Auto	_____	_____	_____
b. Life	_____	_____	_____
c. Medical & dental	_____	_____	_____
5. Other medical	_____	_____	_____
6. Personal	_____	_____	_____
7. Education	_____	_____	_____
8. Taxes (non-housing)	_____	_____	_____
9. Transportation	_____	_____	_____
10. Other (specify): _____	_____	_____	_____
B. Housing			
1. Mortgage	_____	_____	_____
2. Taxes	_____	_____	_____
3. Insurance	_____	_____	_____
4. Utilities	_____	_____	_____
5. Rent	_____	_____	_____
6. Other (specify): _____	_____	_____	_____
C. Total monthly expenses	_____	_____	_____

Worksheet 2: Assets and Liabilities

I. ASSETS (Cash or Market Value)	Borrower ($)	Co-Borrower ($)	Total ($)
A. Cash and cash equivalents			
1. Cash			
2. Deposits (list):			
B. Marketable securities			
1. Stocks/bonds (bid price)			
2. Other securities			
3. Mutual funds			
4. Life insurance			
5. Other (specify):			
C. Total Cash & Marketable Securities			
D. Non-liquid assets			
1. Real estate			
2. Retirement funds			
3. Business			
4. Motor vehicles			
5. Other (specify):			
E. Total non-liquid assets			
F. Total all assets			

II. LIABILITIES			
A. Debts			
1. Real estate loans			
2. Student loans			
3. Motor vehicle loans			
4. Child or spousal support			
5. Personal loans			
6. Credit cards (specify):			
7. Other (specify):			
B. Total liabilities			

III. NET WORTH

(Total assets minus total liabilities) _____ _____ _____

Monthly Carrying Costs Worksheet

1. Estimated purchase price $ _____

2. Down payment $ _____

3. Loan amount (line 1 minus line 2) $ _____

4. Interest rate _____ %

5. Mortgage payment factor   _____

6. Monthly mortgage payment
   (multiply line 3 by line 5) $ _____

7. Homeowner's insurance (monthly) $ _____

8. Property taxes (monthly) $ _____

9. Total monthly carrying costs
   (add lines 6-8) $ _____

10. Long-term debts (monthly payments)

    _____ $ _____

    _____ $ _____

    _____ $ _____

    _____ $ _____

    Total long-term debts (monthly payments) $ _____

11. Private mortgage insurance $ _____

12. Homeowners' association fee $ _____

13. Total monthly carrying costs and
    long-term debts (add lines 9-12) $ _____

14. Lender qualification (between .28 and .38)   _____ %

15. Monthly income to qualify (divide line 13 by line 14) $ _____

16. Yearly income to qualify (multiply line 15 by 12 (months)) $ _____

Mortgage Rates and Terms Worksheet

Lender: _____ _____ _____

Loan agent: _____ _____ _____

Phone number: _____ _____ _____

Date: _____ _____ _____

1. General Information

Fixed or adjustable	☐ F	☐ A	☐ F ☐ A		☐ F ☐ A
Fixed interest rate	_____ %		_____ %		_____ %
Government financing	☐ Y	☐ N	☐ Y ☐ N		☐ Y ☐ N
Minimum down payment	_____ %		_____ %		_____ %
PMI required	☐ Y	☐ N	☐ Y ☐ N		☐ Y ☐ N
Impound account	☐ Y	☐ N	☐ Y ☐ N		☐ Y ☐ N
Term of mortgage	_____ Years		_____ Years		_____ Years
Assumable	☐ Y	☐ N	☐ Y ☐ N		☐ Y ☐ N
Prepayment penalty	☐ Y	☐ N	☐ Y ☐ N		☐ Y ☐ N
Negative amortization	☐ Y	☐ N	☐ Y ☐ N		☐ Y ☐ N
Rate lock-in available	☐ Y	☐ N	☐ Y ☐ N		☐ Y ☐ N
Cost to lock-in	21 Days $_____		21 Days $_____		21 Days $_____
	30 Days $_____		30 Days $_____		30 Days $_____
	45 Days $_____		45 Days $_____		45 Days $_____

2. Debt-to-Income Ratios Information

Allowable monthly carrying costs as
% of income _____ % _____ % _____ %

Allowable monthly carrying costs plus
long-term debts as % of monthly income _____ % _____ % _____ %

Maximum loan you qualify for
based on debt-to-income ratios $ _____ $ _____ $ _____

3. Loan Costs

Number of points $ _____ $ _____ $ _____

Cost of points $ _____ $ _____ $ _____

PMI $ _____ $ _____ $ _____

Additional loan fee	$ _____	$ _____	$ _____
Credit report	$ _____	$ _____	$ _____
Application fee	$ _____	$ _____	$ _____
Appraisal fee	$ _____	$ _____	$ _____
Miscellaneous fees	$ _____	$ _____	$ _____
Estimated total loan costs	$ _____	$ _____	$ _____

4. Time Limits

Credit/employment check	_____ Days	_____ Days	_____ Days
Lender appraisal	_____ Days	_____ Days	_____ Days
Loan approval	_____ Days	_____ Days	_____ Days
Loan funding	_____ Days	_____ Days	_____ Days
Loan due date each month	_____	_____	_____
Grace period	_____ Days	_____ Days	_____ Days
Late fee	_____ %	_____ %	_____ %

5. Other Features

[such as a discount for having an account
with a certain bank, or a lender discount
of interest rate on initial payments]

_____   _____   _____   _____

_____   _____   _____   _____

_____   _____   _____   _____

6. Fixed Rate Two-Step Loans

Initial annual interest rate	_____ %	_____ %	_____ %
Over how many years	_____ Years	_____ Years	_____ Years

7. Fixed Rate Balloon Payment Loans

Interest rate	_____ %	_____ %	_____ %
Monthly payment	$ _____	$ _____	$ _____
Term of loan	_____ Years	_____ Years	_____ Years
Amount of balloon payment	$ _____	$ _____	$ _____

8. Adjustable Rate Mortgages (ARMs)

Index: 11th District COFI □ _____ % □ _____ % □ _____ %

    6 Mo. T-Bills □ _____ % □ _____ % □ _____ %

    1 Yr. T-Bills □ _____ % □ _____ % □ _____ %

    Other _____ □ _____ % □ _____ % □ _____ %

Margin _____ % _____ % _____ %

Initial interest rate

  How long ____ Mos. ___ Yrs. _____ Mos. ____ Yrs. _____ Mos. ____ Yrs.

Interest rate cap
(with negative amortization) or _____ % _____ % _____ %

Interest rate cap
(without negative amortization) _____ % _____ % _____ %

Adjustment period _____ Months _____ Months _____ Months

Life-of-loan (overall) cap _____ % _____ % _____ %

Initial payment _____ Months _____ Months _____ Months

Payment cap _____ % _____ % _____ %

Payment cap period _____ Months _____ Months _____ Months

Highest payment or interest rate in:

  6 months ____% $ _____ ____% $ _____ ____% $ _____

  12 months ____% $ _____ ____% $ _____ ____% $ _____

  18 months ____% $ _____ ____% $ _____ ____% $ _____

  24 months ____% $ _____ ____% $ _____ ____% $ _____

  30 months ____% $ _____ ____% $ _____ ____% $ _____

  36 months ____% $ _____ ____% $ _____ ____% $ _____

9. Hybrid Loans

Initial interest rate _____ % _____ % _____ %

Term as a fixed rate loan _____ Years _____ Years _____ Years

Interest rate at first adjustment period _____ % _____ % _____ %

Moving Checklist

[Not all items on this list will apply to you. If you're moving within the same town, you probably won't have to transfer your kids to a new school, get references for a new job or have your car serviced for travel. So just focus on the applicable items.]

I. Two Weeks Before Moving

☐ Transfer school records and transcripts.

☐ Close bank and safe deposit box accounts.

☐ Cancel deliveries—newspaper, diapers, laundry.

☐ Cancel utilities—gas, electric, cable, phone, water, garbage; transfer services (if possible) or arrange new services; request deposit refunds.

☐ Get recommendations or find in advance (especially if a medical condition needs regular attention) new doctors, dentist and veterinarian. If possible, photocopy key medical records to have with you.

☐ Get reference letters, if you'll need to find a job.

☐ Cancel membership (or transfer membership, if relevant) in religious, civic and athletic organizations.

☐ Have car serviced for travel.

☐ Arrange for moving pets.

☐ Finalize arrangements with moving company. (You should have gotten bids and made preliminary arrangements weeks earlier.)

☐ Tell close friends and relatives your schedule.

II. Things to Remember While Packing

☐ Before you pack, take the time to do a good inventory and sort through things. This way you can move less and won't end up throwing things away at your new home or taking up storage space.

☐ Label boxes on top and side—your name, new city, room of house, contents.

☐ Pack phone books.

☐ Assemble moving kit—hammer, screwdriver, pliers, tape, nails, tape measure, scissors, flashlight, cleansers, cleaning cloths, rubber gloves, garbage bags, light bulbs, extension cords. If you're driving to your new home, pack a broom and pail in your car. Larger items that are handy when moving in, such as a step stool or vacuum cleaner, should go in the moving van, unless your new house is nearby and you're moving lots of things by car.

☐ Keep the basics handy—comfortable clothes, toiletries, towels, alarm clock, disposable plates, cups and utensils, can opener, one pot, one pan, sponge, paper towels, toilet paper, plastic containers and toys for kids.

☐ Consider carrying jewelry, extremely fragile items, currency and important documents.

☐ Make other arrangements if moving company won't move antiques, art collections, crystal, other valuables or plants.

III. Whom to Send Change of Addresses

- ☐ Friends and relatives.
- ☐ Subscriptions.
- ☐ Government agencies you regularly deal with—Veterans' Administration, Social Security Administration, etc.
- ☐ Charge and credit accounts.
- ☐ Installment debt—such as student loan or car loan.
- ☐ Frequent flyer programs.
- ☐ Brokers and mutual funds.
- ☐ Insurance agent/companies.
- ☐ Medical providers—if you'll be able to use them after moving.
- ☐ Catalogues you want to keep receiving.
- ☐ Charities you wish to continue donating to.
- ☐ Post office. (If you're trying to get off of catalogue and other direct mailing lists, only have first-class mail forwarded. Give your new address to those catalogue companies on whose lists you want to remain, and don't forget to tell them not to trade or sell your name.)

IV. Things to Do After Moving In

- ☐ Open bank accounts.
- ☐ Open safe deposit box account.
- ☐ Begin deliveries—oil, newspaper, diapers, laundry.
- ☐ Register to vote.
- ☐ Change (or get new) driver's license.
- ☐ Change auto registration.
- ☐ Install new batteries in existing smoke detectors (and install any additionally needed smoke detectors); buy fire extinguisher.
- ☐ Hold party for the people who helped you find your house and your moving helpers, and take yourself out for a congratulatory dinner!

If Owner is unable to deliver possession of the premises to Tenant for any reason not within Owner's control, including but not limited to partial or complete destruction of the premises, Tenant will have the right to terminate this Agreement upon proper notice as Clause 23. Validity of Each Part

Motor Vehicle Bill of Sale

Seller 1: _____

Address: _____

Seller 2: _____

Address: _____

Buyer 1: _____

Address: _____

Buyer 2: _____

Address: _____

If there is more than one buyer or seller, the use of the singular incorporates the plural.

1. Seller hereby sells the Vehicle described here to Buyer *[specify vehicle year, make and model]*: _____

   _____

   Its body type is: _____.

   It carries the following vehicle identification number (VIN): _____.

   Vehicle includes the following personal property items: _____

   _____.

2. The full purchase price for Vehicle is $ _____ . In exchange for Vehicle, Buyer has paid Seller *[choose one]:*

   ☐ single payment of the full purchase price.

   ☐ $ _____ as a down payment, balance of the purchase price due by _____ *[date].*

   ☐ $ _____ as a down payment and has executed a promissory note for the balance of the purchase price.

3. Seller warrants that Seller is the legal owner of Vehicle and that Vehicle is free of all legal claims (liens or encumbrances) by others except: _____

   _____

   Seller agrees to remove any lien or encumbrance specified in this clause with the proceeds of this sale within _____ days of the date of the bill of sale.

4. Vehicle ☐ has been ☐ has not been   inspected by an independent mechanic at Buyer's request. If an inspection has been made, the inspection report ☐ is attached ☐ is not attached   to and made part of this bill of sale.

5. Seller believes Vehicle to be in good condition except for the following defects: _____

_____

_____

6. Other than the warranty of ownership in Clause 3 and the representations in Clause 5, Seller makes no express warranties. **Buyer takes Vehicle as is.** Seller hereby disclaims the implied warranty of merchantability and all other implied warranties which may apply to the extent disclaimers are permitted in the state having jurisdiction over this bill of sale.

7. The odometer reading for Vehicle is: _____ .

8. Additional terms of sale for Vehicle are as follows: _____

_____

_____

_____

_____   _____
Seller 1's signature   Date

_____   _____
Seller 2's signature   Date

_____   _____
Buyer 1's signature   Date

_____   _____
Buyer 2's signature   Date

Boat Bill of Sale

Seller 1: _____

Address: _____

Seller 2: _____

Address: _____

Buyer 1: _____

Address: _____

Buyer 2: _____

Address: _____

If there is more than one buyer or seller, the use of the singular incorporates the plural.

1. Seller sells the boat (Boat) described here to Buyer:

   Year: _____ Make: _____

   Model: _____ Length: _____

   Serial or Hull ID number: _____ General type: _____

   Registration, CF or Document number: _____

2. Boat has the following types of engine(s) (Engines) *[provide details on any engines including year, make, type, model, hours and serial number]*:

   _____

   _____

   _____

   _____

   _____

   _____

3. Boat contains the following equipment (Equipment) included in this sale *[list and describe all that apply, including sails and rigging, safety equipment, electronics and navigation equipment and deck equipment]*:

   _____

   _____

   _____

   _____

   _____

   _____

4. Seller believes Boat, Engines and Equipment to be in good condition except for the following defects:

_____

_____

5. Boat and Engines ☐ have been ☐ have not been independently inspected or surveyed at Buyer's request. If an independent inspection or Marine Survey has been made, the inspection report or Marine Survey ☐ is attached ☐ is not attached to and made part of this bill of sale.

6. The full purchase price for Boat, Engines and Equipment is $ _____ . In exchange for Boat, Engines and Equipment, Buyer has paid Seller [choose one]:

☐ single payment of the full purchase price.

☐ $ _____ as a down payment, balance of the purchase price due by _____ [date].

☐ $ _____ as a down payment and has executed a promissory note for the balance of the purchase price.

7. Seller warrants that Seller is the legal owner of Boat, Engines and Equipment and that Boat, Engines and Equipment are free of all liens and encumbrances except _____

_____

Seller agrees to remove any lien or encumbrance specified in this clause with the proceeds of this sale within _____ days of the date of the bill of sale.

8. Other than the warranty of ownership in Clause 7 and the representations in Clause 4, Seller makes no express warranties. **Buyer takes Boat, Engines and Equipment as is.** Seller hereby disclaims the implied warranty of merchantability and all other implied warranties which may apply to the extent that such disclaimers are permitted in the state having jurisdiction over this bill of sale.

9. Additional terms of sale for Boat, Engines and Equipment are as follows: _____

_____

_____

_____   _____
Seller 1's signature   Date

_____   _____
Seller 2's signature   Date

_____   _____
Buyer 1's signature   Date

_____   _____
Buyer 2's signature   Date

Computer System Bill of Sale

Seller 1: _____

Address: _____

Seller 2: _____

Address: _____

Buyer 1: _____

Address: _____

Buyer 2: _____

Address: _____

If there is more than one buyer or seller, the use of the singular incorporates the plural.

1. Seller sells the goods (Goods) described here to Buyer:

    Hardware *[provide the brand name and, wherever possible, the serial number]*:

    ☐ computer (boards, cpu, bus, I/O ports): _____

    _____

    ☐ monitor: _____

    _____

    _____

    _____

    ☐ external floppy disk drive: _____

    _____

    ☐ external hard drive: _____

    _____

    ☐ CD-ROM: _____

    _____

    ☐ external mass storage device: _____

    _____

    ☐ printer: _____

    _____

    ☐ modem: _____

    _____

    ☐ multimedia system: _____

    _____

    ☐ furniture or other items as follows: _____

    _____

Software *[provide the titles of the software and, wherever possible, the serial number]:*

_____

_____

_____

_____

_____

2. The full purchase price for Goods is $_____. In exchange for Goods, Buyer has paid Seller
   [choose one]:

   ☐ the single payment of the full purchase price.

   ☐ $ _____ as a down payment, balance of the purchase price due by _____ *[date].*

   ☐ $ _____ as a down payment and has executed a promissory note for the balance of the
   purchase price.

3. Seller warrants that Seller is the legal owner of Goods and that Goods are free of all liens and

   encumbrances except _____

   _____

   Seller agrees to remove any lien or encumbrance specified in this clause with the proceeds of this

   sale within _____ days of the date of the bill of sale.

4. Seller believes Goods to be in good condition except for the following defects: _____

   _____

5. Other than the warranty of ownership in Clause 3 and the representations in Clause 4, Seller makes no
   express warranties. **Buyer takes Goods as is.** Seller hereby disclaims the implied warranty of
   merchantability and all other implied warranties which may apply to the extent that such disclaimers
   are permitted in the state having jurisdiction over this bill of sale.

6. Additional terms of sale for Goods are as follows: _____

   _____

   _____

_____   _____
Seller 1's signature   Date

_____   _____
Seller 2's signature   Date

_____   _____
Buyer 1's signature   Date

_____   _____
Buyer 2's signature   Date

General Bill of Sale

Seller 1: _____

Address: _____

Seller 2: _____

Address: _____

Buyer 1: _____

Address: _____

Buyer 2: _____

Address: _____

If there is more than one buyer or seller, the use of the singular incorporates the plural.

1. Seller sells the goods (Goods) described here to Buyer: _____

   _____

   _____

   _____

2. The full purchase price for Goods is $_____ . In exchange for Goods, Buyer has paid Seller *[choose one]:*

   ☐ single payment of the full purchase price.

   ☐ $ _____ as a down payment, balance of the purchase price due by _____ *[date]*.

   ☐ $ _____ as a down payment and has executed a promissory note for the balance of the purchase price.

3. Seller warrants that Seller is the legal owner of Goods and that Goods are free of all liens and encumbrances except _____

   _____

   Seller agrees to remove any lien or encumbrance specified in this clause with the proceeds of this sale within _____ days of the date of the bill of sale.

4. Seller believes Goods to be in good condition except for the following defects: _____

   _____

   _____

5. Other than the warranty of ownership in Clause 3 and the representations in Clause 4, seller makes no express warranties. **Buyer takes all goods as is.** Seller hereby disclaims the implied warranty of merchantability and all other implied warranties which may apply to the extent that such disclaimers are permitted in the state having jurisdiction over this bill of sale.

6. Goods shall be delivered to Buyer in the following manner *[choose one]:*

  ☐ Buyer shall take immediate possession of Goods.

  ☐ Buyer assumes responsibility for picking up goods from_____

    within _____ days.

  ☐ In exchange for an additional delivery charge of $ _____ , receipt of which is hereby

    acknowledged, Seller will deliver Goods within _____ days to the following location:

    _____ .

7. Additional terms of sale for Goods are as follows:_____

_____

_____

_____   _____

Seller 1's signature   Date

_____   _____

Seller 2's signature   Date

_____   _____

Buyer 1's signature   Date

_____   _____

Buyer 2's signature   Date

Bill of Sale for Dog

Seller 1: _____

Address: _____

Seller 2: _____

Address: _____

Buyer 1: _____

Address: _____

Buyer 2: _____

Address: _____

If there is more than one buyer or seller, the use of the singular incorporates the plural.

1. Seller sells to Buyer the Dog described as follows:

   Name: _____

   Breed: _____ Sex: _____

   Birthdate *[estimate if specific date not known]*: _____

2. The full purchase price for Dog is $_____.

3. Buyer has paid Seller *[choose one]*:

   ☐ single payment of the full purchase price

   ☐ a down payment of $_____ with the balance of $_____ due

   _____ *[date]*, or

   ☐ other: _____ *[explain]*.

4. Seller warrants that

   a. Seller is the legal owner of the Dog.

   b. The Dog has had the following vaccinations *[list all the vaccinations the Dog has received, including the date the vaccination was given and the name of the vet who gave it]*: _____

   _____

   _____.

   c. Dog was *[choose one]*:

      ☐ bred by the Seller

      ☐ bought from a breeder _____ *[name of breeder]*

      on_____ *[date]*.

   d. The Dog has had the following special training: _____

   _____.

e. The Dog ☐ is or ☐ is not purebred.

f. Dog is *[check one]*:

   ☐ registered with the American Kennel Club or another entity *[provide details as appropriate]*

   _____ .

   ☐ not registered with the American Kennel Club or another entity and is not eligible to be registered, or

   ☐ not registered with the American Kennel Club or another entity but is eligible to be registered *[explain]* _____ .

5. Seller believes that the Dog is healthy and in good condition, except for the following known problems: _____ .

6. If a licensed veterinarian certifies, in writing, that the Dog has a serious disease or congenital defect that was present when Buyer took possession of the Dog, Buyer may, within 14 days of taking possession of the Dog *[choose one]*:

   ☐ return the Dog to Seller. In this case, Seller will refund the purchase price and reimburse Buyer for the cost of reasonable veterinary services directly related to the examination that showed the Dog was ill, and emergency treatment to relieve suffering.

   ☐ keep the dog. In this case, Seller will refund the purchase price and reimburse Buyer for the cost of reasonable veterinary services directly related to the examination that showed the Dog was ill, and emergency treatment to relieve suffering.

7. Dog will be delivered to Buyer in the following manner *[choose one]*:

   ☐ Buyer will take immediate possession of the Dog.

   ☐ Buyer assumes responsibility for picking up Dog from _____

   _____ by _____ *[date]*.

   ☐ In exchange for an additional delivery charge of $ _____ , Seller will deliver Dog by

   _____ *[date]* to the following location: _____

   _____ .

8. Additional terms: _____

_____ .

_____   _____
Seller 1's signature   Date

_____   _____
Seller 2's signature   Date

_____   _____
Buyer 1's signature   Date

_____   _____
Buyer 2's signature   Date

Personal Property Rental Agreement

Owner's name: _____

Address: _____

Renter's name: _____

Address: _____

If there is more than one owner or renter, the use of the singular incorporates the plural.

1. Property Being Rented

Owner agrees to rent to Renter, and Renter agrees to rent from Owner, the following Property: _____

_____

_____

_____

2. Duration of Rental Period

This rental will begin at _____ o'clock a.m./p.m. on _____ , _____

and will end at _____ o'clock a.m./p.m. on _____ , _____ .

3. Rental Amount

The rental amount will be $ _____ per *[specify hour, day, week or month].*

4. Payment

Renter has paid $ _____ to Owner to cover the rental period specified in Clause 2.

☐ **Security deposit** *[optional].* In addition to the rent, Renter has deposited $_____ with Owner. This deposit will be applied toward any additional rent and any amounts owed for damage to or loss of the Property, which Owner and Renter agree has the current value stated in Clause 8. Owner will return to Renter any unused portion of the deposit.

5. Delivery

☐ Renter will pick up the Property from Owner at *[specify address]* _____

_____ .

☐ Owner will deliver the Property to Renter ☐ at no charge ☐ for a fee of $ _____

on _____ , _____ at: _____

_____ *[specify address]*

☐ Other delivery arrangements: _____

_____

_____ .

6. Late Return

If Renter returns the Property to Owner after the time and date when the rental period ends, Renter will pay Owner a rental charge of $_____ per day for each day or partial day beyond the end of the rental period until the Property is returned. Owner may subtract this charge from the security deposit (if any).

7. Condition of Property

Renter acknowledges receiving the Property in good condition, except for the following defects or

damages: _____

_____ .

. _____

8. Damage or Loss

Renter will return the Property to Owner in good condition except as noted in Clause 7. If the Property is damaged while in Renter's possession, Renter will be responsible for the cost of repair, up to the current value of the Property. If the Property is lost while in Renter's possession, Renter will pay Owner its current value. Owner and Renter agree that the current value of the Property is *[list value of items individually as well as total]* $ _____ .

9. Disputes

[choose one]:

☐ **Litigation.** If a dispute arises, either Owner or Renter may take the matter to court.

☐ **Mediation and Possible Litigation.** If a dispute arises, Owner and Renter will try in good faith to settle it through mediation conducted by *[choose one]:*

☐ _____ *[name of mediator].*

☐ a mediator to be mutually selected.

Owner and Renter will share the costs of the mediator equally. If the dispute is not resolved within 30 days after it is referred to the mediator, either Owner or Renter may take the matter to court.

☐ **Mediation and Possible Arbitration.** If a dispute arises, Owner and Renter will try in good faith to settle it through mediation conducted by *[choose one]:*

☐ _____ *[name of mediator].*

☐ a mediator to be mutually selected.

Owner and Renter will share the costs of the mediator equally. If the dispute is not resolved within 30 days after it is referred to the mediator, it will be arbitrated by *[choose one]:*

☐ _____ *[name of arbitrator].*

☐ an arbitrator to be mutually selected.

Judgment on the arbitration award may be entered in any court that has jurisdiction over the matter. Costs of arbitration, including lawyers' fees, will be allocated by the arbitrator.

_____   _____

Owner's signature   Date

_____   _____

Renter's signature   Date

Notice of Termination of Personal Property Rental Agreement

To *[name of person to whom notice is being sent]*:

1. Notice of Termination

This is a notice that as of _____ , _____ ,

I am terminating the following rental agreement:

Name of Owner: _____

Name of Renter: _____

Property covered by agreement: _____

_____

Date agreement signed: _____ , _____

2. Reason for Termination

The reasons for the termination are as follows *[optional, unless a reason to terminate is required by the rental agreement]*: _____

_____

_____

_____

_____

3. Return of Property

[choose one]:

☐ I will return the Property to Owner on or before _____ , _____ *[for renters]*.

☐ Please return the Property to Owner on or before _____ , _____ *[for owners]*.

4. Return of Security Deposit

☐ Renter has deposited $ _____ with Owner. Owner agrees to inspect the Property for damage and refund Renter any unused portion of the security deposit. Within 24 hours of the return of the Property, owner will deposit in the U.S. mail a refund check made out to Renter at the following address: _____

_____ .

_____   _____
Signature   Date

_____   ☐ Owner   ☐ Renter
Print name

Storage Contract

Property Owner: _____

Address: _____

Property Custodian: _____

Address: _____

If there is more than one owner or custodian, the use of the singular incorporates the plural.

1. Property

Owner desires to store with Custodian and Custodian agrees to accept and store for Owner the

following Property: _____

_____

_____

_____

_____

_____

2. Storage Location

The Property shall be stored at the following location: _____

_____

Custodian agrees that the Property will not be removed from this location without prior written notice
to and written consent of Owner.

3. Storage Term and Payment

[choose one]:

☐ Custodian agrees to store the Property on a _____ *[daily, weekly or monthly]* basis

in exchange for payment of $ _____ per _____ , payable on

the first day of each such period.

☐ Custodian agrees to store the Property for payment of $_____ . Payment shall be

made on or before_____ , _____ .

4. Beginning and Ending Dates

[choose one]:

☐ Storage will begin on _____ , _____ , and will continue until Owner claims

the Property or Custodian serves Owner with a _____ day written notice terminating this

storage agreement.

☐ Storage will begin on _____ , _____ , and will continue until

_____ , _____ , or until Owner claims the Property, whichever

occurs first.

5. Failure to Reclaim Property

If Owner fails to reclaim the Property on or before the last day of storage indicated in the notice or in Clause 4, Custodian shall *[choose one]:*

☐ continue to store the Property at the rate of $ _____ per _____ until Owner reclaims the Property.

☐ send to Owner's last known address by first-class mail a notice to reclaim the Property, and wait 30 days; if Owner does not make arrangements to reclaim the Property, Custodian may deem the Property abandoned, sell it to pay for outstanding storage fees and hold the balance for Owner.

6. Early Reclaiming

If Owner reclaims the Property during a period for which payment has been made, no pro rata refund shall be made.

7. Delivery to Someone Other Than Owner

Custodian shall not deliver the Property to any person other than Owner without prior written permission from Owner.

8. Value of the Property

Owner and Custodian agree that the approximate ☐ replacement value ☐ fair market value of the Property on the date this agreement is signed is $ _____ .

9. Condition of the Property

Property being stored appears to be in good condition except for the following defects or damage

[provide details on each item of property being stored]: _____

_____

_____

_____

_____

_____

10. Care During Storage Period

[choose one]:

☐ Custodian agrees to exercise reasonable care to protect the Property from theft or damage. Responsibility for theft or damage to the Property that doesn't result from Custodian's negligence shall be borne by Owner.

☐ In exchange for the compensation paid by Owner, Custodian agrees to (a) be fully responsible for returning the Property to Owner in the same condition as it was when the storage commenced; and (b) obtain insurance to protect the Property against all commonly insurable losses, except _____

_____

_____

_____

11. Title to the Property

The title to the Property shall remain at all times in Owner.

12. Disputes

[choose one]:

☐ **Litigation.** If a dispute arises, either Owner or Custodian may take the matter to court.

☐ **Mediation and Possible Litigation.** If a dispute arises, Owner and Custodian will try in good faith to settle it through mediation conducted by *[choose one]:*

☐ _____ *[name of mediator].*

☐ a mediator to be mutually selected.

Owner and Custodian will share the costs of the mediator equally. If the dispute is not resolved within 30 days after it is referred to the mediator, either Owner or Custodian may take the matter to court.

☐ **Mediation and Possible Arbitration.** If a dispute arises, Owner and Custodian will try in good faith to settle it through mediation conducted by *[choose one]:*

☐ _____ *[name of mediator].*

☐ a mediator to be mutually selected.

Owner and Custodian will share the costs of the mediator equally. If the dispute is not resolved within 30 days after it is referred to the mediator, it will be arbitrated by *[choose one]:*

☐ _____ *[name of arbitrator].*

☐ an arbitrator to be mutually selected.

Judgment on the arbitration award may be entered in any court that has jurisdiction over the matter. Costs of arbitration, including lawyers' fees, will be allocated by the arbitrator.

13. Modification of This Agreement

All agreements between the parties related to storage of the Property are incorporated in this contract. Any modification to this contract shall be in writing.

14. Additional Terms

Additional terms for the storage of the Property are as follows: _____

_____

_____

_____

_____

_____   _____

Owner's signature   Date

_____   _____

Custodian's signature   Date

Home Maintenance Agreement

Homeowner's name: _____

Address: _____

_____ Phone number: _____

Contractor's name: _____

Address: _____

_____ Phone number: _____

Homeowner desires to contract with Contractor to perform certain work on property located at:

_____

1. Work to Be Done

The work to be performed under this agreement consists of the following:

_____

_____

_____

_____

_____

_____

_____

_____

2. Payment

In exchange for the work specified in Clause 1, Homeowner agrees to pay Contractor as follows
[choose one and check appropriate boxes]:

☐ $ _____ , payable upon completion of the specified work by ☐ cash ☐ check.

☐ $ _____ , payable one half at the beginning of the specified work and one half at the completion of the specified work by ☐ cash ☐ check.

☐ $ _____ per hour for each hour of work performed, up to a maximum of $ _____ , payable at the following times and in the following manner: _____

_____

_____ .

3. Time

The work specified in this contract shall *[check the boxes and provide dates]*:

☐ begin on _____ , _____ .

☐ be completed on _____ , _____ .

4. Additional Terms

Homeowner and Contractor additionally agree that: _____

_____

_____

_____

_____

_____

_____

All agreements between Homeowner and Contractor related to the specified work are incorporated in this contract. Any modification to the contract shall be in writing.

_____   _____
Homeowner's signature   Date

_____   _____
Contractor's signature   Date

Home Repairs Agreement

Homeowner's name: _____

Address: _____

_____ Phone number: _____

Contractor's name: _____

Address: _____

_____ Phone number: _____

Homeowner desires to contract with Contractor to perform certain work on property located at:

_____

1. Work to Be Done

The work to be performed under this agreement consists of the following:

_____

_____

_____

_____

_____

_____

2. Payment

In exchange for the work specified in Clause 1, Homeowner agrees to pay Contractor as follows
[choose one and check appropriate boxes]:

☐ $ _____ , payable upon completion of the specified work by ☐ cash ☐ check.

☐ $ _____ , payable by ☐ cash ☐ check as follows:

_____ % payable when the following occurs: _____

_____ % payable when the following occurs: _____

_____ % payable when the following occurs: _____ .

☐ $ _____ per hour for each hour of work performed, up to a maximum of $ _____ ,

payable at the following times and in the following manner: _____

_____

_____ .

3. Time

The work specified in Clause 1 shall *[check the boxes and provide dates]:*

☐ begin on _____ , _____ .

☐ be completed on _____ , _____ .

Time is of the essence.

4. Licensing and Registration Requirements

Contractor shall comply with all state and local licensing and registration requirements for type of activity involved in the specified work *[check one box and provide description]*:

☐ Contractor's state license or registration is for the following type of work and carries the following number: _____

_____ .

☐ Contractor's local license or registration is for the following type of work and carries the following number: _____

_____ .

☐ Contractor is not required to have a license or registration for the specified work, for the following reasons: _____

_____ .

5. Permits and Approvals

[check all appropriate boxes]:

☐ Contractor ☐ Homeowner shall be responsible for determining which permits are necessary and for obtaining those permits.

☐ Contractor ☐ Homeowner shall pay for all state and local permits necessary for performing the specified work.

☐ Contractor ☐ Homeowner shall be responsible for obtaining approval from the local homeowner's association, if required.

6. Injury to Contractor

Contractor will carry his or her own insurance. If Contractor is injured in the course of performing the specified work, Homeowner shall be exempt from liability for those injuries to the fullest extent allowed by law.

7. Additional Terms

Homeowner and Contractor additionally agree that: _____

_____

_____

_____

_____

_____

All agreements between Homeowner and Contractor related to the specified work are incorporated in this contract. Any modification to the contract shall be in writing.

_____   _____
Homeowner's signature   Date

_____   _____
Contractor's signature   Date

Daily Expenses

Week of _____

Sunday's Expenses	Cost	Monday's Expenses	Cost	Tuesday's Expenses	Cost	Wednesday's Expenses	Cost
_____	_____	_____	_____	_____	_____	_____	_____
_____	_____	_____	_____	_____	_____	_____	_____
_____	_____	_____	_____	_____	_____	_____	_____
_____	_____	_____	_____	_____	_____	_____	_____
_____	_____	_____	_____	_____	_____	_____	_____
_____	_____	_____	_____	_____	_____	_____	_____
_____	_____	_____	_____	_____	_____	_____	_____
_____	_____	_____	_____	_____	_____	_____	_____
_____	_____	_____	_____	_____	_____	_____	_____
_____	_____	_____	_____	_____	_____	_____	_____
_____	_____	_____	_____	_____	_____	_____	_____
_____	_____	_____	_____	_____	_____	_____	_____
Daily Total:	_____	**Daily Total:**	_____	**Daily Total:**	_____	**Daily Total:**	_____

Thursday's Expenses	Cost	Friday's Expenses	Cost	Saturday's Expenses	Cost	Other Expenses	Cost
_____	_____	_____	_____	_____	_____	_____	_____
_____	_____	_____	_____	_____	_____	_____	_____
_____	_____	_____	_____	_____	_____	_____	_____
_____	_____	_____	_____	_____	_____	_____	_____
_____	_____	_____	_____	_____	_____	_____	_____
_____	_____	_____	_____	_____	_____	_____	_____
_____	_____	_____	_____	_____	_____	_____	_____
_____	_____	_____	_____	_____	_____	_____	_____
_____	_____	_____	_____	_____	_____	_____	_____
_____	_____	_____	_____	_____	_____	_____	_____
_____	_____	_____	_____	_____	_____	_____	_____
_____	_____	_____	_____	_____	_____	_____	_____
Daily Total:	_____	**Daily Total:**	_____	**Daily Total:**	_____	**Daily Total:**	_____

Total for the Week $_____

Monthly Income

Source of Income		Amount of each payment	Time period covered by each payment	Monthly income

A. Wages or Salary

Job 1: _____ Gross pay, including overtime: $ _____ _____

Subtract:

Federal taxes _____

State taxes _____

Social Security (FICA) _____

Union dues _____

Insurance payments _____

Child support withholding _____

Other deductions _____

(specify): _____ _____

Subtotal Job 1 $_____ _____ $ _____

Job 2: _____ Gross pay, including overtime: $ _____ _____

Subtract:

Federal taxes _____ _____ $ _____

State taxes _____ _____ $ _____

Social Security (FICA) _____ _____ $ _____

Union dues _____ _____ $ _____

Insurance payments _____ _____ $ _____

Child support withholding _____ _____ $ _____

Other deductions _____ _____ $ _____

(specify): _____ _____ _____ $ _____

Subtotal Job 2 $_____ _____ $ _____

Job 3: _____ Gross pay, including overtime: $ _____ _____

Subtract:

Federal taxes _____ _____ $ _____

State taxes _____ _____ $ _____

Social Security (FICA) _____ _____ $ _____

Union dues _____ _____ $ _____

Insurance payments _____ _____ $ _____

Child support withholding _____ _____ $ _____

Other deductions _____ _____ $ _____

(specify): _____ _____ _____ $ _____

Subtotal Job 3 $_____ _____ $ _____

Total Wages or Salary $ _____

B. Self-Employment Income

Job 1: _____   Gross pay, including overtime: $_____ _____

                                     Subtract:

                                             Federal taxes   _____

                                             State taxes   _____

                                             Social Security (FICA)   _____

                                             Union dues   _____

                                             Insurance payments   _____

                                             Child support withholding   _____

                                             Other deductions   _____

                                             (specify): _____   _____

                                          Subtotal Job 1 $_____ _____ $_____

Job 2: _____   Gross pay, including overtime: $_____ _____

                                       Subtract:

                                             Federal taxes   _____

                                             State taxes   _____

                                             Social Security (FICA)   _____

                                             Union dues   _____

                                             Insurance payments   _____

                                             Child support withholding   _____

                                             Other deductions   _____

                                             (specify): _____   _____

                                          Subtotal Job 2 $_____ _____ $_____

                              Total Self-Employment Income $_____

C. Investment Income   Dividends $_____ _____ $_____

                                   Interest $_____ _____ $_____

                                   Leases $_____ _____ $_____

                                   Licenses $_____ _____ $_____

                                   Rent $_____ _____ $_____

                                   Royalties $_____ _____ $_____

                                   Other (specify): _____ $_____ _____ $_____

                                   _____ $_____ _____ $_____

                              Total Investment Income $_____

D. Other Income   Bonuses $_____ _____ $_____

                                   Note or trust income $_____ _____ $_____

                                   Alimony or child support $_____ _____ $_____

                                   Pension/retirement income $_____ _____ $_____

                                   Social Security $_____ _____ $_____

                                   Other public assistance $_____ _____ $_____

                                   Other (specify): _____ $_____ _____ $_____

                                   _____ $_____ _____ $_____

                              Total Other Income $_____

                              Grand Total Monthly Income $_____

Monthly Budget

	Proj.	Jan.	Feb.	Mar.	April	May	June	July	Aug.	Sept.	Oct.	Nov.	Dec.
Home													
rent/mortgage													
property taxes													
renter's ins.													
homeowner's ins.													
homeowner's association dues													
telephone													
gas & electric													
water & sewer													
cable TV													
garbage													
household supplies													
housewares													
furniture & appliances													
cleaning													
yard or pool care													
maintenance & repairs													
Food													
groceries													
breakfast out													
lunch out													
dinner out													
coffee/tea													
snacks													
Wearing Apparel													
clothing & accessories													
laundry, dry cleaning & mending													
Self Care													
toiletries & cosmetics													
haircuts													
massage													
health club membership													
donations													
Health Care													
insurance													
medications													
vitamins													
doctors													
dentist													
eyecare													
therapy													
Transportation													
insurance													
road service club													
registration													
gasoline													
maintenance & repairs													

	Proj.	Jan.	Feb.	Mar.	April	May	June	July	Aug.	Sept.	Oct.	Nov.	Dec.
car wash													
parking & tolls													
public transit & cabs													
parking tickets													
Entertainment													
music													
movies & video rentals													
concerts, theater & ballet													
museums													
sporting events													
hobbies & lessons													
club dues or membership													
film development													
books, magazines & newspapers													
software													
Dependent Care													
child care													
clothing													
allowance													
school expenses													
toys													
entertainment													
Pet Care													
grooming													
vet													
food													
toys & supplies													
Education													
tuition or loan payments													
books & supplies													
Travel													
Gifts & Cards													
holidays													
birthdays & anniversaries													
weddings & showers													
Personal Business													
supplies													
photocopying													
postage													
bank & credit card fees													
lawyer													
accountant													
taxes													
savings													
Total Expenses													
Total Income													
Difference													

Statement of Assets and Liabilities

(as of _____)

Assets	Date of Purchase	Account Number (if relevant)	Current Market Value ($)
Cash and Cash Equivalents			
Cash	_____	_____	_____
Checking accounts	_____	_____	_____
Savings accounts	_____	_____	_____
Money market accounts	_____	_____	_____
Other	_____	_____	_____
Subtotal			_____
Real Estate			
House/condo/coop	_____	_____	_____
Vacation home	_____	_____	_____
Income properties	_____	_____	_____
Unimproved lot	_____	_____	_____
Other lot	_____	_____	_____
Subtotal			_____
Personal Property			
Motor vehicles	_____	_____	_____
Furniture	_____	_____	_____
Home furnishings	_____	_____	_____
Electronic equipment	_____	_____	_____
Computer system	_____	_____	_____
Jewelry	_____	_____	_____
Clothing	_____	_____	_____
Collections (coin, stamp)	_____	_____	_____
Animals	_____	_____	_____
Other	_____	_____	_____
Subtotal			_____
Investments			
Life ins. (term cash value)	_____	_____	_____
Life ins. (whole policies)	_____	_____	_____
Stocks	_____	_____	_____
Bonds	_____	_____	_____
Mutual funds	_____	_____	_____
Annuities	_____	_____	_____
IRAs	_____	_____	_____
Keoghs	_____	_____	_____
401k Plans	_____	_____	_____
Other retirement plans	_____	_____	_____
Partnerships	_____	_____	_____
Accounts receivable	_____	_____	_____
Other	_____	_____	_____
Subtotal			_____

Liabilities	Date Incurred	Account Number	Total Balance Due ($)
Secured			
Mortgage	_____	_____	_____
Mortgage	_____	_____	_____
Deeds of trust	_____	_____	_____
Home equity loans	_____	_____	_____
Liens	_____	_____	_____
Motor vehicle loans	_____	_____	_____
Bank loans	_____	_____	_____
Personal loans	_____	_____	_____
Other	_____	_____	_____
Subtotal			_____
Unsecured			
Student loans	_____	_____	_____
Bank loans	_____	_____	_____
Personal loans	_____	_____	_____
Credit card balances	_____	_____	_____
Judgments	_____	_____	_____
Taxes	_____	_____	_____
Support arrears	_____	_____	_____
Other	_____	_____	_____
Subtotal			_____

Net Worth Summary

Total Assets

Cash Subtotal	$ _____
Real Estate Subtotal	_____
Personal Property Subtotal	_____
Investments Subtotal	_____
Total Assets	$ _____

Total Liabilities

Secured Subtotal	_____
Unsecured Subtotal	_____
Total Liabilities	$ _____

Net Worth

(Assets minus liabilities)	$ _____

Assignment of Rights

Assignor 1's name: _____

Address: _____

Assignor 2's name: _____

Address: _____

Assignee 1's name: _____

Address: _____

Assignee 2's name: _____

Address: _____

If there is more than one assignor or assignee, the use of the singular incorporates the plural.

1. Assignor transfers to Assignee all of the following rights of Assignor *[describe the rights you are assigning]*:

   _____

   _____

   _____

   _____ .

2. Evidence of Assignor's rights can be found in the following document *[describe the document, such as a promissory note, providing details of document name, parties and date]*:

   _____

   _____ .

   Evidence of Assignor's right ☐ is ☐ is not attached to this Assignment of Rights form.

3. This assignment takes effect on: _____ .

4. This assignment lasts until: _____ *[specify date or event that ends assignment]*.

_____   _____

Assignor 1's signature   Date

_____

Print name

_____

Location *[city or county where signed]*

_____

Address

_____   _____
Assignor 2's signature   Date

_____
Print name

_____
Location *[city or county where signed]*

_____
Address

_____   _____
Assignee 1's signature   Date

_____
Print name

_____
Location *[city or county where signed]*

_____
Address

_____   _____
Assignee 2's signature   Date

_____
Print name

_____
Location *[city or county where signed]*

_____
Address

Notice to Terminate Joint Account

Date: _____

_____

_____

_____

_____

[name and address of creditor]

Names on account: _____

Account number: _____

To Whom It May Concern:

With this letter, I am requesting that you close the account referenced above, effective immediately.

I am requesting a "hard close" of the account so that neither party to the account may incur new charges. If you do not hard close the account, please be informed that as of the date of this letter, I will not be responsible for any new charges made to this account.

If my account has an outstanding balance, you may keep the account open for billing purposes only. Nevertheless, I request that you keep the account inactive so that neither party to the account can incur new charges.

Please acknowledge receipt of this notice by signing the duplicate of this letter and returning it to me in the enclosed stamped, self-addressed envelope

Thank you for your assistance with this matter.

_____   _____
Signature   Date

_____
Printed or typed name

_____
Address

_____

_____   _____
Home phone   Work phone

- -

Receipt acknowledged by:

_____   _____
Signature   Date

_____
Printed or typed name

_____
Title

Outstanding balance: _____   As of: _____

_____

Notice to Stop Payment of Check

Date: _____

_____

_____

_____

_____

[name and address of financial institution]

Re: Stop payment of check

To Whom It May Concern:

This letter is to confirm my telephone request of _____ *[date]* that you stop payment on the following check:

Name(s) on account: _____

Account number: _____ Check number: _____

Payable to: _____

Date written: _____ Amount of check: _____

  Please acknowledge receipt of this notice by signing the duplicate of this letter and returning it to me in the enclosed stamped, self-addressed envelope.

  Thank you for your assistance.

_____
Signature

_____
Printed or typed name

_____
Address

_____

_____   _____
Home phone   Work phone

. . . .

Receipt acknowledged by:

_____   _____
Signature   Date

_____
Printed or typed name

_____
Title

Request for Credit Report

Date: _____

_____

_____

_____

_____

[name and address of credit bureau]

To Whom It May Concern:

Please send me a copy of my credit report.

Full name: _____

Date of birth: _____ Social Security number: _____

Spouse's name: _____

Telephone number: _____

Current address: _____

_____

Previous address: _____

_____

[check one]:

☐ I was denied credit on _____ by _____

_____. Enclosed is a copy of the rejection letter.

☐ I hereby certify that I am unemployed and intend to apply for a job within the next 60 days. Enclosed is a copy of a document verifying my unemployment.

☐ I hereby certify that I receive public assistance/welfare. Enclosed is a copy of my most recent public assistance check as verification.

☐ I hereby certify that I believe there is erroneous information in my file due to fraud.

☐ I live in _____ .

I am requesting my annual complimentary credit report. Enclosed is a copy of a document identifying me by my name and address.

☐ I am not entitled to a free copy of my report. Enclosed is a copy of a document identifying me by my name and address and a check for $ _____ .

Thank you for your attention to this matter.

Sincerely,

_____

Signature

Challenge Incorrect Credit Report Entry

Date: _____

_____

_____

_____

_____

[name and address of credit bureau]

This is a request for you to reinvestigate the following items which appear on my credit report:

☐ The following personal information about me is incorrect:

Erroneous Information	Correct Information
_____	_____
_____	_____
_____	_____

☐ The following accounts are not mine:

Creditor's Name	Account Number	Explanation
_____	_____	_____
_____	_____	_____
_____	_____	_____

☐ The account status is incorrect for the following accounts:

Creditor's Name	Account Number	Correct Status
_____	_____	_____
_____	_____	_____
_____	_____	_____

☐ The following information is too old to be included in my report:

Creditor's Name	Account Number	Date of Last Activity
_____	_____	_____
_____	_____	_____
_____	_____	_____

☐ The following inquiries are older than two years:

Creditor's Name		Date of Inquiry
_____		_____
_____		_____
_____		_____

☐ The following accounts were closed by me and should say so:

Creditor's Name   Account number

_____   _____

_____   _____

_____   _____

☐ Other errors:

Explanation

_____

_____

_____

_____

_____

_____

_____

I understand that you will check each item above with the credit grantor reporting the information, and remove any information the credit grantor cannot verify. I further understand that under the federal Fair Credit Reporting Act, 15 United States Code §1681i(a), you must complete your reinvestigation and issue me and anyone who has requested a copy of my credit report within the previous one year (two years if requested for employment purposes) a new credit report within 30 days of receipt of this letter. Thank you.

Sincerely,

_____
Signature

_____
Print name

_____
Address

_____   _____
Home phone   Social Security number

Dispute Credit Card Charge

Date: _____

_____

_____

_____

_____

[name and address of the company or financial institution that issued credit card]

Re: Account number: _____

To Whom It May Concern:

I am writing to dispute the following charge that appears on my billing statement dated_____.

Merchant's name: _____

Amount in dispute: _____

I am disputing this amount for the following reason(s):

_____

_____

_____

_____

_____

As required by law, I have tried in good faith to resolve this dispute with the merchant.

[For purchases made with a credit card, such as Visa or MasterCard, not issued by the seller]:

☐ This purchase was for more than $50 and was made in the state in which I live or within 100 miles of my home.

Please verify this dispute with the merchant and remove this item, and all late and interest charges attributed to this item, from my billing statement.

Sincerely,

_____

Signature

_____

Print name

_____

Address

_____

_____

Home phone

Demand Collection Agency Cease Contact

Date: _____

_____

_____

_____

_____

[name and address of collection agency, including name of individual collector, if known]

Name(s) on account: _____

Account number: _____

Creditor: _____

To _____ :

Since_____ *[date]*, I have received several phone calls and letters from you concerning my overdue account with the above-named creditor.

Accordingly, under 15 U.S.C. § 1692c, this is my formal notice to you to cease all further communications with me except for the reasons specifically set forth in the federal law.

Sincerely,

_____

Signature

_____

Print name

_____

Address

_____

Home phone

Notice to Remove Name From List

Date: _____

_____

_____

_____

_____

[name and address of list maintainer]

To Whom It May Concern:

Please permanently remove all members of this household from all lists you maintain, sell, trade, share or use in any other capacity for direct marketing, telemarketing, credit card pre-screening or any other promotional opportunity.

_____

Name 1

_____

Address

_____

_____

Name 2

_____

Address

_____

_____

Name 3

_____

Address

_____

_____

Sincerely,

_____

Signature

_____

Print name

Notice to Add or Retain Name but Not Sell or Trade It

Date: _____

_____

_____

_____

_____

[name and address of list maintainer]

To Whom It May Concern:

Please ☐ add ☐ retain   my name on your mailing list. ***Please do not sell, trade or share my name or address with any other company or business.***

☐ I will accept telemarketing phone calls from your company.

☐ I do not wish to receive telemarketing phone calls from your company. That is, put me on your "do not call" list.

Sincerely,

_____
Signature

_____
Print name

_____
Address

_____

Telemarketing Phone Call Log

Date	Time	Company	Telemarketer's name	Product	Said "Put me on a 'do not call' list"	Followed up with letter
Example:						
9/11/XX	6:15pm	AT&T	Terri	Long Distance	✔	✔

Notice to Put Name on "Do Not Call" List

Date: _____

_____

_____

_____

_____

[name and address of list maintainer]

To Whom It May Concern:

This letter is a follow up to the telemarketing phone call I received from _____

[name of person who placed the call to you] from your company on _____ *[date].*

As I stated at that time, I do not wish to receive telemarketing phone calls from your company. That is, please immediately put me on your "do not call" list.

Signature

_____

Print name

_____

Address

_____

_____

Demand for Damages for Excessive Calls

Date: _____

_____

_____

_____

_____

[name and address of list maintainer]

To Whom It May Concern:

Since _____ *[date]*, I have received multiple phone calls from telemarketers calling on behalf of your company. I am giving your company the opportunity to settle my claim against you before I sue you in small claims court.

On or about _____ *[date]*, I received a telephone call at my home from a telemarketer by the name of _____,
who stated that ☐ he ☐ she was calling on behalf of your company. I told this person that I was not interested in your company's product, and asked that my name be placed on a "do not call" list. I was assured that this would be done.

On or about _____ *[date]*, I received a second telephone call at my home from a telemarketer by the name of _____,
who stated that ☐ he ☐ she was calling on behalf of your company. I told this person that I was not interested in your company's product, and asked that my name be placed on a "do not call" list. Again, I was assured that this would be done.

[Repeat the above paragraph as needed, changing the word "second" to "third," "fourth," etc.]

Section 64.1200(e)(2)(iii) of Title 47 of the Code of Federal Regulations states, in pertinent part:

> If a person or entity making a telephone solicitation (or on whose behalf a solicitation is made) receives a request from a residential telephone subscriber not to receive calls from that person or entity, the person or entity must record the request and place the subscriber's name and telephone number on the do-not-call list at the time the request is made. If such requests are recorded or maintained by a party other than the person or entity on whose behalf the solicitation is made, the person or entity on whose behalf the solicitation is made will be liable for any failures to honor the do-not-call list.

A violation of this regulation is actionable under 47 U.S.C. § 227(c)(5). That section provides that:

> A person who has received more than one telephone call within any 12-month period by or on behalf of the same entity in violation of the regulations prescribed under this subsection may … bring in an appropriate court of that state—
>
> (A) an action based on a violation of the regulations prescribed under this subsection to enjoin such violation,

(B) an action to recover for actual monetary loss from such a violation, or to receive up

to $500 in damages for each such violation, whichever is greater, or

(C) both such actions.

In addition, treble damages are available for knowing and willful violations.

Your company clearly violated the law on _____ separate occasions. I am entitled to $500 for each violation, for a total of $ _____ .

[Optional] Your company also violated state law. I am entitled to damages and/or civil penalties for those violations as well.

I am willing to forego my right to seek an injunction and treble damages against your company if you send me a cashier's check for the amount stated above within the next 30 days. If I do not hear from you within that time, I will seek all appropriate remedies in a court of law.

Sincerely,

_____

Signature

_____

Print name

_____

Address

_____

_____

_____

Home phone

Child Care Agreement

1. Parent or Legal Guardian

Parent(s)' name(s): _____

Address(es): _____

_____

Home phone number(s): _____

Work phone number(s): _____

Other contact number(s) (cell phone, pager, Email): _____

_____

2. Child Care Provider

Child Care Provider's name: _____

Address: _____

_____ Home phone number: _____

Other contact number(s) (cell phone, pager, Email): _____

_____

3. Children

Parent(s) desire(s) to contract with Child Care Provider to provide child care for: _____

_____ *[names and birthdates of the children].*

4. Location and Schedule of Care

Care will be provided at: _____

_____ *[your address or other location where care is to be given].*

Days and hours of child care will be as follows: _____

_____ .

5. Beginning Date

Employment will begin on _____ *[date].*

6. Training or Probation Period

There will be a training/probation period during the first_____ *[length of training period]*
of employment.

7. Responsibilities

The care to be provided under this agreement consists of the following responsibilities *[describe and*

provide details]: _____

_____

_____

_____ .

8. Wage or Salary

Child Care Provider will be paid as follows:

☐ $ _____ per hour

☐ $ _____ per month

☐ other: _____

9. Payment Schedule

Child Care Provider will be paid on the following intervals and dates:

☐ once a week on every _____

☐ twice a month on _____

☐ once a month on _____

☐ other: _____

10. Benefits

Parent(s) will provide Child Care Provider with the following benefits: *[describe and provide details]:*

_____

_____

_____

_____

11. Termination Policy

Either Parent(s) or Child Care Provider may terminate this agreement at any time, for any reason, without notice.

12. Additional Provisions

Parent(s) and Child Care Provider agree to the following additional terms: _____

_____

_____ .

13. Modifications in Writing

To be binding, any modifications to this contract must be in writing and signed by both parties to the agreement.

Signatures

_____   _____
Parent(s)' Signature(s):   Date

_____   _____
Child Care Provider's Signature   Date

Child Care Instructions

1. Home and Family Information

Parent(s)' name(s) *[list any parents who live at this address; other parents may be listed under Emergency Contacts]*: _____

Names of Children: _____

Address: _____

_____ Home phone number: _____

Other contact numbers at home (cell phone, pager, Email): _____

_____

2. Parent(s)' Work Information

[list name and address of employer, work phone number and regular work hours for each parent]

_____

_____

3. Temporary Contact Information

[specify the address and phone number where you can be reached at a temporary location, such as a restaurant, movie or friend's house, plus the times you will be at each location]

_____

_____

4. Child's Personal and Care Information

[provide the following information for each child]

Name of child: _____

Date of birth: _____

Allergies and other medical conditions: _____

Medications: _____

Meals, naps and bedtime schedule: _____

Other comments: _____

_____

5. Child's Healthcare Providers

[list names, addresses and phone numbers]

Doctor: _____

Dentist: _____

Other medical providers: _____

6. Emergency Contacts

[list names, addresses and phone numbers of people that babysitter can contact if they can't reach you in case of emergency; specify their relationship to your family, such as children's aunt or neighbor]

_____

IN CASE OF EMERGENCY, CALL 911.

7. Other Important Information _____

_____

_____

_____

Elder Care Agreement

1. Employer

Employer(s)' name(s): _____

Address(es): _____

_____

Home phone number(s): _____

Work phone number(s): _____

Other contact number(s) (cell phone, pager, Email): _____

_____

2. Elder Care Provider

Elder Care Provider's name: _____

Address: _____

_____ Home phone number: _____

Other contact number(s) (cell phone, pager, Email): _____

_____

3. Older Adult(s) to Be Cared For

Employer(s) desire(s) to contract with Elder Care Provider to provide elder care for: _____

_____

_____ *[names and birthdates of person(s) in need of elder care].*

4. Location and Schedule of Care

Care will be provided at: _____

_____*[your address or other location where care is to be given].*

Days and hours of elder care will be as follows: _____

_____ .

5. Beginning Date

Employment will begin on _____ *[date].*

6. Training or Probation Period

There will be a training/probation period during the first_____

[length of training period] of employment.

7. Responsibilities

The care to be provided under this agreement consists of the following responsibilities *[describe and*

provide details]: _____

_____

_____

_____

_____ .

8. Wage or Salary

Elder Care Provider will be paid as follows:

☐ $ _____ per hour

☐ $ _____ per month

☐ other: _____

9. Payment Schedule

Elder Care Provider will be paid on the following intervals and dates:

☐ once a week on every _____

☐ twice a month on _____

☐ once a month on _____

☐ other: _____

10. Benefits

Employer(s) will provide Elder Care Provider with the following benefits: *[describe and provide details]:*

_____

_____

_____ .

11. Termination Policy

Either Employer(s) or Elder Care Provider may terminate this agreement at any time, for any reason, without notice.

12. Additional Provisions

Employer(s) and Elder Care Provider agree to the following additional terms: _____

_____

_____

_____ .

13. Modifications in Writing

To be binding, any modifications to this contract must be in writing and signed by both parties to the agreement.

Signatures

_____   _____

Employer(s)' Signature(s):   Date

_____   _____

Elder Care Provider's Signature   Date

Housekeeping Services Agreement

1. Employer

Employer(s)' name(s): _____

Address(es): _____

_____

Home phone number(s): _____

Work phone number(s): _____

Other contact number(s) (cell phone, pager, Email): _____

_____

2. Housekeeper

Housekeeper's name: _____

Address: _____

_____ Home phone number: _____

Other contact number(s) (cell phone, pager, Email): _____

_____

3. Location and Schedule of Work

Employer desires to contract with Housekeeper to work at: _____

_____ [your address].

Days and hours of cleaning will be as follows: _____

_____

4. Beginning Date

Employment will begin on _____ [date].

5. Housecleaning Responsibilities

The responsibilities to be provided under this agreement consist of cleaning the following rooms and areas

[describe and provide details]: _____

_____

_____

_____

6. Other Responsibilities

Housekeeper also agrees to do the following types of work [describe and provide details regarding

cooking, laundry and other non-cleaning responsibilities]: _____

_____

_____

_____

7. Wage or Salary

Housekeeper will be paid as follows:

☐ $ _____ per hour

☐ $ _____ per month

☐ other: _____

8. Payment Schedule

Housekeeper will be paid on the following intervals and dates:

☐ once a week on every _____

☐ twice a month on _____

☐ once a month on _____

☐ other: _____

9. Benefits

Employer(s) will provide Housekeeper with the following benefits: *[describe and provide details]* _____

_____

_____

_____

_____

_____.

10. Termination Policy

Either Employer(s) or Housekeeper may terminate this agreement at any time, for any reason, without notice.

11. Additional Provisions

Employer(s) and Housekeeper agree to the following additional terms: _____

_____

_____

_____

_____

_____.

12. Modifications in Writing

To be binding, any modifications to this contract must be in writing and signed by both parties to the agreement.

Signatures

_____   _____

Employer(s)' Signature(s):   Date

_____   _____

Housekeeper's signature   Date

_____

Agreement to Keep Property Separate

Partner 1's name: _____

Partner 2's name: _____

We agree as follows:

1. This contract sets forth our rights and obligations toward each other. We intend to abide by them in a spirit of cooperation and good faith.

2. All property owned by either of us as of the date of this agreement shall remain the separate property of its owner and cannot be transferred to the other person unless this is done in writing. We have each attached a list of our major items of separate property to this contract.

3. The income each of us earns—as well as any items or investments either of us purchases with our income—belongs absolutely to the person who earns the money unless there is a written joint ownership agreement as provided in Clause 6.

4. We shall each maintain our own separate bank, credit card, investment and retirement accounts, and neither of us shall in any way be responsible for the debts of the other (if we register as domestic partners in a community that makes this option available and, by so doing, the law requires us to be responsible for each other's basic living expenses, we agree to assume the minimum level of reciprocal responsibility required by the law).

5. Expenses for routine household items and services, which include groceries, utilities, rent and cleaning supplies, shall be equally divided.

6. From time to time, we may decide to keep a joint checking or savings account for a specific purpose (for example, to pay household expenses), or to own some property jointly (for example, to purchase a television). If so, the details of our joint ownership agreement shall be put in writing (either in a written contract or a deed, title slip or other joint ownership document).

7. Should either of us receive real or personal property by gift or inheritance, the property belongs absolutely to the person receiving the gift or inheritance and cannot be transferred to the other except in writing.

8. In the event we separate, each of us shall be entitled to immediate possession of our separate property.

9. Any dispute arising out of this contract shall be mediated by a third person mutually acceptable to both of us. The mediator's role shall be to help us arrive at our solution, not to impose one on us. If good-faith efforts to arrive at our own solution to all issues in dispute with the help of a mediator prove to be fruitless, either of us may pursue other legal remedies.

10. This agreement represents our complete understanding regarding our living together and replaces any and all prior agreements, written or oral. It can be amended, but only in writing, and must be signed by both of us.

11. If a court finds any portion of this contract to be illegal or otherwise unenforceable, the remainder of the contract is still in full force and effect.

_____   _____
Partner 1's signature   Date

_____   _____
Partner 2's signature   Date

[Notary Seal]

Attachment A

Separate personal property of _____ :

_____

_____

_____

_____

_____

_____

_____

_____

_____

_____

_____

_____

_____

_____

_____

_____

Attachment B

Separate personal property of _____ :

_____

_____

_____

_____

_____

_____

_____

_____

_____

_____

_____

_____

_____

_____

_____

_____

_____

Agreement for a Joint Purchase

Partner 1's name: _____

Partner 2's name: _____

We agree as follows:

1. We will jointly acquire and own _____

   _____ *[describe the property]* at a cost of $ _____ .

2. We will own the Property in the following shares:

   Partner 1 will own _____% of the Property and Partner 2 will own _____% of the Property.

3. Should we separate and cease living together, one of the following will occur:

   (a) If one of us wants the Property and the other doesn't, the person who wants the Property will pay the other fair market value (see Clause 4) of the Property.

   (b) If both of us want the Property, the decision will be made in the following way *[choose one]:*

   ☐ Right of First Refusal. _____

   _____ *[specify either Partner 1 or 2]* shall have the right of first refusal

   and may purchase _____

   _____ 's *[specify either Partner 1 or 2]* share of the Property for its fair

   market value (see Clause 4). _____

   _____ *[specify either Partner 1 or 2]* will then become sole owner of the Property.

   ☐ Coin Toss Method. We will flip a coin to determine who is entitled to the Property. The winner, upon paying the loser his or her share of ownership, will become the sole owner of the Property.

   ☐ Other: _____ .

4. Should either of us decide to end the relationship, we will do our best to jointly agree on the fair current market value of the Property. If we can't agree on a price, we will jointly choose a neutral appraiser and abide by his or her decision.

5. Should we separate and neither of us want the Property—or if we can't agree on a fair price—we will advertise it to the public, sell it to the highest bidder and divide the money according to our respective ownership shares as set forth in Clause 2.

6. Should either of us die while we are living together, the Property will belong absolutely to the survivor. (If either of us makes a will or other estate plan, this agreement shall be reflected in that document.)

7. This agreement can be changed, but only in writing, and must be signed by both of us.

8. Any dispute arising out of this contract shall be mediated by a third person mutually acceptable to both of us. The mediator's role shall be to help us arrive at our solution, not to impose one on us. If good-faith efforts to arrive at our own solution to all issues in dispute with the help of a mediator prove to be fruitless, either of us may pursue other legal remedies.

9. If a court finds any portion of this contract to be illegal or otherwise enforceable, the remainder of the contract is still in full force and effect.

_____   _____
Partner 1's signature   Date

_____   _____
Partner 2's signature   Date

Agreement to Share Property

Partner 1's name: _____

Partner 2's name: _____

We agree as follows:

1. This contract sets forth our rights and obligations toward each other. We intend to abide by them in a spirit of cooperation and good faith.

2. All earned income received by either of us after the date of this contract and all property purchased with this income belongs in equal shares to both of us with the following exceptions:_____
   _____
   _____
   _____ .

3. All real or personal property earned or accumulated by either of us prior to the date of this agreement (except jointly owned property listed in Attachment C of this agreement), including all future income this property produces, is the separate property of the person who earned or accumulated it and cannot be transferred to the other except in writing. Attached to this agreement in the form of Attachments A, B and C are lists of the major items of property each of us owns separately and both of us own jointly.

4. Should either of us receive real or personal property by gift or inheritance, that property, including all future income it produces, belongs absolutely to the person receiving the gift or inheritance and cannot be transferred to the other except in writing.

5. In the event we separate, all jointly owned property shall be divided equally.

6. Any dispute arising out of this contract shall be mediated by a third person mutually acceptable to both of us. The mediator's role shall be to help us arrive at our solution, not to impose one on us. If good-faith efforts to arrive at our own solution to all issues in dispute with the help of a mediator prove to be fruitless, either of us may pursue other legal remedies.

7. This agreement represents our complete understanding regarding our living together and replaces any and all prior agreements, written or oral. It can be amended, but only in writing, and must be signed by both of us.

8. If a court finds any portion of this contract to be illegal or otherwise unenforceable, the remainder of the contract is still in full force and effect.

_____   _____
Partner 1's signature   Date

_____   _____
Partner 2's signature   Date

[Notary Seal]

Attachment A

Separate property of _____ :

_____

_____

_____

_____

_____

_____

_____

_____

Attachment B

Separate property of _____ :

_____

_____

_____

_____

_____

_____

_____

_____

Attachment C

Jointly owned property acquired prior to _____ *[date of this Agreement]:*

_____

_____

_____

_____

_____

_____

_____

_____

_____

Declaration of Legal Name Change

I, the undersigned, declare that I am 18 years of age or older and further declare:

1. I, _____ [name presently used],

   was born _____ [name on birth certificate]

   in the County of _____ [county where born]

   in the State of _____ [state where born]

   on _____ [birthdate, including year].

2. I HEREBY DECLARE my intent to change my legal name, and be henceforth exclusively known as

   _____ [new name].

3. I further declare that I have no intention of defrauding any person or escaping any obligation I may presently have by this act.

4. NOTICE IS HEREBY GIVEN to all agencies of the State of _____ [state where you reside], all agencies of the federal government, all creditors and all private persons, groups, businesses, corporations and associations of said legal name change.

I declare under penalty of perjury under the laws of the State of _____ [state where you reside] that the foregoing is true and correct.

_____   _____

Signature, new name   Date

_____   _____

Signature, old name   Date

[Notary Seal]

Demand Letter

Date: _____

_____

_____

_____

_____

[name and address of party with whom you have a dispute]

I am seeking redress for the following problem:

[Describe in your own words exactly what happened. Specify dates, names of people with whom you dealt and the damages you have suffered.]

_____

_____

_____

_____

_____

_____

_____

_____

_____

_____

_____

_____

_____

_____

_____

Please send me a check or money order in the amount of: $ _____

on or before _____ *[specify date].*

If I don't receive payment by this date, I will promptly take this case to court unless you notify me that you are willing to attempt to resolve this dispute through mediation. In that case I am willing to promptly meet with a neutral third party agreed to by both of us in a good-faith attempt to mutually resolve this dispute without court action.

Thank you for your immediate attention to this matter.

Sincerely,

_____

Signature

_____   _____   _____

Daytime phone   Evening phone   Email

Request for Refund or Repair of Goods Under Warranty

Date: _____

_____

_____

_____

[name and address of seller or manufacturer]

ATT: Customer Service Department

Re: _____ *[description of item purchased, including serial number, if any]*

To Whom It May Concern:

I am writing to request compensation for the above-named item which I purchased for $ _____

on _____ *[date]* from _____

[specify place of purchase].

My reason for demanding redress is as follows *[describe the reason you are dissatisfied with your purchase, in as much detail as possible. List anything included with this request, such as a copy of the warranty, purchase receipt or the item itself]:* _____

_____

_____.

Specifically, I would like to request the following compensation *[explain what you want, such as a refund of the full purchase price, a replacement item or a repair]:* _____

_____

_____.

Please process this request by _____ *[specify a deadline for processing this request, such as date within 30 days].* If I don't receive redress by then, I will take further action, which may include filing a court action.

Thank you for your immediate attention to this matter.

Sincerely,

_____

Signature

_____

Address

_____

_____ _____ _____
Daytime phone   Evening phone   Email

Accident Claim Worksheet

What Happened

Description of Accident: _____

_____

Names of parties involved: _____

_____

Names of witnesses: _____

_____

Location of accident: _____

Time of accident: _____

Names of witnesses: _____

Weather condition (if outside): _____

_____

_____

People Responsible for the Accident

Name: _____

Address: _____

_____

Telephone (work): _____ (home): _____

Insurance company: _____

Policy number: _____ Auto license: _____

What person did: _____

_____

_____

_____

_____

· ·

Name: _____

Address: _____

_____

Telephone (work): _____ (home): _____

Insurance company: _____

Policy number: _____ Auto license: _____

What person did: _____

_____

_____

_____

_____

Name: _____

Address: _____

_____

Telephone (work): _____ (home): _____

Insurance company: _____

Policy number: _____ Auto license: _____

What person did: _____

_____

_____

_____

_____

Witnesses

Name: _____

Address: _____

_____

Telephone (work): _____ (home): _____

Date of first contact: _____

Written statement: ☐ yes ☐ no

What person saw: _____

_____

_____

_____

_____

_____

Name: _____

Address: _____

_____

Telephone (work): _____ (home): _____

Date of first contact: _____

Written statement: ☐ yes ☐ no

What person saw: _____

_____

_____

_____

_____

_____

· ·

Name: _____

Address: _____

_____

Telephone (work): _____ (home): _____

Date of first contact: _____

Written statement: ☐ yes ☐ no

What person saw: _____

_____

_____

_____

_____

_____

Medical Treatment Providers

Name: _____

Address: _____

_____Telephone: _____

Date of first visit: _____ Date of most recent or last visit: _____

Person to be contacted for medical records: _____

Date requested: _____ Date received: _____

Person to be contacted for medical billing: _____

Date requested: _____ Date received: _____

Reason for treatment and prognosis: _____

_____

_____

_____

· ·

Name: _____

Address: _____

_____ Telephone: _____

Date of first visit: _____ Date of most recent or last visit: _____

Person to be contacted for medical records: _____

Date requested: _____ Date received: _____

Person to be contacted for medical billing: _____

Date requested: _____ Date received: _____

Reason for treatment and prognosis: _____

_____

_____

_____

Name: _____

Address: _____

_____ Telephone: _____

Date of first visit: _____ Date of most recent or last visit: _____

Person to be contacted for medical records: _____

Date requested: _____ Date received: _____

Person to be contacted for medical billing: _____

Date requested: _____ Date received: _____

Reason for treatment and prognosis: _____

_____

_____

_____

Other Party's Insurance Company (First Party)

Company name: _____

Address: _____

_____

Telephone: _____ Claim number: _____

Insured: _____

Adjuster: _____

Date demand letter was sent: _____

Settlement amount: _____ Date accepted: _____

Other Party's Insurance Company (Second Party)

Company name: _____

Address: _____

_____

Telephone: _____ Claim number: _____

Insured: _____

Adjuster: _____

Date demand letter was sent: _____

Settlement amount: _____ Date accepted: _____

Communications With Insurer

Date: _____

If oral, what was said: _____

_____

_____

_____

Communications With Insurer

Date: _____

If oral, what was said: _____

_____

_____

Communications With Insurer

Date: _____

If oral, what was said: _____

_____

_____

Communications With Insurer

Date: _____

If oral, what was said: _____

_____

_____

Communications With Insurer

Date: _____

If oral, what was said: _____

_____

_____

Losses

Describe damage to your property: _____

_____

Do you have photos showing damage? ☐ yes ☐ no

If Repairable

Estimates for repairs (name of repair shop and amounts of estimates): _____

_____

Actual

Repair bills (name of repair shop and amounts of bills): _____

_____

If totaled:

Value at the time destroyed: _____

Documentation of value: _____

General Release

Releasor: _____

Address: _____

Releasee: _____

Address: _____

1. Releasor voluntarily and knowingly signs this release with the express intention of eliminating Releasee's legal liabilities and obligations as described below.

2. Releasor hereby releases Releasee from all claims, known or unknown, that have arisen or may arise from the following occurrence: _____

   _____

   _____

3. In exchange for granting this release, Releasor has received the following payment or other consideration: _____

   _____

   _____

4. By signing this release, Releasor additionally intends to bind his or her spouse, heirs, legal representatives, assigns and anyone else claiming under him or her. Releasor has not assigned any claim covered by this release to any other party. Releasor intends that this release apply to the heirs, personal representatives, assigns, insurers and successors of Releasee as well as to the Releasee.

_____   _____
Releasor's signature   Date

_____   _____
Print name   County of residence

_____   _____
Releasor's spouse's signature   Date

_____   _____
Print name   County of residence

_____   _____
Releasee's signature   Date

_____   _____
Print name   County of residence

_____   _____
Releasee's spouse's signature   Date

_____   _____
Print name   County of residence

General Mutual Release

Party 1: _____

Address: _____

Party 2: _____

Address: _____

1. We voluntarily and knowingly sign this mutual release with the express intention of eliminating the liabilities and obligations described below.

2. Disputes and differences that we mutually desire to settle have arisen between us with respect to the following: _____

   _____

   _____

   _____

3. The value (consideration) for this mutual release consists of our mutual relinquishment of our respective legal rights involved in the disputes described above.

4. In addition, either party will receive the following payment or other consideration from the other [check and explain any that apply]:

   ☐ Party 1 will receive from Party 2: _____

   _____.

   ☐ Party 2 will receive from Party 1: _____

   _____.

5. By signing this release, we both intend to bind our spouses, heirs, legal representatives, assigns, and anyone else claiming under us, in addition to ourselves.

_____   _____
Party 1's signature   Date

_____   _____
Print name   County of residence

_____   _____
Party 1's spouse's signature   Date

_____   _____
Print name   County of residence

_____   _____
Party 2's signature   Date

_____   _____
Print name   County of residence

_____   _____
Party 2's spouse's signature   Date

_____   _____
Print name   County of residence

Release for Damage to Real Estate

Releasor: _____

Address: _____

Releasee: _____

Address: _____

1. Releasor is the owner of certain property (Property) located at _____
_____, which specifically consists of the following:
_____

2. Releasor voluntarily and knowingly signs this release with the intention of eliminating Releasee's liabilities and obligations as described below.

3. Releasor hereby releases Releasee from all claims, known or unknown, that have arisen or may arise from the transaction described in Clause 4.

4. Releasor has alleged that Property suffered damage in the approximate amount of $ _____
as a result of the following activity of Releasee:_____
_____
_____

5. By signing this release, Releasor additionally intends to bind his or her spouse, heirs, legal representatives, assigns and anyone else claiming under him or her. Releasor has not assigned any claim arising from the transaction described in Clause 4 to another party. Releasor intends that this release apply to the heirs, personal representatives, assigns, insurers and successors of Releasee as well as to the Releasee.

6. Releasor has received good and adequate value (consideration) for this release in the form of:
_____
_____

_____   _____
Releasor's signature   Date

_____   _____
Print name   County of residence

_____   _____
Releasor's spouse's signature   Date

_____   _____
Print name   County of residence

_____   _____
Releasee's signature   Date

_____   _____
Print name   County of residence

_____   _____
Releasee's spouse's signature   Date

_____   _____
Print name   County of residence

Release for Property Damage in Auto Accident

Releasor: _____

Address: _____

Releasee: _____

Address: _____

1. Releasor voluntarily and knowingly signs this release with the express intention of eliminating Releasee's liabilities and obligations as described below.

2. Releasor hereby releases Releasee from all liability for claims, known and unknown, arising from property damage sustained by Releasor in an automobile accident that occurred on _____ [date] at _____ [location] involving a vehicle owned by Releasee or driven by Releasee or his/her agent.

3. By signing this release Releasor does not give up any claim that he or she may now or hereafter have against any person, firm or corporation other than Releasee and those persons and entities specified in Clause 6.

4. Releasor understands that Releasee does not, by providing the value described below, admit any liability or responsibility for the accident described in Clause 2 or its consequences.

5. Releasor has received good and adequate value (consideration) for this release in the form of:

   _____

   _____

6. By signing this release, Releasor additionally intends to bind his or her spouse, heirs, legal representatives, assigns and anyone else claiming under him or her. Releasor has not assigned any claim arising from the accident described in Clause 2 to any other party. This release applies to Releasee's heirs, legal representatives, insurers and successors, as well as to Releasee.

_____	_____
Releasor's signature	Date
_____	_____
Print name	County of residence
_____	_____
Releasor's spouse's signature	Date
_____	_____
Print name	County of residence
_____	_____
Releasee's signature	Date
_____	_____
Print name	County of residence
_____	_____
Releasee's spouse's signature	Date
_____	_____
Print name	County of residence

Release for Personal Injury

Releasor: _____

Address: _____

Releasee: _____

Address: _____

1. Releasor voluntarily and knowingly executes this release with the intention of eliminating Releasee's liabilities and obligations as described below.

2. Releasor hereby releases Releasee from all liability for claims, known and unknown, arising from injuries, mental and physical, sustained by Releasor as follows: _____

   _____

   _____

3. Releasor has been examined by a licensed physician or other health care professional competent to diagnose [choose one or both]:

   ☐ physical injuries and disabilities.

   ☐ mental and emotional injuries and disabilities.

   Releasor has been informed by this physician or health care professional that the injury described in Clause 2 has completely healed without causing permanent damage.

4. By executing this release Releasor does not give up any claim that he or she may now or hereafter have against any person, firm or corporation other than Releasee and those persons specified in Clause 7.

5. Releasor understands that Releasee does not, by providing the value described in Clause 6 below, admit any liability or responsibility for the above described injury or its consequences.

6. Releasor has received good and adequate value (consideration) for this release in the form of:

   _____

   _____

7. By signing this release, Releasor additionally intends to bind his or her spouse, heirs, legal representatives, assigns and anyone else claiming under him or her. Releasor has not assigned any claim arising from the accident described in Clause 2 to any other party. This release applies to Releasee's heirs, legal representatives, insurers and successors, as well as to Releasee.

_____   _____
Releasor's signature   Date

_____   _____
Print name   County of residence

_____   _____
Releasor's spouse's signature   Date

_____   _____
Print name   County of residence

_____   _____
Releasee's signature   Date

_____   _____
Print name   County of residence

_____   _____
Releasee's spouse's signature   Date

_____   _____
Print name   County of residence

Mutual Release of Contract Claims

Party 1: _____

Address: _____

Party 2: _____

Address: _____

1. We voluntarily and knowingly sign this mutual release with the intention of eliminating the liabilities and obligations described below.

2. Disputes and differences have arisen between us with respect to an agreement entered into between us on _____ [date], under which we agreed to the following:

   _____

   _____

   _____

      This agreement is hereby made a part of this release and incorporated by reference. A copy of the agreement (if written) is attached to this release.

3. We each hereby expressly release the other from all claims and demands, known and unknown, arising out of the agreement specified in Clause 2.

4. This release additionally applies to our heirs, legal representatives and successors and is binding on our spouses, heirs, legal representatives, assigns and anyone else claiming under us. Neither of us has assigned to another party any claim arising under or out of the contract specified in Clause 2.

5. The value (consideration) for this mutual release binds our mutual agreement to forgo our respective legal rights with reference to the disputes and differences described above.

6. We also agree that the contract specified in Clause 2 shall be and is hereby rescinded, terminated, and canceled as of _____ [date].

_____   _____
Party 1's signature   Date

_____   _____
Print name   County of residence

_____   _____
Party 1's spouse's signature   Date

_____   _____
Print name   County of residence

_____   _____
Party 2's signature   Date

_____   _____
Print name   County of residence

_____   _____
Party 2's spouse's signature   Date

_____   _____
Print name   County of residence

Complaint Letter

Date: _____

_____

_____

_____

_____

[name and address of consumer protection office]

To Whom It May Concern:

I wish to lodge a complaint about the following company:

Name: _____

Address: _____

_____

Phone number: _____

Name of person with whom I dealt: _____

The details of my complaint are as follows *[attach additional sheets if necessary]*:

_____

_____

_____

_____

_____

_____

Please investigate this matter and inform me of the results.

Sincerely,

_____
Signature

_____
Printed name

_____
Address

_____

_____ _____ _____
Daytime phone   Evening phone   Email

cc: _____

_____

_____

_____

Notice of Insurance Claim

Date: _____

_____

_____

_____

_____

[name and address of insurance company]

Name of your insured: _____

Policy number: _____

To Whom It May Concern:

Please be advised that ☐ I received injuries ☐ I sustained property damage   in an accident on

_____, _____, at the following location: _____

_____ .

The accident was of the following nature:

☐ two or more motor vehicles

☐ motor vehicle and pedestrian

☐ motor vehicle and bicycle

☐ motor vehicle and property

[for all motor vehicles involved other than your own, give]:

Make, model, year and color of vehicle: _____

License plate number and state of issuance: _____

Vehicle identification number: _____

Name or driver (if different from name of insured above): _____

Driver's license number and state of issuance: _____

☐ slip and fall

☐ animal bite, claw, knockdown, etc.

☐ dangerous or defective product

☐ other (specify): _____

Please confirm in writing to the address below your liability coverage of the insured identified above. Please also advise whether your insured contends that anyone other than your insured may be in whole or in part legally responsible for accidents on or near the premises.

As requested, please respond in writing. If necessary, I may be reached by telephone at the below number.

Thank you for your prompt attention to this matter.

Sincerely,

_____   _____
Signature   Date

_____
Printed name

_____
Address

_____   _____
                                                                                 Phone

Notice to Cancel Certain Contracts

To Whom It May Concern:

This letter constitutes written notice to you that I am canceling the following contract:

Seller: _____

Address: _____

Buyer: _____

Address: _____

Contract pertains to the following goods/services purchased: _____

_____ .

Date contract signed for these goods/services: _____ , _____

Please acknowledge receipt of this letter by signing below and returning the acknowledgment to me in the enclosed envelope. I understand that under the law, you must refund my money within _____ days. Furthermore, if applicable, I understand that you must either pick up the items purchased, or reimburse me within _____ days for my expense of mailing the goods back to you. If you do not pick up the goods within that time, I am entitled to keep them.

_____   _____
Buyer signature   Date

_____   _____
Print name

. . . .

Acknowledgment

_____   _____
Seller's signature   Date

_____   _____
Print name

Cancel Membership or Subscription Notice

Date: _____

_____

_____

_____

_____

[name and address of publication or organization; include name of department if available]

Re: _____ *[subscription or membership number]*

This letter is to notify you that I would like to cancel my _____

_____ *[specify what you are canceling, such as a subscription to publication or*

membership in organization] effective _____ *[date of cancellation].*

The reason for this cancellation is _____

_____ *[specify reason for cancellation].*

Thank you for your prompt assistance.

_____

Signature

_____

Address

_____

_____

Subscription or account number

Request to Begin Special Education Process

Date: _____

_____

_____

_____

_____

[name and address of special education administrator]

Re: _____ *[name of child]*

Child's school: _____

Child's teacher: _____ Child's grade: _____

I am writing because my child is experiencing difficulties in school, including *[describe difficulties]*

_____

_____

_____

I am formally requesting that the school's special education process begin at once, including initial assessment for eligibility. I understand that you will send me an assessment plan that explains what tests may be given to my child. Because I realize that assessment can take some time, I would appreciate receiving the assessment plan within ten days. I would also appreciate any other information regarding the assessment process, how eligibility is determined and the general IEP process.

I am also requesting that you make available to me a complete copy of my child's school file, including all tests, reports, assessments, grades, notes by teachers or other staff members and any other information contained in the file. I understand I am entitled to access the complete file under the Family Educational Rights and Privacy Act (FERPA) (20 U.S.C. Section 1232 (g)). I would greatly appreciate having these files within the next five days. I will call you to confirm the details of getting copies.

Thank you very much for your assistance. I look forward to working with you and your staff.

Sincerely,

_____
Signature of parent

_____
Printed name

_____
Address

_____

_____ _____ _____
Daytime phone   Evening phone   Email

Request for Birth Certificate

Date: _____

_____

_____

_____

_____

[insert name and address of vital statistics office]

Birth name of person on birth certificate: _____

Father's name: _____

Mother's maiden name: _____

Date of birth: _____ Sex: _____

Place of birth: *[if hospital, specify name, if known]* _____

Place of birth: *[list city, county, state]* _____

Reason for request: _____

_____ .

Please send me _____ *[number of copies]* certified copy[ies] of the birth certificate of the above-named

person. I have enclosed a check in the amount of $ _____ and a stamped, self-addressed envelope.

Thank you for your assistance.

Signature: _____

Printed or typed name: _____

Relationship to person on birth certificate: _____

Address: _____

_____

Home phone: _____ Work phone: _____

INDEX

P

R

S

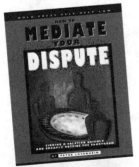

& Give Us Your 2 cents

Your comments make a big difference in the development and revision of Nolo books and software. Please take a few minutes and register your Nolo product—and your comments—with us. Not only will your input make a difference, you'll receive special offers available only to registered owners of Nolo products on our newest books and software. Register now by:

PHONE
1-800-728-3555

FAX
1-800-645-0895

EMAIL
cs@nolo.com

or **MAIL** us
this registration card

REMEMBER:
Little publishers have big ears. We really listen to you.

fold here

REGISTRATION CARD

NAME	DATE

ADDRESS

CITY	STATE	ZIP

PHONE	E-MAIL

WHERE DID YOU HEAR ABOUT THIS PRODUCT?

WHERE DID YOU PURCHASE THIS PRODUCT?

DID YOU CONSULT A LAWYER? (PLEASE CIRCLE ONE)   YES   NO   NOT APPLICABLE

DID YOU FIND THIS BOOK HELPFUL?   (VERY)   5   4   3   2   1   (NOT AT ALL)

COMMENTS

WAS IT EASY TO USE?   (VERY EASY)   5   4   3   2   1   (VERY DIFFICULT)

DO YOU OWN A COMPUTER? IF SO, WHICH FORMAT? (PLEASE CIRCLE ONE)   WINDOWS   DOS   MAC

We occasionally make our mailing list available to carefully selected companies whose products may be of interest to you.

❑ If you do not wish to receive mailings from these companies, please check this box.

❑ You can quote me in future Nolo promotional materials. Daytime phone number _____.

SPOT 2.0

**N O L O
IN THE
NEWS**

"Nolo helps lay people perform legal tasks without the aid—or fees—of lawyers."

—USA TODAY

Nolo books are ..."written in plain language, free of legal mumbo jumbo, and spiced with witty personal observations."

—ASSOCIATED PRESS

"...Nolo publications...guide people simply through the how, when, where and why of law."

—WASHINGTON POST

"Increasingly, people who are not lawyers are performing tasks usually regarded as legal work... And consumers, using books like Nolo's, do routine legal work themselves."

—NEW YORK TIMES

"...All of [Nolo's] books are easy-to-understand, are updated regularly, provide pull-out forms...and are often quite moving in their sense of compassion for the struggles of the lay reader."

—SAN FRANCISCO CHRONICLE

fold here

- -

nolo
950 Parker Street
Berkeley, CA 94710-9867

Attn: SPOT 2.0